That was the plan. But while the revenues came, the company never realized the scale economies for which it had planned. Its costs continued to rise, and moreover, rise at an increasing pace: *the geometric growth of complexity costs.* The board had been growing impatient and was now seeking a quick fix to the situation.

For the head of strategy, the penny had dropped, but it didn't seem to have brightened his mood. He knew a path to profitability meant wrestling with the complexity in his organization.

"I wish I had this chart 10 years ago," he said.

We thought, *and your investors are probably wishing the same.* But the meeting got us thinking. *How could this happen? Why do companies' growth strategies so frequently lead them to crash on the rocks? How should companies think about growth in a complex world?* Since the publication of *Waging War on Complexity Costs,* we have focused on answering and expanding upon these questions. But the original spark was that day.

At the end of the meeting, we left the head of strategy with some words of encouragement, and the two of us made our exit out into the chilly mountain air. We were still consumed by what we had heard. The implication had hit us both like a thunderbolt: a group of very smart people had invested more than $10 billion in a business plan that was based on an *out-of-date understanding of the world.* No one had accounted for the impact of complexity on profitable growth. No one had accounted for how, in today's complex world, companies needed new rules for attaining and sustaining profitable growth. And it made us wonder: *How many other companies are in a similar situation today, about to embark on a growth journey built on shaky foundations?*

We were both thinking the same thing. We had another book to write.

D1049572

A New Framework for Global Growth

For brevity in this book we'll make two assumptions. The first is a reasonable starting point: that your business has a good set of customers, a portfolio of products and services, dedicated management, and the usual mix of positives and negatives that touch global companies. The second is that your primary interest is in the new and the different. So we'll be concise with our treatment of traditional elements of growth strategy. We'll train our eye for the most part on the new knowledge and insights that have emerged around growth and complexity through our research and client work.

At this point in time, the stakes couldn't be higher. Many companies—including, most likely, your own—are fully engaged in new growth initiatives, and setting sail on a voyage to find scale and profitability. *Now is the time to assess your growth strategy!* One degree of difference in direction at the outset, a slight shift of emphasis on different disciplines within your business, may be all that determines whether you reach safe harbor or end in a shipwreck.

This book provides a new framework for profitable growth. And while you'll find plenty of books on growth, this is the first book to address what it means to achieve *breakaway growth and profitability* in this new age.

In this book, we will prepare you for charting a new course through these dangerous waters. In the chapters that follow we will introduce you to the new landscape, the traps that can lure you onto the rocks, and the tools and perspective you will need to find profitable growth in the *Age of Complexity.** Anchors aweigh!

---

* Age of Complexity[SM] is a service mark of Wilson Perumal & Company, Inc.

PART I

The New Growth Challenge

CHAPTER 1

The Paradox of Growth

"I am prepared to go anywhere, provided it be forward"
—DR. DAVID LIVINGSTONE[1]

Growth is rarely in a straight line. It is tempting to think otherwise, particularly when looking in the rearview mirror, but anyone faced with plotting the coordinates for a company's growth knows the fallacy of this notion. As much as we like to think of corporate leaders executing surefire growth strategies, the truth is far messier: growth is more often the outcome of an informed set of hunches (called strategies), a lot of tenacity and resolve, some experimentation, and yes, a little bit of luck—more an act of exploration and discovery than a step-by-step process.

Over the last several years, we have worked with dozens of companies as they seek to recover from the recession, stabilize their business, and plot a course for growth. Many had to undo, or cut through, a knot of complexity, which had slowly crept into the business over a decade or longer and strangled the company's ability to serve customers and create profits. Many others were looking at the issue from a different end: how to grow, and how to do so profitably, delighting customers while preserving critical economies of scale.

Behind this tension, we realized, there lay a fundamental paradox, one that was impacting and hurting many companies and that seemed worthy of attention. We found in fact that *many of the* *actions that companies were taking in a bid to drive growth were fundamentally impeding their ability to grow.* We named this the Growth Paradox^SM,* and we found examples everywhere we looked.

Consider the technology company that had launched hundreds of R&D projects, with a commitment to accelerate growth and create a customer-focused organization. The result: a clogged R&D pipeline, with nothing coming to market yet significant product proliferation, impairing manufacturing scale and efficiencies and overall on-time delivery rates—a key customer metric.

Or consider the industrial manufacturing company struggling to survive after losing nearly half of its sales in the economic downturn. If only, it was hoped, it could get back the volume, it would recover its profitability. But the volume it captured was different in nature from the volume it had lost. The company took on whatever bits of business it could get—scraps of revenue that saddled operations with greater product variety and smaller order sizes. The result: poorer service levels, reduced product availability, unhappy customers, ultimately lower profits, and a cap on growth.

Across industries we saw the same dynamic: companies chasing growth in a way that creates complexity, which inhibits growth: the Growth Paradox.

But companies need growth, and many are operating in a particularly unforgiving environment. "If we don't cannibalize ourselves, someone else will," said Steve Jobs, who made iPods obsolete by bringing iPhones to market. And the pace of creative destruction in the market is accelerating. The average tenure of companies on the S&P 500 (a proxy for company life span) was 60 years in 1958 but shortened to 25 years in 1980 and just 18 years today.[2]

---

* The Growth Paradox^SM and The Paradox of Growth^SM are service marks of Wilson Perumal & Company, Inc. The first public presentation of The Growth Paradox concept was by the authors at the CEO and CFO Forums, Sydney, Australia in May 2010.

As corporate leaders, this may be unsettling. But it is great news for consumers—a dynamic marketplace where there is always a new entrant looking for innovative ways to improve the lives of people and disrupt the status quo. Still, it creates a challenging dynamic for established companies, particularly incumbents, with legacy products, processes, and organizational structures.

Consider a specific industry that barely existed 10 years ago and is now is a $400 billion market: smartphones. Figure 1.1 shows how market leadership has shifted over the last several years in response to the rapid pace of innovation and an explosion in product choice.

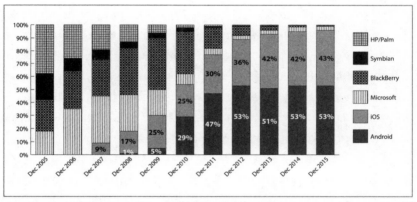

FIGURE 1.1: The Changing Face of the Smartphone Market (Platform Market Share)
Source: comScore's 2016 US Cross Platform Future In Focus

BlackBerry (on the RIM operating system) at first dismissed the iPhone due to its lack of a physical keyboard. This was an easy perception to have in 2007, when Apple (on iOS) had just 9 percent of the market. What no one foresaw was that the virtual keyboard was good enough and the apps and versatility that the iPhone brought with it would more than compensate. BlackBerry virtually disappeared from the market by 2014 and in September 2016 announced it would cease making phones altogether.

Companies as Complex Systems

The pace of change in markets and companies' efforts to stay in step have led to unprecedented increases in complexity—to the point that most organizations have truly become *complex systems*—ones with a very large number of interrelated parts.

Complex systems are difficult to understand, harder to manage, and often surprise us because of nonlinear dynamics, vicious cycles (booms and busts), and emergent properties (properties that arise, or emerge, from the interactions across smaller elements that themselves do not exhibit that property). Examples include the human body, the climate, and our economy. They exhibit a complex web of cause-and-effect instead of the linear causal chains with which we are familiar.

Our key point is that complex systems are highly prone to unintended consequences, and as companies and markets become more complex, we begin to see certain paradoxes. We see actions taken to reduce costs that inadvertently lead to more costs, and actions taken to grow that ultimately impede the company's ability to grow.

In our earlier book, *Waging War on Complexity Costs*, we examined the issue of cost reduction through the complexity lens, and came up with new insights and frameworks for attacking the complexity costs that lurk in all companies, inflating cost structures and eroding profits. We wrote that book in 2009, shortly after the economic downturn when so many companies were facing challenges around cost reduction. With so many companies now facing the challenge of growth, we now look at growth through the complexity lens, and find that complexity has changed the dynamics around growth as well.

Not Only Cost and Growth, but Risk as Well

Complexity has not just changed the nature of cost and growth, but also that of risk. Complexity was the major underlying factor behind catastrophic events from BP's Deepwater Horizon oil spill in the Gulf of Mexico in 2010 (Figure 1.2) to JPMorgan's $2 billion trading loss in 2012. Even highly regarded technical organizations have struggled to manage complexity and risk—for example, NASA and the Space Shuttle *Challenger* and *Columbia* accidents; TEPCO and the Fukushima Daiichi nuclear power plant accident; the USAF loss of accountability of nuclear missile components.

FIGURE 1.2: Deepwater Horizon Oil Rig Explosion and Fire

Operational risk grows geometrically with complexity, to levels that in many cases now exceed the capabilities of traditional risk management programs. Technology is more complex, processes are more complex, organizations are more complex, government regulations are more complex, and so on; and with more complexity, there are more ways a system can fail. The more complex, the more difficult to anticipate the potential combinations of events that can result in a disaster. Unfortunately, the typical response to complexity is to add even more complexity—more people, more management systems, more protocols, more oversight—which often compounds the problem.

The root issue is that business leaders are trying to manage a complex system using old approaches. It is not a matter of an executive's capability and intent; rather it is because the tools, approaches, frameworks, mental models, and paradigms we have acquired in our lives are no longer applicable. Complexity has changed the game.

What Is Complexity?

We all know when something is complex, but a definition is much more difficult. Our simplest definition is that *complexity is the number of different things you have in your business.* This includes the number of products and services you offer, the number of steps in a process, the number of regions you operate in, the number of different store formats you may have, the number of production facilities in your footprint, the number of suppliers you use, the number of different systems you maintain, and on and on.

In our previous book, we introduced the Complexity Cube. This simple diagram has continued to be a helpful framework for explaining the nature of complexity (see Figure 1.3), in part because it illustrates the relationship between complexity and complexity

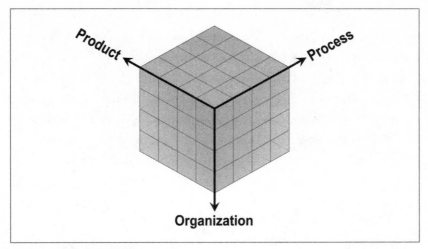

FIGURE 1.3: Complexity Cube

costs. By understanding this relationship you will be much more able to spot it at work in your company and manage its impact.

In our work we define complexity across three dimensions:

- **Product dimension.** The variety of goods and services you offer to your customers, as well as the variety of components that make up those goods and services.
- **Process dimension.** The number of processes, process steps, and handoffs in the production of your goods and services and operation of your business.
- **Organizational dimension.** The variety of resources involved in carrying out your processes. This includes your people, facilities, equipment, suppliers, systems, reports, the number of entities, and so on.

While it is possible to define *complexity* across these three dimensions, we assess the impacts or costs of complexity by considering the interactions between these dimensions. For example, recall the manufacturing company cited earlier in the chapter: the additional product complexity led to issues in its processes, with the result being poor service levels (we refer to this as "product-process complexity").

The larger point is, as you start to consider the impacts of complexity on costs and growth, it is necessary to take a broader than normal view of the business. *Complexity lives in the interactions.*

The more things you have, and the more different and interconnected they are, the more complex your organization is. In this sense complexity is akin to variety. But variety sounds good, and complexity sounds bad, and indeed, there is *good* and *bad* complexity.

Good complexity is simply defined as the variety in your business that customers value and *will pay for.* If customers aren't interested in paying for a feature or additional product variety, and all that goes into that, then at the level that matters it's truly not important to them. Bad complexity is the complexity that customers *can't see or won't pay for.* By definition, internal complexity is bad complexity; customers don't value an overly complicated internal process.

What the Complexity Cube Tells Us About Complexity

First, since complexity is really a multidimensional issue, with costs residing on the faces of the cube, looking at any one dimension alone will understate the magnitude of the issue. For example, if looking at each dimension of the cube we were to say that half our complexity was good, value-adding complexity, and the other half was bad, non-value-adding complexity, then by looking at each face we would see that three-quarters of our complexity costs were non-value-add (NVA). Further by looking across the entire cube, we would see that seven-eighths of my complexity costs are NVA.

Second, if you really want to attack the impacts of complexity (on costs, on risk, and on performance), then you must attack the issue across at least two and often all three dimensions. You need to, so to speak, put *more in play.* Contrast that with a typical approach to attacking complexity. Many times the approach is to take a broad issue and winnow it down to a "manageable" scope of work—and in so doing, putting the opportunity for truly unlocking the problem out of reach.

Finally, the cube tells us that since complexity costs grow geometrically, at some point, as you continue to add complexity, the cost of that complexity will rise at such a geometric rate that it will eventually outpace your revenue growth. At this point, complexity is clearly destroying value. Most companies are well past this point, with significant impact not just on their cost structure but also their ability and prospect for growth.

Your organization (1) uses its resources to (2) execute a set of processes to (3) deliver your portfolio of goods and services to your customers. When defined this way, it is clear that complexity isn't necessarily bad—certainly, no one would want to return to a world with little or no variety, *but at some point, too much complexity certainly is bad, meaning it does not add value (non-value-added or bad complexity).*

What does bad complexity look like?

- On the **product dimension** it can look like a bloated product portfolio that the business struggles to deliver. Inventory levels are high and product availability is low. The sales force struggles to stay abreast of the ever-expanding variety of products and services. Even worse, customers may suffer from overchoice, feeling unable to make sense of the portfolio and in the end preferring not to buy rather than trying to figure it all out.

- On the **process dimension**, too much complexity looks like duplication, rework, and workarounds. Processes are convoluted, painful, and laborious and have numerous handoffs, resulting in poor process performance (poor quality, long lead-times, poor on-time delivery) and growing internal inefficiencies. People are frustrated.

- On the **organizational dimension**, complexity is perhaps best described by the word *disarray*—disarray in the resources of your company and how those are deployed against your processes to deliver your goods and services. This may be a sprawling footprint of manufacturing and distribution facilities, the weight of multiple IT systems that are difficult to manage, or complex organizational structures that make it difficult to get things done.

Local Benefits, Distributed Costs

Why do so many companies have too much complexity? One reason is that *the benefits from complexity tend to be local, while the costs of complexity tend to be distributed*. When someone adds an item of complexity, whether a new product, an additional process step, a new report, or a new IT system, the reason—the benefit—of adding that complexity is very clear. It is why the item is being added in the first place. The benefits are very proximate and visible to those who want to add the item. They are local.

However, there is typically a much fuzzier and more incomplete view of the costs that will actually result from adding the item, such as the increased costs of sourcing, logistics, sales, and so on. The complexity costs arise due to the interactions throughout the system and are borne across the system—they are distributed. When there is a very good view of local benefits, and a much less complete view of distributed costs, and this happens again and again across the system, the company naturally progresses one step at a time toward too much complexity.

Unfortunately, as the company becomes more complex, the disparity between local benefits and distributed costs grows even more, and it becomes ever more difficult to anticipate the full costs and impact of more complexity on the rest of the system, making it likely that even more complexity will be added, creating a vicious cycle.

The natural dynamic of local benefits and distributed costs, and the vicious cycle it creates, is the most fundamental reason companies have too much complexity and why overly complex companies are the best at adding even more variety.

Most organizations of any size have moderate to high degrees of complexity in all three dimensions, and this at a time when many are facing up to a new dynamic: *the need to do more, do it more quickly, with greater integration required internally and externally, for shorter periods of competitive advantage.* In practice this means a dizzying array of demands on the organization and its leaders, within a globalized and fiercely competitive framework, in the pursuit of transient levels of competitive advantage.

While most leaders will recognize the issue of complexity as we describe it, few have yet to translate their growth strategies—and indeed their operating practices—into the disciplines they need to navigate to profitable growth in a complex world. What we observe is companies doggedly executing traditional growth strategies, with mixed results: no growth, slow growth, or worse, significant value destruction. How is it all coming undone? Because leaders are being led astray by the Sirens of Growth^{SM}.*

The Sirens of Growth

In Greek mythology, the Sirens were the enchanting, yet dangerous creatures that seduced sailors with their beautiful songs, luring them to their deaths when their ships crashed on the rocks.

> *"The Sirens enchant him with their clear song, sitting in the meadow, and all about is a great heap of bones."*
>
> **HOMER, *THE ODYSSEY***

In Part II, we will expand on these Sirens in more detail, but here we will introduce them briefly (see Figure 1.4). Each Siren represents a growth trap—a powerful allure that motivates behaviors—and for each there is a corresponding mental model.

#	Siren		Siren Song
1		The Expanding Portfolio	"More is better than less." "Whatever the customer asks for." "Let's see what sticks."
2		The Greener Pasture	"We won at home; we will do great over there, too." "This is a natural growth adjacency for us." "Competition is less tough elsewhere."
3		The Smash Hit	"A single thing will determine our success." "Bet the farm; this has to succeed." "If we can just find a differentiated product."
4		The Castle Walls	"We like where we are, it has served us well." "Declining margins are a short-term blip." "Customers want quality, not a low-priced knockoff."

FIGURE 1.4: The Sirens of Growth

---

* The Sirens of Growth^{SM} is a service mark of Wilson Perumal & Company, Inc.

Siren #1: The Expanding Portfolio

A medical products company struggles under the weight of a sprawling portfolio with more than 100,000 SKUs, while its sales force believes there is room for further additions. A popular Midwest restaurant chain considers how its multipage menu has expanded over the years with new additions, while customer service and supply chain costs have worsened. In both these situations, the company is facing the consequences of portfolio proliferation. The reason for product proliferation is understandable: *Customers like variety, so the broader the portfolio the better.* It is a powerful Siren because incremental innovation is easier to embrace from a management perspective, and because portfolio expansion *can* drive growth—at least up to a point. But as many companies have found over the past decade, there are unintended consequences to unrestrained portfolio proliferation: the introduction of incremental costs and complexity, negative impacts on key service levels and processes, the cannibalization of existing sales, and most important, lack of focus.

Siren #2: The Greener Pasture

In the research for his book *How the Mighty Fall*, Jim Collins initially assumed that complacency would be a major determinant in a company's downfall. That is, until he looked at the data. In fact, he says, "overreaching much better explains how the once-invincible self-destruct." As an example, he cites Ames Department Stores, which in the 1970s was a competitor to Walmart but made a number of big bets with acquisitions, new ventures, and deviations from its formerly successful formula serving rural markets. The result: the company eventually plunged into bankruptcy, while Walmart went on to successfully and persistently execute its rural strategy.[3] Greener pastures are always tempting, for a couple of reasons—either things look easier elsewhere, or else we assume we can compete as well away from home as we can in our core area. But as we discuss later in the book, to successfully expand from your core business into new markets, new geographies, and new customers requires a candid assessment of your existing capabilities, basis of competition, and the likely increasing complexity of operations. The pursuit of greener pastures can erode the very core you are looking to expand from.

Siren #3: The Smash Hit

"Today, Apple is going to reinvent the phone, and here it is. . . . And boy, have we patented it."[4] Hence came the iPhone, by any measure a gigantic hit, a game-changer in the phone industry, and a disrupter for many other industries. But today Apple is judged as much on its pipeline as by its quarterly iPhone sales; in other words, even a killer product has a limited shelf life. The "Smash Hit" has a powerful allure—like winning the lottery. But the pursuit of it can suck up resources in what amounts to bet-the-farm strategies. An illusion creeps in: *If this works, all our worries will be gone!* But in our more sober states, we all recognize that any big hit will be quickly copied, and commoditized, despite filing 200 patents.[5] Therefore, it's your ability to *repeatedly innovate* on an ongoing basis that matters. The insidious reality is that a myopic focus on the Smash Hit, at the exclusion of all else, inhibits the creation of disciplines that are truly needed for repeatable innovation and differentiation.

Siren #4: The Castle Walls

As Rita Gunther McGrath points out in her book *The End of Competitive Advantage*, "The assumption of sustainable advantage creates a bias toward stability that can be deadly." In our experience, many advantages that companies describe as "sustainable" never actually met the bar in the first place. Thus, a common and very destructive Siren is the Castle Walls: deploying resources around a perceived or past competitive advantage in the hope of maintaining or regenerating growth. It is common because while a company and its products or services may represent a *transient* response to a market need, it is very easy to start believing in *permanence*. Companies become institutions, with preservation biases. The required response: reshape your business, to keep pace with or ahead of market shifts, with a cold, dispassionate eye.

Resisting the Sirens

In the *Odyssey*, Homer's eighth-century BC epic poem, Odysseus commanded that all his crew members plug their ears with beeswax to deafen them to the song, and then commanded them to tie him to the mast so he would not himself be at risk of being drawn astray. His discipline saved him.

Organizational leaders are facing a similar choice: either allow themselves to be lured by the Sirens—pursuing growth strategies that too frequently lead to disappointing results—or be like Odysseus and embrace a new set of disciplines to suit the changing conditions of today. The first choice can lead to crashing on the rocks, the latter to successfully reaching your goals.

One of the central questions that drove the development of this book was why and how companies are led astray by the Sirens. Moreover, we wanted to identify and share what these organizations—and you—can do to avoid them and fully realize the ambition of your growth agenda. At the heart of the answer is the fact that many common corporate strategies for growth, while alluring at the outset, do not account for the radically different world we face in the Age of Complexity. In our parlance, the allure of the Sirens has gotten stronger, while the shoreline has gotten rockier and the seas choppier.

By "choppy seas," we are referring to specific changes in the business environment. The world is more complex, more global, and more competitive than ever; and at the same time, today's customers enjoy and expect unprecedented levels of choice. Businesses of every shape and size are struggling with a new set of tensions:

- How to serve the twin masters of customer intimacy and global cost-competitiveness
- How to reconcile the "long tail" with requisite scale
- How to capture new sources of growth without creating a mess of complexity

In the rest of Part I, we will continue to explore the Age of Complexity, while in Part II, we will dive deeper into understanding the Sirens, and how companies can ensure their growth strategies are robust against the Siren Song. If your growth strategy is leading you into a Siren trap, it may be time to raise the red flag.

Parts III and IV discuss the *organizational capabilities* required to find and accelerate profitable growth in today's complex environment. These break down into two categories: the *mindsets* to tap into new sources of growth, combined with the *critical skill sets and disciplines* to separate good from bad complexity, create value, and navigate to profitable growth.

In our experience, the degree that a company has both what we call the Explorer's Mindset and the Navigator's Skill Set in large part determines its ability to find profitable growth in today's complex environment.

Today, companies need to be more innovative and customer-focused than ever, and simultaneously be more productive, efficient, and resilient than ever. For example, no longer can companies ponder a simple choice—*To centralize or not to centralize?*—implying a trade-off between industrial efficiency and customer proximity. The new requirement is *both*, with implications for structure, for strategy, and for operations.

Welcome to the Age of Complexity!

CHAPTER 2

The Age of Complexity

"The historian of science may be tempted to claim that when paradigms change, the world itself changes with them. . . . It is rather as if the professional community had been suddenly transported to another planet where familiar objects are seen in a different light and are joined by unfamiliar ones as well."

—THOMAS S. KUHN, *THE STRUCTURE OF SCIENTIFIC RESOLUTIONS*

As labels go, *the Age of Complexity* may be an understatement. In 2009, we described an example of how choice had exploded in the marketplace:

> *The consumer packaged goods companies, as suppliers to these retailers, have kept apace, launching a volley of new products: new versions of Oreo cookies, an aisle of potato chips, hundreds of types of toothpaste. The retailers, the consumer goods companies, and their suppliers have all rightly rushed to meet consumer demand, but not without considerable adjustment.*[1]

. . . and the unintended impacts on businesses:

Think about the impact of all that change on the sup-
ply chain that "grew up" over many years getting cans of
soup from the supplier to the shelf-edge. That same sup-
ply chain now has also to support flat-screen TVs . . . now
extend across multiple countries . . . now support differ-
ent format stores, and on and on. . . .

Chances are your business has gone through similar
changes. Your business has stretched and grown to meet
a decade of growth but has left in its wake an enormous
burden of complexity costs.

In the last seven years, things have gotten more complex, not less!
Mobile platforms—another channel—were then just emerging. There are now ever more ways to engage with consumers via
social media. And the regulatory environment has become more
stringent, cumbersome, and confusing, not less so. Whatever your
measure, most would agree that our world has become much more
complex.

And this increase has been across different dimensions. A lot of
the issues that we see companies deal with today fit into the realm
of what we call *process-organizational* complexity. For example,
the F-35 Joint Strike Fighter (JSF) program was supposed to save
us money. The concept seemed straightforward: by developing one
aircraft (albeit in three versions) for the Air Force, Marine Corps,
and Navy, as well as many allied nations, development costs would
be spread across larger numbers, gaining scale and achieving cost
savings.

But a December 2013 Rand Corporation report produced for the
U.S. Air Force dismissed the anticipated joint program savings.
Amazingly, the report concluded that "the F-35 Joint Strike Fighter
program will cost more than three single-service programs would
have done."[2]

The study found that the higher cost-growth rate of joint programs more than offsets their expected savings. According to the study, an ideal two-service program, by doubling the number of aircraft produced, would deliver a maximum savings of 13 percent in unit production costs and 20 percent in overall procurement costs (assuming production costs are four times R&D costs). But in practice these "theoretical savings were more than offset by the greater cost increase rates observed in practice" for joint programs, "making the joint program more costly for both parties."*

By not anticipating the impact of increased organizational complexity—the massive coordination required across not just the Air Force, Navy, and Marine Corps, but also across 16 nations—the attempt to reduce one type of rather apparent complexity (the number of different types of aircraft) backfired to lead to a significant increase in a much more insidious type of complexity. Not only is the aircraft more complex itself, but the burgeoning organizational and process complexity has led to significantly higher costs for the overall program.†

---

* According to *Defense News* (April 18, 2016), the 60-year estimate to keep F-35s flying until 2070 is now $1.124 trillion.

† It is ironic that it was Kelly Johnson, founder of Lockheed's famous Skunk Works, who was the leader in understanding the impact of organizational complexity on aircraft development. It is tempting to consider what Johnson would make of the JSF program. One of his 14 rules of management was that "the number of people having any connection with the project must be restricted in an almost vicious manner." It seems that out of the best intentions the JSF program has gone the other way, and highlights the challenge of complexity and the importance of determining where to build scale.

Geometric Growth of Complexity Costs

In the Introduction, we introduced the Complexity Cost Curve (see figure), the curve that captures the notion of systemwide costs introduced as the result of a specific action. Complexity costs are the costs you incur in order to have many things, and are typically unanticipated, inadvertent, and often hidden.

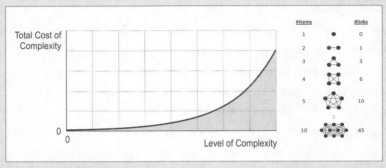

COMPLEXITY COST CURVE

It is this aspect of complexity—that its costs result from the interactions between its dimensions—that drives complexity costs to grow geometrically with complexity.

As we add more complexity to a business, we also increase the potential number of interactions between those items (see figure on the right), and as the complexity of a system grows, the relationships and linkages between the parts becomes ever more important. With only two items, there is only one possible link or interaction between them. Increase this to four items, and the number of possible links grows to six. Make it 10, and we now have as many as 45 links. At 100 items, there are nearly 5,000 links. You see the pattern. This is how complexity costs grow, and it is easy to see how they can get out of hand.

Complexity and Growth

So in this context of burgeoning consumer options, the challenge is twofold for companies: simplify to grow, and grow with scale. The Complexity Cube highlights how complexity drives non-value-add cost into organizations. No less real are the impacts of complexity on growth. In fact, complexity impedes growth in many ways:

- **Impaired service levels.** Product and process complexity lead to issues around service, such as poor on-time delivery, quality, or customer service.
- **Slowing innovation.** A large number of products (or initiatives) actually clog up the development pipeline, slowing time-to-market.
- **Customer confusion.** In the face of higher levels of choice, customers struggle to make purchase decisions and the sales channel is less able to provide support.
- **Higher costs, leading to less margin for reinvestment or higher prices.** Complexity costs creep in and working capital goes up, putting pressure on the business.
- **Profit concentration, and risk.** Complexity breeds cross-subsidizations, often massive ones, that mask the real creators of value in your company.

Islands of Profit in a Sea of Cost

A detailed review conducted by researchers in Europe of product profitability studies undertaken by companies in many industries found that typically the most profitable 20 to 30 percent of a company's products generate more than 300 percent of the company's profits. This of course means that *the remaining 70 to 80 percent of products lose over 200 percent of the profits!*[3]

(See Figure 2.1.) In our own work with clients we have found similar (in many case more acute) situations. This is extraordinarily high profit concentration. On the one hand it highlights the profit opportunity if you are able to identify and focus in on what we call the "islands of profit in a sea of cost." At the same time it exposes a vulnerability. If you are unaware of where these islands are, you cannot protect them, nor build growth strategies around the advantages implicit in their economics.

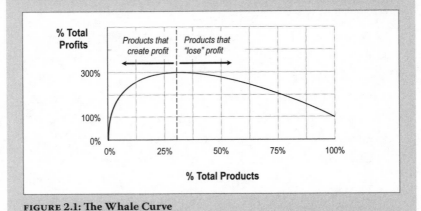

FIGURE 2.1: The Whale Curve

As the above starts to indicate, complexity has many direct and indirect impacts on your ability to grow. It can quietly but devastatingly consume resources that would be better deployed elsewhere. It can increase your cost base, undermining your ability to fund growth. Not surprisingly, costs and growth are inextricably linked, and that means complexity and growth are too.

Complexity Gains Status

A growing number of CEOs are recognizing the significant challenge that complexity represents. Andy Beal, number 42 on the

Forbes 400 list of wealthiest Americans and chairman and CEO of Beal Bank, one of largest and most successful privately owned financial institutions in the United States, says, "Complexity increases costs and risk of failure. It is a cancer that eats away at efficiency and profitability."[4] And the central topic at the 2013 Global Peter Drucker Forum was managing complexity.

- In a recent survey of 1,500 business leaders, complexity was cited as the most significant issue facing leaders today.[5]
- Nearly 80 percent of CEOs in a second survey said they expect higher levels of complexity over the next five years, yet far fewer said they felt prepared.[6]
- In a third survey, out of 1,400 global CEOs, nearly 80 percent of CEOs said they have made reducing unnecessary complexity a personal priority.[7]

Academics are also recognizing this challenge. In 2008 the University of Maryland's Robert H. Smith School of Business launched its *Center for Complexity in Business*. Similarly, in 2011, Suffolk University's Sawyer Business School launched its *Center for Business Complexity and Global Leadership*.

But we are not academics. Our insights come from years in the field actually helping clients across numerous industries attack critical cross-functional and systemic issues in their businesses, and one thing is clear to us: complexity isn't just the latest management fad. This is because complexity isn't just another tool, or discipline, but the fundamental challenge itself—not just an issue for management to contend with, but one that exacerbates all other management challenges. How did it get this way?

To answer this question it will be helpful to first gain some historical perspective, to view today's unique challenge within its larger historical context. There are strong undercurrents that have led us to this moment. To successfully navigate the Age of Complexity, it will be very helpful for you to see these currents, and to those we now turn.

The Preindustrial Age

Consider for a moment the world before the Industrial Age, before the advent of factories, steam power, electric utilities, fossil fuels, and the power, mobility, and efficiency that they allow. This was not that long ago. You just need to go back about 200 years, relatively recent in historical terms.

Consider not just what the preindustrial world was, but what it was like to live and work in that world (for many of us, it is difficult to think of life without the Internet, much less the steam engine). For almost everyone it was a hard, backbreaking world. Maury Klein, in his book *The Power Makers*, provides a vivid description:

> *Human existence had always been an unrelenting struggle against nature, pitting limited sources of energy against a seemingly endless series of tasks. In early America most people lived on farms that had taken them years to wrench from the wilderness. The farmer had to first clear his land of dense forest by girdling trees, chopping them, pulling up their stumps, and then cutting up the wood for use in building a home and outbuildings as well as for fuel. Rocks and boulders had to be pried up and hauled away to make a fence or simply dumped. . . .*
>
> *Once a field was cleared, the new farmer could begin his real work. For tools he had a hoe, a plow, and a scythe—staples that would remain in use until the mid-1800s. With a horse or ox as his helper, the farmer spent an exhausting day pushing against the soil to plow maybe an acre. Then he spent the season planting his crop,*

cultivating it, and finally harvesting it and preparing it for storage. Afterward some crops had to be ground or milled, often by pounding the grain with a mallet....

For his pains the farmer got a simple meal of meat and cornbread washed down with homemade cider or milk if the family had a cow. All of it had to be prepared in tedious rituals: the animals slaughtered, butchered, and salted; the apples picked, dumped into a press, and squeezed. Water had to be hauled in a bucket from a stream or well. The family wore the simplest of garments made from wool or flax. The women of the house toiled for hours spinning, weaving, and cutting clothes for their family, using thread made by twisting short fibers together. Through the long winter months the numbing process of spinning and weaving went on seemingly without end.

Life in the one-room house revolved around the fireplace, which provided heat for warmth and cooking.... Feeding the fireplace became one of the most laborious chores of all. A farmer had to cut down an acre of trees to supply enough fuel for a year, and every year the trees were farther away from him. The wood had to be chopped and split to fit the fireplace, hauled to the house, and stacked. Kindling had to be gathered and stored. By one estimate a farmer spent a third of his time during the year doing the chores that provided fuel for the house—and over time the supply around him dwindled rapidly.[8]

The defining characteristic of the preindustrial world was that work was done through muscle power, whether that of man or beast. In this world, efficiency was driven by the strength or speed of the individual working unit, and this only varied within a narrow biological range from person to person, or from animal to animal.

Relying on muscle power meant that costs therefore were largely variable, meaning that they were proportional to volume of work. For example, 10 horses could do 10 times the work of one horse, but also cost 10 times as much. Hence, *the preindustrial world was a variable cost world* (see Figure 2.2). This meant that larger companies did not necessarily have significant cost advantages over smaller ones, as there were no significant economies of scale to be had (exceptions existed, of course, but these were largely political and not industrial in nature).

Then the world changed. It began with the Industrial Revolution, a transformation the level of which the world has rarely seen, perhaps akin to the discovery of fire millennia before.*

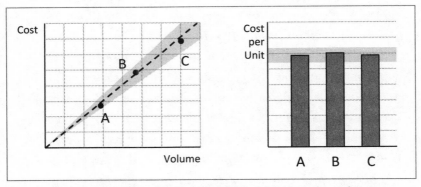

FIGURE 2.2: Cost Curve in the Preindustrial Age. In the Preindustrial Age costs were largely variable, rising in proportion to volume, as shown in the chart on the left. Three companies (A, B, and C) of very different volumes are shown. The chart on the right shows the unit cost for each of these same companies, which only vary within a narrow range despite the relative size differences of these companies (shaded area shown on each chart).

---

* Historians debate the precise dates for the beginning and end of the Industrial Revolution, but it was generally between 1760 and 1830.

The Industrial Age

The Industrial Age brought with it a level of change that touched almost every aspect of daily life. "Industrialization was not some master plan to remove workers from their century-old tasks. Instead it was *a complete reengineering of life* based on the ability to provide daily staples at much lower costs" (emphasis added).[9]

In a relatively short period of time, the steam engine, electricity, and fossil fuels provided significant new sources of power, which offered a whole new world of possibilities. "All the achievements of humanity down to about the eighteenth century were constrained by the inability to find more efficient ways to do things beyond the capacity of muscle and tools that, however ingenious, still required muscle to operate them."[10]

The world was finally released from the confining limits of muscle power. Steam, electricity, and fossil fuels enabled new machines and massing of production in the factory. In the factories, massing of production, interchangeable parts, and later the assembly line combined to create ever greater economies of scale. Larger volumes meant more repetitive tasks, which meant greater worker productivity. Larger machines were physically more efficient than smaller ones. Greater productivity and efficiency meant lower prices, which drove greater demand and even larger volumes. Increasing volumes meant ever larger factories, even more powerful machines, and even greater efficiency. Power and production combined in a virtuous cycle that rapidly changed Europe and America.

Samuel Insull's Self-Perpetuating Cycle

On July 1, 1892, Samuel Insull, until then one of Thomas Edison's right-hand men, left a plum position as second vice-president of the General Electric Company to take the helm of a small, relatively unknown electric utility in Chicago.

Four years earlier, the Chicago Edison Company had opened the city's first central generating station on Adams Street, with a capacity of 3,200 kilowatts, serving wealthy nearby customers. Electricity was at this time still too costly for the vast majority of people, but Samuel Insull had big plans.

Insull began construction at once of a much larger generating station on Harrison Street, which would open two years later with 16,400 kilowatts of capacity. At the same time he began to quickly acquire all of the other central generating stations in Chicago's central business district.

However, Insull didn't create a monopoly to raise prices, but to lower them. By aggregating volume he was able to support much larger, more efficient generating stations. In fact, the new Harrison Street station required only one-third the coal that the Adams Street station did to produce the same amount of electricity.

By pooling demand, Insull was also able to achieve a much higher load factor (the percentage of time the plant was in use). Insull himself pointed out that the greatest cost of electricity was the interest on the money borrowed to construct the power station. The higher load factor helped to further reduce costs by spreading the interest costs across more kilowatts, thereby further reducing prices.

Lower prices allowed Insull to offer electricity to new previously untapped customers. More customers meant even larger and more efficient generators, with even higher load factors, which drove costs and prices down even further.

At a time when the prevailing wisdom was to maintain a small pool of customers and induce them to pay more, the key according to Insull was more customers to achieve a "self-perpetuating cycle of rising consumption and falling rates." When asked how small a customer he would take, Insull was said to have declared that he would accept a customer with a single 25-watt bulb![11]

The key takeaway is that the Industrial Age story was one dominated by fixed costs. Significant fixed-cost investment was required to build ever larger factories and machines, but greater volumes meant greater ability to spread those costs (fixed cost leverage). The result: cost no longer rose proportionately with volume, but improved with volume (see Figure 2.3).

This was a dramatic and fundamental change. With economies of scale, larger companies now had significant cost advantages over smaller ones! Bigger was now better, and companies such as U.S. Steel, Standard Oil, Westinghouse, and GE raced to be the biggest. This was the story of the Industrial Age.

But the Industrial Age didn't just shape our world, it shaped how we think. America in particular came "of age" during this era, and the dynamics it brought forth (economies of scale, bigger is better, and so on) were stamped on our psyche. We continue to see the world through this lens, and it is hard to change our wiring. The world has evolved, but our thinking has not kept up.

The Industrial Age did not just stamp itself on how Americans think, but people throughout the West, throughout where the Industrial Revolution spread, and more recently the East, where the Industrial Revolution has played out all over again. (China, in particular, has just experienced its own Industrial Revolution at an incredibly accelerated rate, compressing about 100 years into just a decade.)

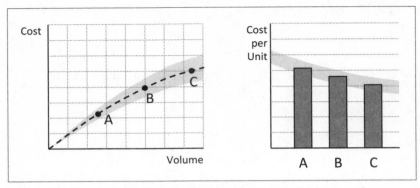

FIGURE 2.3: Cost Curve in the Industrial Age. In the Industrial Age, with economies of scale, costs did not rise as fast as volume, as shown in the chart on the left; three companies (A, B, and C) of very different volumes are shown. Unit cost therefore dropped as volumes grew, as shown in the right-hand chart. Productivity differences were driven by volume more than by differences in the skill of individual workers, as was the case in the Preindustrial Age. Larger companies therefore were naturally more cost competitive than smaller ones.

America!

The Industrial Revolution began in Great Britain, but took particular root in America. (It was Englishman James Watt who made the first practical steam engine, but American Eli Whitney who made the cotton gin.) America was a young country, a relatively new canvas with vast resources, industrious energy, a willingness to take risks, and a tendency to dream big. (Perhaps it is no small coincidence that Adam Smith's *The Wealth of Nations*, discussing division of labor and free markets, was first published in 1776.)

The Industrial Revolution transformed America more than any other country. The steamboat and the railroad connected America, enabling the country to tap its vast lands. Industrialization found its most fertile soil in the hustle and bustle of America. After his visit to America in 1831–1832, French political scientist Alexis de Tocqueville wrote in his book *Democracy in America*, "One is struck by a most extraordinary sight: there all is activity and bustle . . . improvement and progress are all that matter . . . no sooner do you set foot in America than you find yourself in a sort of tumult; a confused clamor rises on every side; a thousand voices reach your ears at once. Everything stirs about you."

The Postindustrial Age—"The Age of Complexity"

We have seen that the world before the Industrial Revolution was dominated by variable costs, with all the limitations that brought. Then in the Industrial Age, fixed-cost leverage became so significant that it became dominant over all else. Strangely, in a way, this simplified things. In the Preindustrial Age, winning depended on nuances. In the Industrial Age, however, winning primarily came down to size. It took initiative, of course, but the first to be the biggest tended to become much bigger.

To understand the Industrial Age, you just have to understand fixed and variable costs. Larger companies were simply more cost efficient than smaller ones, creating a virtuous cycle that reduced prices, accelerated volumes, and carried some companies to amazing heights.

Today, however, we see industry after industry where the largest company is not the most cost efficient, and often quite the opposite. What has changed is that the world has become fantastically more complex—more products, more segments, more channels, more regulations, more sophisticated technology, more complicated processes and organizations, and more sophisticated and demanding customers. This has added to the mix a third category of cost: *complexity costs.*

The most important characteristic of complexity costs is that they grow geometrically with complexity. When you double the level of complexity, you more than double the cost of that complexity. Lee Coulter, former SVP of Kraft Foods' global shared services group, calls complexity a "cube function." He says, "If I have 10 applications, I may be able to manage them all. If I have 100 applications, managing them is not simply 10 times the complexity—it's more like 30 times the complexity."

The exponential nature of complexity costs is what makes them so different, and much more insidious and difficult to manage, than the other types of cost (see Figure 2.4). Traditional variable costs are rather linear—costs tend to rise proportionally with volume. With a linear cost, the unit cost is simply the slope of the line ($/volume), making it very easy to think in terms of unit costs.

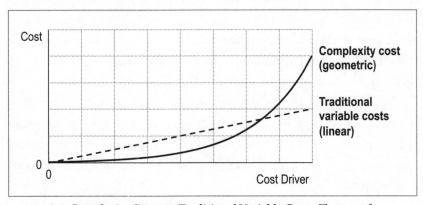

FIGURE 2.4: Complexity Costs vs. Traditional Variable Costs. The cost of complexity to a company doesn't grow proportionally with the level of complexity in the company; it grows geometrically or exponentially with the level of complexity. The unit cost of complexity therefore grows as more complexity is added. Traditional variable costs, on the other hand, tend to grow proportionally with volume; and the unit cost remains roughly constant as volume is added.

But with complexity the dynamic is very different: *The unit cost of complexity depends on the overall level of complexity* (the slope of the line is no longer constant, but changes along the curve), making it much more difficult to think in terms of unit cost. The unit cost of complexity depends on how much complexity has come before it. It also means that the cost of today's complexity tomorrow will depend on how much more complexity you add.

Just as *fixed costs* dominated the Industrial Age, and *variable costs* the age before that, complexity costs dominate our current age (see Figure 2.5). This is more difficult to get your head around than a simple fixed/variable view of the world, but it is nonetheless our reality today. Failure to recognize the three types of cost can lead to potentially devastating outcomes.

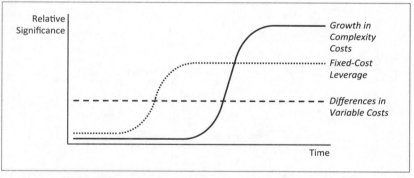

FIGURE 2.5: Three Types of Cost. There are three types of cost: variable (i.e., proportional with volume), fixed, and complexity costs. They have each always existed, but the relative importance of each has changed significantly over history. In the Preindustrial Age, fixed cost leverage was small, and there was relatively little complexity, leaving differences in variable costs, which were small, to determine companies' cost structures. In the Industrial Age, fixed cost leverage and resulting economies of scale were the largest determinants of a company's cost structure. In the Postindustrial Age, with the dramatic rise of complexity, complexity costs tend to be the top driver of a company's cost structure.

Banking: Bigger No Longer Better

In our study of the top 100 bank holding companies, we found larger banks were not necessarily more efficient and profitable than their smaller peers. Using the banks' efficiency ratio (non-interest expense over net interest income + total noninterest income, essentially what a bank must spend to make one dollar) as a measure of operational productivity, we found there is no positive correlation between the sizes (assets) of the banks and the efficiency ratios—bigger is not necessarily better. In fact, the opposite is true; 7 out of the top 10 largest banks in the United States have worse efficiency than the average bank.

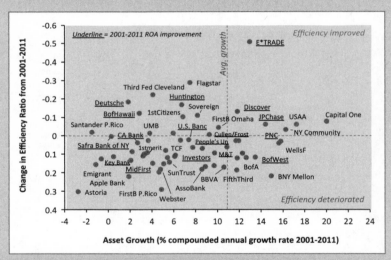

FIGURE 2.6: Change in Efficiency Ratio vs. Asset Growth
Note: Includes bank holding companies with assets over $10 billion
Source: FDIC; National Information Center, United States Federal Reserve System; Company annual reports and press releases; Wilson Perumal & Company Analysis

Of course, many macro- and microeconomic factors come into play to determine efficiency. Comparing one particular bank's efficiency ratio to another may not represent an industry trend. However, comparing banks to themselves over a period

THE AGE OF COMPLEXITY / 37

of 10 years, and looking at the relationship between their asset changes and their change in efficiency (see Figure 2.6), shows that less than 30 percent of the top banks we studied were able to improve their efficiency while maintaining healthy growth (banks above the zero line). When we overlay profitability, the percentage is reduced to 11 percent (the underlined banks above the zero line).

Periods of history can be defined by their dominant characteristics. In each age we discussed, the dynamics themselves were not new, but the relative importance among them certainly was, with significant impact on how companies would compete.

The Preindustrial Age, the Industrial Age, and the Age of Complexity were each very different. Viewed over the span of history, however, the Industrial Age was truly an exception, a remarkably unique and relatively brief period unlike any before or since. Because of its tremendous impact on our world it has stamped itself on how we think—but nonetheless it was an exception.

For a relatively short period of time, a unique combination of technological, political, social, and financial forces came together to launch a self-perpetuating cycle of lower costs and greater consumption (sure, we can still find this trend at work today, certainly in areas such as genomic sequencing and data storage, but these are remarkable stories, not the dominant story of this age). We were freed for the first time on a broad scale from the stifling constraint of muscle power; we enjoyed powerful new forms of energy; social changes released significant amounts of human capital; and financial capital followed suit to lubricate the machine of this new world. *Yet the complexity that would ultimately result had not yet arrived.* For a brief moment in time, the world had scale, but not complexity.

But complexity has arrived, and the world has changed, yet our minds are still stuck in that brief period of time.

Complexity not only affects cost structures, but also how companies compete, which means how they innovate and grow. Yet many companies continue to use outmoded paradigms and frameworks not suited to the present age—akin to navigating dangerous waters with an outdated chart. The tragedy is that despite the best efforts, many companies crash on the rocks.

Just as economy of scale had such a pronounced impact in the Industrial Age, the Complexity Cost Curve, with its exponential growth, has a substantial impact on companies today. It explains why many companies' cost structures have grown faster than their top line, and it goes to the heart of how complexity is eroding a company's ability to grow: complexity sucks up resources that can and should be better focused on higher-growth opportunities.

The complexity curve isn't new, it has always existed, but 50 years ago companies were still on the flat left-hand side of the curve so it could reasonably be ignored. Today however, companies are on the much steeper right-hand side of the curve. This is the new dynamic, the defining dynamic of our time. The Industrial Age was all about economies of scale. The Age of Complexity has brought complexity costs. And these two curves are in a tug of war, with huge implications on both your cost structure and your ability to grow.

CHAPTER 3

Rediscovering Scale

"Concentrate your energies, your thoughts, and your capital."

—ANDREW CARNEGIE

The Industrial Age was a moment in history—a singular, transformative flash—yet it still frames how we look at the world.

Many of us may romanticize the period as a simpler time. It was the era of industrial titans: Carnegie, Rockefeller, J. P. Morgan. Sure it took vision, ambition, and capital, but if you brought just the right ingredients together, and added just enough hard work, you just might create a spark and ride a virtuous cycle of scale economies to amazing heights.

It is tempting to think we are still there, a less ambiguous time when bigger was better, and the rules of the game were much clearer. In the Industrial Age, with its low levels of complexity, it was generally sufficient to think of scale as the overall volume or overall revenue of the business. Profitability was a function of revenue—in fact, it was driven by it. There were economies of scale to be had, and as revenue increased so did profitability. In this age, the thinking was that:

Profitability ≈ Revenue

So, bigger is better. It is tempting to think this way, but it will lead us astray. Take for example the industrial tool company that had lost 40 percent of its sales volume (and all of its profitability) after the economic downturn. With such a devastating shock to its business, management was keenly aware of the direness of the situation. If only it could get its volume back, management thought, the company could recover, regain its profitability, and survive the crisis.

So management did everything it could to capture every revenue dollar possible. In a desperate act, it rapidly expanded the product portfolio. Anything customers might want to buy, it quickly added to the catalog—even including clothing and toys.

But the expansion backfired. Category managers and salespeople struggled to keep up with the ever-expanding product line. The supply chain struggled to deliver ever greater variety of small-volume products. Product availability and on-time delivery performance fell short. Service suffered and customers became unhappy. Profitability dropped through the floor. In a well-intended quest for growth, the company saddled itself with so much complexity that it impaired its ability to execute and deliver. What customers prized was *product availability.* What the company focused on was *portfolio breadth.* The Industrial Age mindset suggested: if we add revenue, we will become more profitable. Instead they just became more complex. They confused revenue with scale.*

This is an all too common a story: we still operate with an Industrial Age rulebook. But of course the rules have changed. The world is also more crowded. We have passed the Age of Exploration where European nations raced to claim greater portions of the new world. Today, the landscape is full, with every gain being someone else's loss.

---

* Fortunately, the story didn't end there. The company began to regain its focus. Under new leadership, it developed a coherent product strategy and reversed course to rationalize its catalog. It stripped complexity out of its product line and its processes, and it was able over time to bring back up its service levels.

Similarly, much of the world has passed the point where a self-perpetuating cycle of consumption created amazing levels of new opportunity; where companies and entrepreneurs raced to capture a piece of a rapidly growing pie with seemingly room for all. Sure, there will continue to be amazing innovations and substantial gains, and likely at an ever accelerating pace, but along with these will be staggering losses for others, also likely at an ever accelerating pace.

In some regards, the world today better resembles the Preindustrial Age, where economies of scale were not so significant, where scale tended to fall under its own weight, and where instead of sparking and riding a virtuous cycle of growth and profits, one had to slog it out one step at a time and fight for each foot of ground.

A Return to a More Feudal World

In many ways the world is returning to its historical mainstream—to its roots.

The peak of the nation-state was arguably during World War II and the Cold War that followed, when it took the resources of a nation, and the largest economy at that, to develop the atomic bomb and to put a man on the moon—a period when the Cold War gripped not just the two most powerful nations, but the whole world. Resources (both economic and human capital) meant power, and similar to the factory and the Industrial Age, the ability to mass and concentrate power fueled the rise of great nations.

While great nations are certainly still powerful, today they are increasingly threatened by lesser nations and even nonstate actors. In the Postindustrial Age, technology has distributed power, democratized it even. We all saw what 19 misguided young zealots were able to inflict on the world's most powerful nation on September 11, 2001; and today we see organizations like ISIS and international drug cartels threatening national sovereignties. After the Islamic terrorist attack at the *Charlie Hebdo* newspaper office in Paris in January 2015, it was Anonymous, an international network of hacktivists, that declared war on ISIS, al-Qaeda, and other terrorist organizations, pledging to track and shut down the terrorists' online activities—in this case one non–nation-state actor being perhaps one of the more potent checks against another. Indeed in 2006, *Foreign Affairs* ran a piece by John Rapley titled "The New Middle Ages" which claimed that "The Middle Ages ended when the rise of capitalism on a national scale led to powerful states with sovereignty over particular territories and populations. Now that capitalism is operating globally, those states are eroding and a new medievalism is emerging, marked by multiple and overlapping sovereignties and identities."[1]

We also see a similar pattern in warfare. National security analyst Ralph Peters in his many books and articles has argued that we have passed the "Age of Ideology" and have returned to a period of "blood and faith." Peters argues that the Age of Ideology ran from 1789 to 1991, the French Revolution to the collapse of the Soviet Union—"a blip" in historical terms. Peters describes ideology as the notion that "one man or a small cabal [can] sit down and design a better system of social, economic, and political organization," which resulted in ideas such as Marxism, National Socialism, and fascism. In the nineteenth century and particularly the twentieth century, wars were fought over such ideas.[2]

The broad theme is that the world has dramatically changed, in many ways returning to its roots, but our thinking has not adjusted accordingly. Across business, economics, social and political organization, and even warfare, after the historically short and roughly concurrent periods of the Industrial Age, the rise of nationalism, and the Age of Ideology, the world is returning to its normative state, for which many are not prepared.

A Framework for Scale in the Twenty-First Century

Scale still matters. In fact, the primary management challenge today can be summarized as: *grow your revenue faster than you grow complexity*. But to do so requires a more nuanced understanding of scale, and what erodes it. If you fail to understand or manage the complexity in your business, you will find the fruits of scale frustratingly out of reach.

The relationship between revenue, complexity, and profitability is captured in the following useful rule of thumb: adding complexity faster than revenue will reduce your profitability, whereas adding revenue faster than complexity will increase your profitability. This rule of thumb is helpful for separating out good from bad complexity.

Compare two companies, both with a total sales volume of one million units. The first company has one product. The second company has 1,000 different products. In terms of true scale, these two companies are worlds apart. So, variety becomes just as important as volume, and the previous relationship becomes:

$$\text{Profitabilty} \approx \frac{\text{Revenue}}{\text{Complexity}}$$

What this means is that today you can no longer focus on revenue more than you think about your level of complexity, as they both have an equal impact on profitability. Revenue can be a misleading indicator of scale—a "false scale." It is a paradox of growth that focusing just on the numerator (growth) but not the denominator (complexity) will impede not just your profitability *but also your ability to grow.* Whereas focusing on complexity in conjunction with revenue will not only protect your profitability, but improve your ability to dramatically and sustainably grow.

Economies of scale certainly still exist today, but they are often less defined by the overall size of the company or business unit. Rather, real scale exists at much lower levels within the company, for example in the sales per a particular product, the volume of a particular task, or the volume with a particular customer or supplier. *Real scale is now found more at the micro level than the macro level.* Offerings, processes, organizational structures, resource allocations, work practices, and technology all affect real scale, and some useful metrics like inventory turns are a measure of real scale.

At this point it is helpful to introduce the notion of *density*. Just as in physics where density is mass per volume (such as grams per cubic centimeter), in businesses we think of density in terms such as sales per store, volume per product, or revenue per region. Density is volume (or sales or size) divided by complexity. *Today, it is more effective to think of economies of scale as economies of density*, where real scale is found in the pockets of density within and across a company. Introducing the notion of density updates our expression to:

$$\text{Profitablity} \approx \text{Density} \approx \frac{\text{Revenue}}{\text{Complexity}}$$

Think of a company as a pile of rocks (intending no offense to anyone). In the Industrial Age a bigger pile of rocks had more scale than a smaller pile of rocks. Today, however, it is instructive to ask whether a smaller pile of rocks has more real scale than a much larger pile of sand (see Figure 3.1).

But there are many good reasons to want to grow the size of your pile of rocks. First, it is often true that if you are not moving forward,

FIGURE 3.1: Which Has More Scale? In many industries today the largest companies (the "larger pile of sand") are less profitable than many smaller ones (the "smaller pile of rocks").

you are moving backward. In this sense, growth is a defensive strategy to ensure continued existence. Second, growth also reflects a natural and commendable human desire to create and to build, and in this sense growth is very satisfying. Third, as Berkshire Hathaway's Annual Report from 1992 points out, "The best business to own is one that over an extended period can employ large amounts of capital at very high rates of return." Certainly a larger company with a healthy rate of return is preferable to a smaller company with the same rate of return. In this sense, growth is a means to creating greater economic value.

In the Industrial Age there was also fourth reason for growth: as a means to become more profitable. And becoming more profitable reinforced the first three reasons, making growth an even more effective defensive strategy, more satisfying, and more economically valuable.

In the Age of Complexity, however, growth itself can no longer be counted upon as a means to greater profitability. Unfortunately, the opposite is more often realized, making growth less sustainable, less satisfying, and less valuable. In the current age, the challenge has become *how to grow while retaining profitability, as only profitable growth is truly sustainable over the longer term*,[3] and behind that question is the question of how and where to build real scale, meaning how and where to build density.

Today, profits beget growth, more than the other way around.

Economies of Density

With nearly half a trillion dollars of annual revenue, Wal-Mart Stores, Inc. is the world's largest retailer and one of the world's largest companies by revenue. Only the largest oil and gas companies are bigger.

If you were to sum up what has made Walmart so successful, most would point to its overwhelming size, deep pockets, and ability to beat price discounts out of its suppliers. A few admirers would point to its sophisticated technology and operations. *But the competitive advantages most of us associate with Walmart were not the drivers of Walmart's success, but rather the fruits of it.* We tend to view Walmart through an Industrial Age lens, seeing its size as the source of its competitive strength, as some sort of virtuous cycle. But Walmart was already highly successful, and *more profitable*, long before it was bigger than its competitors. Indeed, Walmart was more profitable than KMart even when Walmartwas just one-tenth KMart's size, long before it would have the clout to allegedly beat up suppliers. Further, Walmart's high-water mark for profitability was in the mid-1980s, when it had just around 860 stores versus its more than 11,000 today.

It wasn't Walmart's size that made it so successful. Rather it was Walmart's strategy of concentration—its *economies of density*. In their excellent book *Competition Demystified*, Columbia Business School professor Bruce Greenwald and investment manager Judd Kahn show how, after eliminating other explanations, Walmart's success resulted primarily from its strategy of concentration and the significant "local economies of density" it afforded.[4] Their thorough analysis, which they refer to as "Big Where It Counts" and "From Great to Good," goes into much more detail than we can cover here, but to summarize from their work:

> *For the three years ending January 31, 1987, Walmart had average operating earnings of 7.4 percent; Kmart's were 4.8 percent. The difference was due entirely to much lower overhead costs. As a percentage of sales, Kmart had lower cost of goods sold . . . but it dissipated this advantage by spending more, per dollar of sales, on selling, general, and administrative expenses (SGA) . . .*
>
> *What accounts for [Walmart's] thrift? . . . the geography of market concentration. We have seen that in 1985, more than 80 percent of its stores were in Arkansas, adjacent states, or their immediate neighbors. Though much smaller than Kmart overall, it was far larger in its home territory. Kmart had its own area of concentration in the Midwest, but any benefits it might have derived from this regional strength were diluted by its lower density in other parts of the country. Walmart, by contrast, was able to make the most of its strategy of concentration, which accounts for most of its superior profitability. . . .*
>
> *The superior efficiencies in these three functions were due to* local economies of scale. [emphasis in the original]*

---

* The lower costs of Walmart's concentration strategy came from three areas: inbound logistics, advertising, and executive supervision. As Greenwald and Kahn explain: (1) with its greater density of stores and proximity to distributions centers, trucks didn't travel as far and could carry goods on both routes (from vendors to distribution centers and from centers to stores), (2) for retailers, advertising is local, so with three times the *local* sales of competitors, Walmart's advertising costs, as percentage of sales, were about one-third that of competitors, and (3) greater store density meant that management spent more time in stores and less time driving between them—to supervise the same number of stores, a Kmart or Target executive had to cover a territory three to four times as large.

Kmart's sales were actually three times those of Walmart in those years, the authors reported. But that sales number was an amalgamation of national and international stores, with "little bearing on the physical movement of goods, on advertising designed to reach the customers who shopped in their stores, or on the supervision the company employed to manage its retail operations."

As Walmart began its aggressive national expansion in the mid-1980s, returns on sales and on capital declined steadily. By the mid-1990s, when Walmart was a national institution, but with less regional concentration than it had had in its golden days, returns bottomed out at around 15 percent of invested capital. Then, as Walmart added density by filling in the gaps, returns began to recover. The exception to this pattern was the international division, where Walmart was widely dispersed across many countries. As we would expect, international returns on sales and capital appear to have been only about one-half to one-third those of the core U.S. supercenter business.

The Temporal Dimension of Scale

A core strategic issue is that we have more data at our fingertips that at any point in history, yet we have less knowledge about the future. This unpredictability hampers our ability to build scale, as scale investments usually take some time to pay off.

In his book *Team of Teams*, General Stanley McChrystal illuminated the issue:

> *While we might think our increased ability to track, measure and communicate ... would improve our precise "clockwork universe" management, the reality is the opposite: these changes produce a radically different climate—one of unpredictable complexity—that stymies organizations based on Taylorist efficiency.*

Taylorism refers to the notion of Scientific Management, developed by Frederick Taylor in the 1880s, with a focus on the analysis of work flows and in particular labor productivity in manufacturing. It rested on a foundation of stability: incrementally removing seconds or minutes of waste in a (stable) production line for a stable demand. So while it is tempting to see technology as the means to perfect the machine, outside the world is no longer Taylorist. So scale today also requires adaptability:

$$Profitability \approx (Density \times Adaptability)$$

Adaptability means that companies need to leverage different strategies for rapidly creating scale, such as *network orchestration*—a business model where companies coordinate the participation of a network of providers, rather than providing all the value themselves. In fact, if the factory is a symbol of scale in the Industrial Age, then network orchestration may be the equivalent for today's world. Given how quickly any advantage can quickly be competed away— in combination with rapid geopolitical, demographic, and economic changes—the expected *life span* and versatility of investments must be considerations as any organization aspires to build scale.

Network orchestrators create value by forming partnerships with multiple parties—networks—to extend their organization in a low-cost, flexible, and valuable way. By leveraging the network, a company can access lower costs in the value chain, by allowing each subnetwork or individual actor to identify opportunity, structure in a cost-efficient manner, and leverage economies of scale where possible. Empty capacity becomes someone else's problem. It also offers much greater market flexibility, as the organization is longer defined by its assets—it can extend reach through the network. Global sourcing titan Li & Fung, by its own definition, is a network orchestrator in the purest form. The company owns no factories and employs no factory workers. It started as a trading broker in

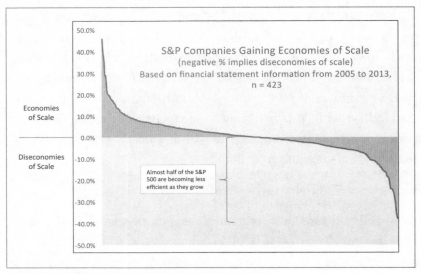

FIGURE 3.2: Winners and Losers in the S&P 500
Note: Here we are defining scale as the change in revenue CAGR (2005–13) and operating income (OI) growth over the same time period. This means that companies that saw profit growth (as measured by OI) exceed revenue growth the most rank the highest.
Source: Company financial statements; WP&C analysis

Canton, China, in 1906 and over the next hundred years grew into an exporter, then a multinational corporation, then finally into its role as an orchestrator. It now orchestrates 15,000 suppliers in more than 40 countries to produce more than $18 billion in garments, consumer goods, and toys.

Winners and Losers

The data suggests that companies are struggling to build scale. According to our analysis, almost half of S&P 500 companies are actually seeing less scale as they grow (see Figure 3.2). What is striking here is that this is not driven by industry. Dissecting the data (see Figure 3.3) reveals that that in most industries there are scale winners and scale losers. Some companies seem able to improve

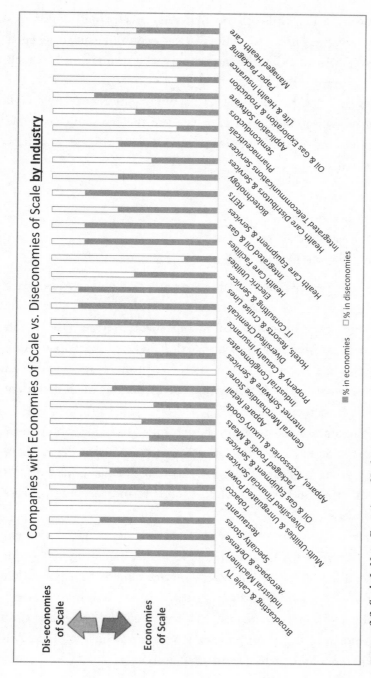

FIGURE 3.3: Scale Is Not a Function of Industry

Source: Company financial statements; WP&C analysis

economies of scale, while others don't. And this includes industries where you would expect to uniformly see economies of scale, such as software-related industries, and others where you wouldn't, such as the restaurant industry.

Let's consider the restaurant industry for a moment. If we look at where a few notable brand names fall in the economies of scale ranking (out of 423 companies), you'll see significant disparity among them:

- #28 Chipotle
- #118 McDonald's
- #289 Yum! Brands
- #359 Darden Restaurants

Yes, they are organizations with substantive differences. Some are relative upstarts while others are very established. Some have many brands and some have just a few. But that's precisely the point. Some of these differences—complexity factors—end up driving their ability to achieve scale, and therefore profitability. As you can see from Figure 3.4, there is a strong correlation between drivers of complexity and their ranking.

To understand what's behind these rankings, consider how these complexity factors are multiplicative, not additive. With more products going to more brands with more formats, the amount of coordination and associated cost tends to increase and process issues multiply.

McDonald's, for example, expanded its menu by 70 percent between 2007 and 2013 to include 145 items, including new products like the McWrap. As a result, service slowed to a point that some franchisees called their stores "operational nightmares."[5] Drive-through times increased by 13 percent in the same time period and were about 20 percent longer than those of Taco Bell and 30 percent longer than those of Wendy's.

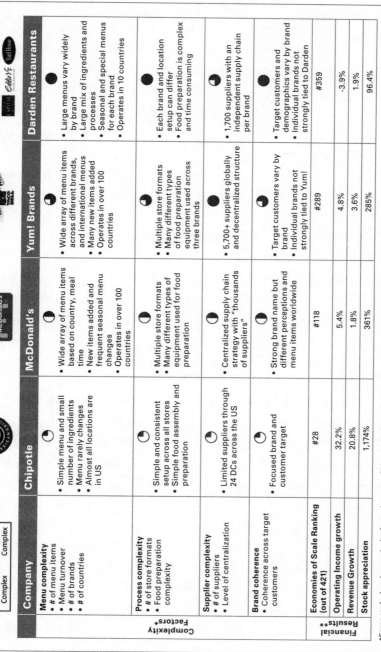

		Company	Chipotle	McDonald's	Yum! Brands	Darden Restaurants
Complexity Factors*		**Menu complexity** • # of menu items • Menu turnover • # of brands • # of countries	• Simple menu and small number of ingredients • Menu rarely changes • Almost all locations are in US	• Wide array of menu items based on country, meal time • New items added and frequent seasonal menu changes • Operates in over 100 countries	• Wide array of menu items across different brands, and international menus • Many new items added • Operates in over 100 countries	• Large menus vary widely by brand • Large mix of ingredients and processes • Seasonal and special menus for each brand • Operates in 10 countries
		Process complexity • # of store formats • Food preparation complexity	• Simple and consistent setup across all stores • Simple food assembly and preparation	• Multiple store formats • Many different types of equipment used for food preparation	• Multiple store formats • Many different types of food preparation equipment used across three brands	• Each brand and location setup can differ • Food preparation is complex and time consuming
		Supplier complexity • # of suppliers • Level of centralization	• Limited suppliers through 24 DCs across the US	• Centralized supply chain strategy with "thousands of suppliers"	• 5,700+ suppliers globally and decentralized structure	• 1,700 suppliers with an independent supply chain per brand
		Brand coherence • Coherence across target customers	• Focused brand and customer target	• Strong brand name but different perceptions and menu items worldwide	• Target customers vary by brand • Individual brands not strongly tied to Yum!	• Target customers and demographics vary by brand • Individual brands not strongly tied to Darden
Financial Results**		**Economies of Scale Ranking** (out of 421)	#28	#118	#289	#359
		Operating Income growth	32.2%	5.4%	4.8%	-3.9%
		Revenue Growth	20.8%	1.8%	3.6%	1.9%
		Stock appreciation	1,174%	361%	285%	96.4%

Less Complex → More Complex

*Force ranked each complexity factor between Chipotle, McDonald's, Yum!, and Darden based on WP&C qualitative and quantitative analysis.

**From 2005–2015 except for Chipotle 2006–2016

FIGURE 3.4: Scale in the Quick-Serve Restaurant Industry

Source: WP&C analysis

"It's gotten to the point where the operation has kind of broken down and that's all a symptom of the complication of the menu," said Richard Adams, a San Diego–based restaurant franchisee consultant and former McDonald's store owner. "They can't make the food fast enough."[6]

In fact, a vast menu may not be the top priority in fast food, according to research from *Nation's Restaurant News* and consultant WD Partners. In the study, menu variety ranked *below* food quality, cleanliness, value, and service in terms of important attributes. This is borne out in the experience—and growth—of Chipotle Mexican Grill Inc., which has a very limited menu and saw its revenue grow by 9.6 percent in 2015.[7]

"Part of the reason why Chipotle works so well is that it's simple," said Peter Saleh, a New York–based analyst at Telsey Advisory Group.[8] "If they added four more items, it would screw up the entire process."

Less a Growth Than a Complexity Issue

Another striking factor from our research is that lack of scale is usually not a growth problem. In fact, in our analysis we have found that *the companies whose economies of scale were deteriorating the quickest actually had the highest revenue growth!* In the S&P data used, the bottom 20 percent of companies (those with the greatest diseconomies of scale trend) were the ones with the highest CAGR. What is going on here? No doubt every case is different. But to frame it in the context of our experience, what we've seen is that in the pursuit of top-line growth, many companies create more complexity and undermine the economic basis that launched these growth strategies in the first place.

To frame in the context of the rest of the book, these companies are falling prey to the Siren Song, pursuing growth strategies that actually erode profitability and ultimately erode the potential for sustainable growth.

Thomas Kuhn, an American physicist who wrote extensively about science, was of the mind that scientific thought did not progress in a linear fashion. Instead, he asserted, it went through periods of revolutionary transformation, or *paradigm shifts*, which were then followed by periods of "normal science" when scientists returned to work within that paradigm.

We all use mental models and rules of thumb to simplify our lives and remain effective. But Kuhn's observation suggests a trap. These models work only within a period of normal science. But during a period of *shift*, these models can lead you astray and need updating.

Unfortunately, many companies are constructing growth strategies for the Age of Complexity with outmoded mental models. The result is they fall victim to the Sirens of Growth and their alluring Siren Song. We will show how to resist the Siren Song and chart a course for growth in Part II.

 **CALL TO ACTION**

Diagnose the Complexity in Your Business

Opportunity:
Complexity can be the single biggest determinant of your cost competitiveness and a drag on resources and growth. Efforts to drive growth are undermined by high levels of non-value-add complexity that currently exist in many companies. Therefore, it is important to diagnose and attack this complexity to ensure that your top-line initiatives are successful and yield bottom-line impact.

Key questions for discussion:
- Do you have too much complexity in your business? Is it limiting your ability to grow?
- Are you growing revenue faster than complexity, or the other way around?
- Where do you have the biggest issues with complexity? Is it product complexity, process complexity, or organizational complexity?
- How is complexity impacting your ability to serve customers or to react to changes in the market?
- What are the biggest barriers to reducing complexity in your business?
- But what would it mean to your ability to grow if you could reduce your level of complexity?

Areas to investigate:

- Plot the sources of complexity in your business; identifying the impacts of that complexity on your process, organizational, and business performance.
- Quantify the true profitability of your products and services, accounting for complexity costs.[1]
- Understand your customers' true key buying factors and your alignment to those relative to competitors.
- Assess your true scale (revenue/complexity) versus your competitors.

PART II

Charting a Course for Growth

CHAPTER 4

The Sirens of Growth

"To the Sirens first shalt thou come, who bewitch all men, whosoever shall come to them. . . . Whoso draws nigh them unwittingly and hears the sound of the Sirens' voice, never doth he see wife or babes stand by him on his return . . . but the Sirens enchant him with their clear song, sitting in the meadow, and all about is a great heap of bones of men."

—HOMER, *THE ODYSSEY*[1]

As a quick refresher on Greek mythology, the Sirens were the enchanting yet dangerous creatures that seduced sailors with beautiful songs, luring them to their deaths as they crashed on rocky shores. In business, we see a similar dynamic: certain growth strategies come to the fore and lure business leaders onto treacherous paths. These strategies seem attractive at the outset, only to lead to destructive outcomes.

As you read the following pages, consider to what degree these Sirens are at the core of your growth strategy, and to what degree they may they be leading you astray. The next chapter discusses ways to resist the Sirens.

Siren #1: The Expanding Portfolio

Customers like variety, so the broader the portfolio the better. That is the mindset behind this Siren. In a world where customers seek choice, companies are responding by offering more options: different sizes, colors, service packages, and so on. Line extensions, for example, offer predictable incremental revenue because customers are already familiar with the earlier version of the product.

For many, proliferation and ever-expanding portfolios have become a business norm. Retailers press consumer packaged goods manufacturers for distinctive packaging, sizing, and branding to create "difference" against competitors. Consumer goods companies deliver an incremental new product (different flavor, packaging, platform, and so on) to try to drive top-line results.

This is a powerful Siren, with a rational underpinning: the more you segment demand, the more specifically you can match differing customer tastes, and thus the more you'll spur growth.

It sounds reasonable, but is it true? Research suggests that for most situations the answer is no. Rather, it is true up to a *complexity threshold*, the point beyond which product variety actually impairs sales performance. For example, in a study entitled "Too Much of a Good Thing," researchers looked at three years of data from 108 distribution centers of a major soft drink bottler to understand the impact of product variety on sales. The authors looked at the positive and negative impacts of variety and the relationship to sales rates. They conclude: "Product variety initially leads to increases in sales, as increased product variety appeals to variety-seeking consumers. However, the increases in sales are at a diminishing rate due to cannibalization as variety increases."[2]

Once variety reaches a certain optimal level, the negative impacts on fill rates and operations, as well as inherent product cannibalization, outweigh the positive benefits. *"Thus, an increase in product variety actually reduces sales performance beyond this optimal level"* [emphasis ours].

Fifty years ago, most organizations had far smaller portfolios, and were therefore a safe distance from this complexity threshold. During that era, the benefits of expanding the portfolio outweighed the costs. But unfortunately many companies today are well beyond this point (Figure 4.1).

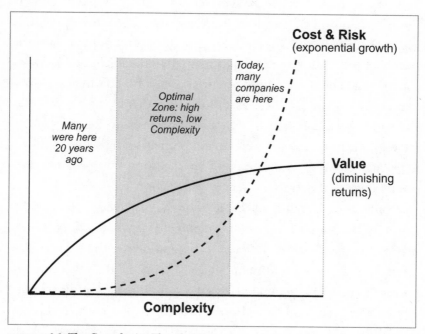

FIGURE 4.1: The Complexity Threshold

There are other organizational impacts to consider as well. Consider a VP of sales contending with hundreds of segments and 200,000 products. Strong product knowledge? Not a chance! An easy buying process for your customers? Very unlikely. Good salespeople will pare down what they pitch to a more manageable breadth. But when every salesperson does this—sampling a different subset of the portfolio—the result is that you carry all the cost of the variety but get none of the benefits. (We call this the *buffet effect*, similar to how you sample certain dishes in the buffet line.) It also effectively delegates portfolio strategy down to the sales force. Thus, proliferating portfolios often take hold in the absence of well-defined customer or product-level strategy.

In our work with industrial companies, it is striking how similar their stories are: a company built around a single engineering innovation that yielded decades of solid growth by responding to specific customer requests, also creating a nice barrier to entry against newcomers who could not compete across such a broad range of items. Then came a moment of crises: falling sales, increasing costs. What changed? Well, being all things to all people is no longer a viable strategy. Customers now have greater choice and greater visibility to pricing, creating a very different buying mindset: *What does this company do uniquely well? That is what I'll pay for.*

Proliferation is a difficult habit to break, for a very good reason: it worked in the past. *One-stop shopping! Everything the customer needs!* Companies that allowed proliferation in their portfolios often accrued some additional sales. That fed into sales targets, bonus plans, and a general sense of accomplishment. But what is less visible is the cannibalization of existing sales and the introduction of the additional costs of complexity. The bias is toward what companies can easily see and measure, so they happily keep on proliferating, cannibalizing existing sales, and increasing their costs. But that way madness lies!

Rubbermaid, the well-known maker of many kitchen items, befell such a fate after a spate of proliferation led to its stumbling and eventual purchase by Newell in late 1998. It was a fall from grace described by *Fortune* as the turning of a "purebred into a howling mutt almost overnight."[3] In fact, rapid portfolio expansion was central to Rubbermaid's strategy: "Our objective is to bury competitors with such a profusion of products that they can't copy us," said then-CEO Wolfgang Schmitt.[4] Unfortunately, it wasn't just the competitors who were buried! As its product line grew to 5,000 SKUs, Rubbermaid's ability to meet customer expectations deteriorated. "They've been such lousy shippers. Not on time, terrible fill rates, and their products cost too much," reported one retailer.[5] Couple this poor performance with additional growth initiatives, ambitious overseas expansion projects, and a severe spike in raw material costs, and the result was the decline of a company that had enjoyed a sterling reputation for almost 80 years.

As Rubbermaid learned, the Siren of the Expanding Portfolio can lead to near-annihilation. Fortunately, such tales of complete disaster are thankfully rare, but the impacts of this Siren are nonetheless crippling to growth, with the resulting complexity impairing critical service levels, confusing customers, and dissipating limited growth resources across an unfocused portfolio.

At what point does *more* become *less*? To what degree are the often hidden impacts of unrestrained portfolio expansion undermining expected benefits and more broadly your growth objectives? In today's increasingly crowded marketplace, how does a strategy of continuously expanding the portfolio of products and services support the goals of differentiation and market leadership?

What Makes Us Susceptible to the Expanding Portfolio Siren?

Contributing mindsets:

- *More is better than less.*
- *Whatever the customer asks for.*
- *Let's see what sticks.*

Contributing conditions:

- Heavy focus on contribution margin—incorrectly assumes that an expanding portfolio has no impact on selling, general, and administrative expenses (SG&A)*
- Revenue rather than profits as basis for sales force compensation
- Lack of strategic focus and customer segmentation
- Siloed organizational structure

Siren #2: The Greener Pasture

How many of us, glancing through the *Wall Street Journal* in the morning, have momentarily wished that we were operating in a different industry—one in which the profits are richer, the growth curve is steeper, or where the competition is (we believe) less fierce than in our own? Or conversely, when business is good, who resists the temptation to consider a neighboring market with a sense of invincibility? We think, *We are doing well here; we can do well over there!*

In both cases, the temptation is to move outside our core markets. Indeed, what better way to drive additional growth and top-line sales than by leveraging current capabilities across a new market, a new product segment, or identifying and capturing an adjacency opportunity? As market competition at home intensifies, new markets appear to be "blue ocean" opportunities—areas that are less crowded with players and therefore offer a better chance for market leadership. Going outside a core market may also represent

---

* Our view is that tactical decisions should be made with a contribution margin focus, and strategic decisions with an operating profit focus. Portfolio decisions are strategic in nature.

the logical expansion of a territory: if you have the leading position at home, why not easily capture new areas abroad?

Unfortunately, great success in one arena is rarely a guarantee of success elsewhere. Only one athlete has been an All-Star in two major American sports.[6] The stacked odds do little to discourage companies, however, particularly when the issue is corporate growth. When faced with a static market, it is often necessary to look outside. Given the challenges frequently experienced on home turf, companies are tempted to think that a new arena will be friendlier.

Thus, the second Siren is the Greener Pasture: the temptation to stray away from core markets and segments into new areas that appear to be more easily or just as winnable—yet ultimately yield dilution and complexity. There is no shortage of businesses that with lots of energy reached beyond their current market only to retrench years later. Best Buy launched in the United Kingdom only to retreat. U.K. grocer Tesco, going the other direction, fared no better with its U.S. venture.

Another case in point: banana producer Chiquita took on a lot of complexity as it looked to new markets. In fact, over a period of 10 years, it lived through a cycle of expansion into new markets, followed by quick retrenchment to the core businesses in the face of poor results.

Under the leadership of CEO Fernando Aguirre, Chiquita expanded its business aggressively into new ventures, including fruit chips, fruit smoothies in Europe, and additional business lines. At the core of this decision was a "grass is greener" moment: looking over at the world of consumer packaged goods and seeing a business better insulated against the commodity cycle. But this diversification strategy, beginning in 2004, required significant R&D, infrastructure, and consumer marketing investment, which diverted funds from the core business, reducing core competitiveness. It also, according to Chiquita, resulted in the business ignoring the private-label salad business and other opportunities in the core.[7] In sum, its diversification strategy, born of a desire to seek out some defense against the commodity cycle of bananas, instead yielded complexity and impaired financial results. Revenues slipped from $3.4 billion in 2009 to $3.0 billion in 2012. Earnings fell from $219 million to just $70 million (Figure 4.2).

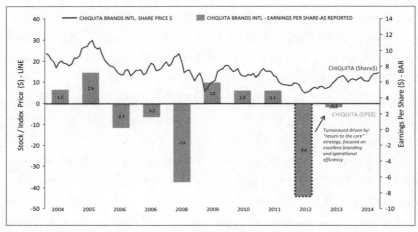

FIGURE 4.2: Chiquita Share Price and EPS Performance, 2004–2014

Source: Stock and Index Prices and EPS AS REPORTED: Datastream (provided by Thomson Reuters), as at 24 November 2014; EPS figures are absolute figures for the period in which the date falls i.e. EPS at 1 May 2013 = Full Year 2013 EPS

In 2012, Chiquita's directors decided to replace Aguirre "due to dissatisfaction over the company's lengthy earnings decline."[8] Aguirre's successor, Ed Lonergan, formerly with Gillette and Diversey, was brought in to reverse the decline and restore focus on the company's core business, bananas and salads.[9] The company has since exited noncore businesses, including grapes and pineapples, and returned the cost structure to a more sustainable level (targeting SG&A, marketing, and value chain costs) as part of a strategic transformation to focus on core business profit growth.

What happened to Chiquita illustrates why this Siren is so seductive. Executives may overestimate the potential market opportunity or underestimate competitive response to a new entry. Frequently, companies do not foresee how new ventures will impact the existing business with the onslaught of increased complexity. But perhaps the most common reason is a lack of understanding or information as to whether the company has the right skills, structures, and assets to win in the new market—or what has made the company successful in its core market in the first place.

In Chapter 1, we introduced the example of Ames Department Stores, which in the 1970s was a competitor to Walmart, but launched a series of acquisitions, new ventures, and deviation from its formerly successful formula serving rural markets. The result: the company eventually fell into bankruptcy, while Walmart went on to successfully and persistently execute its rural strategy.[10]

One could say that while Ames (in the 1970s) had to work hard to overreach, the task nowadays is mind-bogglingly easy. Capital is cheap, enabling the pursuit of acquisitions. The globalization of markets leads us to focus more on the similarities than differences in overseas markets, encouraging geographic expansion. And convergence is leading many organizations to question the boundaries of their industry. So expanding beyond the core is increasingly feasible—and enticing.

What Makes Us Susceptible to the Greener Pasture Siren?

Contributing mindsets:

- *We won at home; we will do great over there, too.*
- *This is a natural growth adjacency for us.*
- *Competition is less tough elsewhere.*

Contributing conditions:

- Top-line focus
- Pursuing M&A for market diversification
- Unclear strategy; fuzzy definition of "where we play" and "how we play"
- Global ambitions

Optimism Bias

A major factor that makes the Siren call of Greener Pastures so powerful is the existence of human cognitive biases. Chief among these is what neuroscientist and author Tali Sharot calls the optimism bias. She concludes that while we think of ourselves as rational creatures, "both neuroscience and social science suggest that we are more optimistic than realistic." People overestimate the chances of success and the potential for failure, she says. We grow more pessimistic in collective terms as a public, but retain private optimism about our future. However, without optimism, she concludes, "our ancestors might never have ventured far from their tribes and we might all be cave dwellers, still huddled together and dreaming of light and heat."[11]

So optimism serves a purpose. In business terms, it gives us the strength to take risks and be bold. But it creates the tendency for us to overweight the positive outcome, and as a result make poor assumptions. We assume that competitors in the new market will be off their game or react slowly to a new entrant; that our current processes and systems are sufficient to compete effectively; that the new arena of competition will be richer and more profitable than our current domain.

Siren #3: The Smash Hit

"I don't think this (failure) is an option. We really have to deliver the product that they expect."

—**BLACKBERRY CEO THORSTEN HEINS AT LAUNCH OF THE BLACKBERRY 10 MOBILE OS**[12]

"The assumption we work to is that every week [that a new phone is in the market], we lose one percent of price."

—**SAMSUNG ELECTRONICS CEO DR. OH-HYUN KWON**[13]

A smash hit, a blockbuster, a knockout! Magic words to any company, whether you happen to be developing new drugs or producing summer movies. But while everyone welcomes the notion of outsized success in response to its offerings, it is dangerous to build a business strategy around winning the lottery.

But some do. Perhaps worse, some find themselves in a position where only a blockbuster will suffice. Discussing the recall of Merck's painkiller drug Vioxx, following the emergence of data that indicated it elevated the risk of heart attack and stroke, Jim Collins said, "My point is not to argue that Merck's leaders were villains seeking profits at the expense of patient lives or, conversely, that they were heroes who courageously removed a hugely profitable product without anyone requiring that they do so. Nor is my point that Merck made a mistake by pursuing a blockbuster. . . . My point, rather, is that Merck committed itself to attaining such huge growth that Vioxx *had* to be a blockbuster."[14]

The problem is clear. In a world where sustainable differentiation is increasingly rare, most companies are operating in a "horse race" where advantage goes to the company that can stay a nose-length ahead. If you frame success around your ability to land a Smash Hit, and if you corral your activities to improve your odds of doing so, *you may neglect other more core activities—the very processes and assets critical for repeatedly finding differentiation.*

Those who bet the farm on a singular smash hit frequently find themselves exposed to rapid commoditization (while they fish for a big hit), disconnected from customers (as an ivory tower mentality takes over), and flat-footed (while other competitors embrace the drumbeat of commoditization and focus on improving their speed to market). It can also lead to an almost indiscriminate lack of focus—*roll the dice in hopes of one success*—conjuring up the Siren of the Expanding Portfolio.

Many fashion retailers, particularly those dubbed "fast fashion" who rapidly bring new designs to stores, have long recognized the futility of chasing a Smash Hit. What matters today is speed to market, the ability to win customer preference, and the capabilities to repeat this time after time. But even in fashion, where the pace has been relentless, the pace is accelerating. The norm used to be that retailers worked to a two-season calendar. Now the focus is on rapid customer feedback and the ability to react to it almost instantaneously. Global retailer Inditex, with many brands including Zara, develops 12,000 different designs each year, 80 percent of which are produced in response to data collected in-store, and none of it driven by a seasonal basis; rather, designs are produced 12 months of the year.[15]

Accelerating life cycles are not the sole domain of this one industry. The pace of commoditization is increasing across myriad industries, due to many macro forces, such as increased consumer power and the growth in online commerce, new competition in the form of nontraditional market entrants, and the "flat world" effects of globalization. In the past, one big hit could secure a nice annuity. In 1978, Sony introduced its first Walkman, a portable audiocassette player, which gained popularity and widespread use through the 1980s and 1990s, only facing technological obsolescence with competition from CDs (still long before the iPod).[16] Today, a 20-year run would be unfathomable, as reflected in Dr. Kwon's assumption (at Samsung Electronics) that "every week . . . we lose one percent of price."

One could argue that today, many more companies need to learn from fast fashion and embrace the notion of the "horse race" marketplace. Very few of us have fully acknowledged the leap in skills, mindsets, and structures required to compete in faster life cycle environments. The Smash Hit still holds great allure; but its ability to provide sustaining advantage has been diminished, requiring a shift to a different way of operating.

What Makes Us Susceptible to the Smash Hit Siren?

Contributing mindsets:

- *A single thing will determine our success; let's roll the dice.*
- *Bet the farm; this has to succeed.*
- *If we can just find a differentiated product.*

Contributing conditions:

- Business legacy, launched around a successful product
- Internal focus—lack of focus on customers
- Lack of strategic clarity
- External pressures, creating go-for-broke mentality

The Many Guises of the Smash Hit

The seductive notion of a panacea extends beyond new product launches. Anytime growth is tagged to a singular new thing, beware. Offshore manufacturing! A new technology platform! Assess any new initiative in terms of how it will improve your operating model, and the tangible ways it will benefit your customers, which is the ultimate acid test.

Siren #4. The Castle Walls

The Middle Ages was a period of warfare-driven innovation. For every fortification enhancement designed to keep the castle impenetrable, invaders were thinking up new ways of breaching it or laying siege. By the thirteenth and fourteenth centuries, the stone castle had become a feature of the European landscape, with its accumulated innovations: the drawbridge and moat, the battlements, towers, and most notably, high and thick stone walls. This was the "Age of Castles."[17] But by the early fifteenth century, changes were afoot in military strategy and the norm shifted to construction of lower walls.

To understand why, it is helpful to understand why walls moved higher in the first place. It was partly the advent of the trebuchet—a type of catapult—and the frequent use of tunneling to destroy castle foundations that led to higher and thicker castle walls in the thirteenth and fourteenth centuries. But once another innovation appeared—the cannon—the walls no longer offered a defense. Niccolo Machiavelli wrote, "There is no wall, whatever its thickness that artillery will not destroy in only a few days."[18] Moreover, high walls imposed vulnerability, as the big walls made generous targets. Frequently, attackers would attack the base of the walls, causing them to collapse on themselves. In addition, given that high walls were generally thinner at the top, there was no place to mount a cannon, and artillery mounted high was less effective than artillery placed at a lower level. *So it was not just that the high castle walls were no longer a good defense against the new technology; the high walls were also a barrier to using that technology offensively.*

The analogy extends to companies today. "The list of once-storied organizations that are either gone or are no longer relevant is a long one," says Rita Gunther McGrath in *The End of Competitive Advantage.* "Their downfall is a predictable outcome of practices that are designed around the concept of sustainable competitive advantage.

The fundamental problem is that deeply ingrained structures and systems designed to extract maximum value from a competitive advantage become a liability when the environment requires instead the capacity to surf through waves of short-lived opportunities."

The dynamic of *creative destruction* is not new, but the challenge in the Age of Complexity is that the pace of it is accelerating dramatically. According to a recent BCG study, businesses are moving through their life cycles twice as quickly as they did 30 years ago.[19] Moreover, this trend was observed across sectors, and neither scale nor experience provided protection. If companies *ambled* toward reinventing themselves in the past (including deconstructing what were formerly sources of advantage), they'd better be *sprinting* today. Even at the best of times, this is an uncomfortable process if you are in the middle of it: How many BU heads will ask for *less* funding for next year because they see diminished market prospects?

Hence, the power of this Siren is rooted in a powerful dynamic: human behavior. "A preference for equilibrium and stability means that many shifts in the marketplace are met by business leaders denying these shifts mean anything negative for them," says McGrath. True, it may be unfair (or at least too easy) to point to these scenarios in hindsight. But the question remains: Who of us is not operating in an industry that is vulnerable to disruption? And how are we each ensuring that normal behavioral tendencies—Optimism bias! Preference for equilibrium!—don't leave us flat-footed. This includes management consulting! In his *Harvard Business Review* article "Consulting on the Edge of Disruption," Clayton Christensen and his coauthors describe how "the consultants we spoke with who rejected the notion of disruption in their industry . . . pointed to the purported impermeability of their brands and reputations. They claimed that too many things could never be commoditized in consulting." And he went on: "We are familiar with these objections—and not at all swayed by them. If our long study of disruption has led us to any universal conclusion, it is that every industry will eventually face it."[20]

What Killed the Monitor Group?

In November 2012, the consulting firm The Monitor Group filed for bankruptcy protection, and was eventually sold to Deloitte. It was a difficult ending for a firm co-founded by the prominent business strategist Michael Porter. What triggered the demise? There were many contributing factors, with insiders citing a complex and costly management structure, a lack of focus, its small size, or the recession. Others point to a more basic tenet: customers were no longer buying what they were selling.

Monitor was formed to monetize the academic platform established by Porter, and in particular the notion that some companies and industries were able to extract "excess profits" due to barriers of entry and competition. Sustainable competitive advantage! The key, the thinking went, was to ensure that you protected these structural barriers. It was then, and is today, an enticing notion both to strategy consultants, who relish this sort of academic challenge, and to CEOs, many of whom were happy to pay large consulting fees in exchange for a shot at extending structural barriers.

But what if this is just a manifestation of Castle Walls? As Forbes contributor Steve Denning wrote in his column: "Why go through the hassle of actually designing and making better products and services, and offering steadily more value to customers and society, when the firm could simply position its business so that structural barriers ensured endless above-average profits?"[21]

What Makes Us Susceptible to the Castle Walls Siren?

Contributing mindsets:

- *We like where we are, it has served us well.*
- *Declining margins are a short-term blip.*
- *Customers want quality, not a low-priced knockoff.*

Contributing conditions:

- Strategic focus on sustaining barriers to entry in your market
- Lack of experimentation and customer focus
- Tolerance for margin erosion

The Need for a New Mental Model

The Sirens are archetypes, the four most common growth traps we see companies succumbing to. In a complex world, we must rely increasingly on mental models and rules of thumb to help us execute against our strategies and wade through a sea of data. We already operate with such rules of thumb, but unfortunately many are out of date, and are rooted in a simpler world: *all revenue is good revenue; more is better than less,* and so on. So an updating of these rules is necessary: we need a different frame of reference, and a new mindset, for a more complex world. Absent this, we fall prey to the Siren Song.

CHAPTER 5

Resisting the Siren Song

"If I beseech and bid you to set me free, then do ye straiten me with yet more bonds."

—HOMER, *THE ODYSSEY*[1]

Odysseus's response to the Siren Song was simple but effective. He anticipated the temptation and made preparations. He commanded that all his crew plug their ears with beeswax to deafen them to the song. At the same time, he had them tie him to the mast—no matter what, he ordered, leave him there until they were safely out of earshot. His strategy saved him.

Resisting the distractions and temptations of modern day Siren Songs requires a similar approach. It requires awareness: recognizing the Sirens as described in the previous chapter is the critical first step, and it requires the right mindset and disciplines to navigate successfully. These we describe in Parts III and IV of the book, respectively.

Before we get to those, however, we want to illustrate how these mindsets and capabilities come together in support of growth strategies that yield not just growth but also profitability. *What does good look like? How have other companies adapted to growth in the age of complexity?*

In other words, *What does it look like to navigate safely around the Sirens, earplugs and all?*

Resisting Siren #1: Smart Variety
(vs. the Expanding Portfolio)

There is an underlying assumption that we frequently come face-to-face with that says, *Complexity is a natural by-product of growth.* While complexity does creep in over time, this assumption is dangerous. It essentially gives free reign to the notion of throwing a lot of things at the wall to see what sticks, on the premise that the cleanup will come later. But in fact, the clean-up rarely happens.

So what's the alternative? In a world where customers demand plentiful options, but companies cannot support infinite choice, *Smart Variety* is the way through, a term we define as "active portfolio management that integrates an understanding of requisite variety (as defined by customers), and the ensuing complexity (and cost)." Essentially, the right customer offer anchors on an understanding of:

- Customer perceived value (the right range of breadth and depth)
- True costs (not just fully burdened or allocated costs, but an understanding of how different variety levels incur different systemic costs, or complexity costs)
- An organization's own complexity threshold (the point beyond which variety destroys value, a point that varies with organizational size and capabilities)

Of course, each of these points represents a significant amount of understanding—and work to achieve that understanding. For example, "customer perceived value" requires an understanding of markets, competition, customer preferences, and segmentation. But given that it's usually better to have an 80 percent answer across different facets of understanding than a 100 percent perspective on just one dimension (and nothing elsewhere), you'd be surprised by how much you can achieve with reasonably available information to get to at least a very directionally informative answer. For example, consider the following list of factors. Anchoring your portfolio around a set of products and services that met this criteria would be a big step forward for many organizations:

- **Strategy.** The portfolio lines up with the company's overall value proposition and areas of strategic focus.
- **Customer coverage.** We are providing requisite breadth and depth in our portfolio to satisfy our core customer segments.
- **Operations and process.** We understand how our portfolio range, and different types of products, impact our operations and process performance. We take into account products that drive disproportionate levels of operational issues when assessing the portfolio.
- **Profitability.** Our products and services are profitable, *once you fully account for complexity costs.*
- **Breakpoints.** We understand how different size portfolios trigger the need for fixed-cost investments (e.g., a new warehouse to store inventory), and we take into account these cost breakpoints when sizing the portfolio.
- **Benefits.** In situations where we are reshaping the portfolio, we are very clear up front around the nature of benefits that we are trying to achieve: fixed cost release, working capital improvements, service level improvements, and so on. Being clear on this will shape how we approach the effort, and keep us focused on the end objective.

Such views at the very least can deliver a motivating snapshot. For example, a global coatings company recognized that it was proliferating its product lines. A quick study revealed that its competitors (for a comparable market coverage) carried approximately half the number of products but had twice the revenues, *which yielded the competitor a 4x scale advantage* (remember that real scale equals revenue divided by complexity).

Such numbers can be a wake-up call for organizations. But despite the compelling need, Smart Variety is difficult to achieve precisely because it requires an integrated view on a sustained basis, yet most organizations tend to struggle with holistic initiatives that require integration across different parts of the business. It can be overwhelming to consider.

Given this challenge, therefore, we find it easier to define the three steps for building out this capability: (1) moving from "bad" to "good" complexity through portfolio optimization, (2) maintaining Smart Variety as you grow, and (3) designing it in as part of your strategy. Think of these as the core building blocks. Master these, and you'll be a long way toward Smart Variety. Here's more detail on all three.

Step 1: Getting to Smart Variety
Through Portfolio Optimization

Portfolio optimization is a powerful means for transforming your business, and can significantly increase your profitability, service levels, and growth prospects. For many companies, it is a first step to spurring growth by returning to what made them great in the first place: the core. Yet too often it becomes downgraded to a tail-cutting exercise, consuming organizational capacity, disrupting customers, and at the end of the day leaving you no better off.

We discuss the approach for portfolio optimization in more detail in Chapter 13, "Reignite Your Core Brands." But for the executive who is considering this strategy as a means to battle back against proliferation, there is a key principle to keep in mind: this is about right-sizing your portfolio after a long period of complexity accumulating in your business. If that is truly your situation, then *you won't drive benefit by cutting 5 percent, 10 percent, or even 15 percent of your product portfolio; you will need to go deeper.*

At the same time, bear in mind that nearly all corporate dynamics are biased toward keeping vs. cutting products. So, absent the right target setting, the prevailing emphasis will be on justifying why we should cut this product. A more productive framework would be to say, *Why would we keep it?* The idea of target-setting is simple: it poses a challenge, based on our understanding of the markets, customers, and our own business, such as: *Is there any reason we can't serve our customers with half the range?* (Many times you may find competitors doing just that!)

Step 2: Maintaining Smart Variety as You Grow

Given that complexity creeps in over time like weeds, it is perhaps not too surprising that part of Smart Variety is some form of pruning and weeding to keep the rest of the garden healthy, and to make room for new growth.

Many organizations conduct an annual portfolio review to help rebalance the portfolio, and ensure that the offering is optimized for the current marketplace. It is necessary tidying up as products commoditize or new products fail to live up to expectations. Skip this step and you will rapidly find yourself burdened by complexity and in need of major rationalization efforts (as described in Step 1).

Two key factors are critical for maintenance: The first is an understanding of your complexity threshold, the point beyond which complexity will overwhelm your organization. Blue Bell Creameries, the producer of the nation's third best-selling ice cream, knows that it is critical to limit the number of flavors it carries at any one time to 25 to 30. Blue Bell knows that above that number its manufacturing and distribution processes start to bog down, and many of its competitive advantages begin to melt. "Our space in the stores dictates how many flavors we can carry," said CEO Paul Kruse. "You start with the big sellers, and then we'll rotate a number of flavors in for 3 to 6 months."[2]

Having this baseline enables you to establish some simple mechanisms which can help with maintenance, such as "one-in-one-out" rules that mandate the elimination of an existing product before the introduction of a new one.

The second key factor is a simple but effective process for periodically reviewing the portfolio. The goal here is less a massive reshaping of the portfolio, as with Step 1, but a health check that the current portfolio is on target and aligned with strategy. Figure 5.1 highlights an example process used for an annual portfolio review.

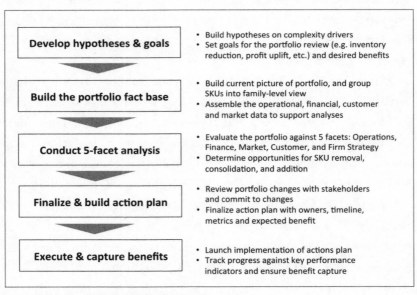

FIGURE 5.1: Example Portfolio Review Process

What matters is that there *actually is* a process! The portfolio management process can be a very analytical and detailed process, incorporating inputs from a wide spectrum of sources. But even absent that level of detail, a company can generate great insights via a series of whiteboard sessions, pulling in key perspectives from market proxies such as marketing and sales. There may be some testing to go and do as a result (to validate assumptions and hypotheses). But what's critical is establishing a platform from which to assess the portfolio, how the market is changing, and how your product development efforts line up (or not) against these emerging trends.

Step 3: "Designing in" Smart Variety

The road to hell is paved with good intentions. This is an apt description for how many portfolios become bloated and out of control. By responding to individual customer requests, or responding to new market opportunities (good intentions), a company can over time find itself burdened with high costs and poor service levels (hell for your customers and your team).

Paramount therefore is the need to design your portfolio, recognizing the sometimes competing needs for economies of scale (and cost effectiveness) and customer responsiveness (and changing customer tastes). But it is often a false choice between the two.

Strategies such as localization offer you the opportunity to scale efficiently, while remaining responsive to customer tastes. McDonald's, with 35,000 restaurants in 120 countries, offers a core menu—items such as the Big Mac and Egg McMuffin—but then tailors elements to suit local tastes: if you fancy a Samurai Pork Burger, go to Thailand; for Spam and Eggs, Hawaii; and the Dutch are fond of their McKrokets. The company can continue to evolve new items in different markets in response to changing customer tastes, as part of a disciplined strategy to localize (within controlled narrow parameters) what is essentially a standard offering. Imagine the chaos if every McDonald's manager could choose his or her own menu!

McDonalds uses a strategy of "localization with scale" to remain simultaneously cost-competitive *and* customer-responsive. That requires the right operating model. As we discuss in later chapters, many operating models have changed little in the last 15 or 20 years, and therefore struggle to support localization and consistent customer experiences. Indeed, one could make the argument that the most notable element of McDonald's is less the Big Mac than the fact that you have a consistent experience anywhere in the world.

Resisting Siren #2: The Winnable New Market (vs. The Greener Pasture)

Companies seek new markets beyond their core business—and opportunities for expansion are plentiful—yet many adjacency expansions end badly. So how best to avoid the Greener Pasture Siren and find new market growth opportunities which don't erode your existing advantages?

First, let's review some of the more common ways companies expand into new markets, and how, in the Age of Complexity, these approaches can backfire.

- **Product line expansion.** *We know customers like our current array of cookies, so launching new flavors will help us attract more sales.* Product and service line expansion is a common form of adjacency expansion, and can help boost or maintain category interest and keep competitors at bay. But as we've discussed elsewhere, it often leads to service issues (for example, out-of-stock issues in retail), unanticipated complexity costs, cannibalization of existing sales, and even overwhelming the customer with too many choices.
- **New customer segments.** *Our current consumers of beef jerky are young males, but we can tap into a young female population by focusing on health (protein snack) and with*

different marketing. Going after additional segments with existing products may seem to limit complexity, but any attempt to target new consumers and/or new consumer needs must consider the ability of the existing brand to stretch into new territory. Does jerky as the high-nutrition snack for women fit alongside the positioning of jerky as the favorite snack of hunters? Or is a different branding required? Attempts to stretch brands beyond the existing brand permission may ultimately lead to the dilution of identity and, with this, a decline in brand strength.

- **New channels.** This has been an area of explosive activity over the last decade. Digital channels are now core to business. But 15 years ago, few were discussing omnichannel strategy in retail (for reference, Walmart.com was founded in 2000, its first online venture). Although digitization has become a basic requirement, the process has surfaced many complications from channel expansion. In a recent survey, 80 percent of retailers said their supply chains were not ready for omnichannel.[3] Few said they were able to handle online returns, and more than half said they do not have the systems in place to provide the required visibility to inventory in each store. This form of channel expansion is notable as it has become mandatory—which means that for many the strategic questions remain unresolved. For example, 75 percent of survey respondents said that e-commerce is cannibalizing existing in-store sales. The question of how to leverage two different channels has not been addressed.

- **Geographic expansion.** Moving overseas can be a great way to boost distribution of your products and services. But as Compass Group discovered, unfettered expansion will dilute your focus and scale. Despite globalization, the differences are frequently bigger than the similarities.

Pursuing Sales Through Geographic Expansion

"When you're *just* focused on revenue growth, you say 'Yes' too often," said Jason Leek, group strategy director of Compass Group, a £17.6 billion contract foodservice and facilities management business.[4]

The company, with operations in 50 countries, today serves more than four billion meals a year in locations such as offices, factories, hospitals, and schools. Back in 1998, however, it was operating solely in the United Kingdom. Then, by 2006 it began operating in more than 100 countries, including East Timor, Eritrea, Costa Rica, and Swaziland, where there were inherent limits on its ability to achieve scale, market leadership, or a cost base to let it compete effectively. This came to a head in 2004 and 2005, when, rocked by profit warnings, it began a process of injecting greater focus and discipline, which included exiting 50 countries. The results for Compass since have been positive from a bottom-line *and* top-line perspective. (See Figure 5.2.)

- Operating profit has risen from 4.5 percent in 2006 to 7.2 percent in 2013.
- In the same period, free cash flow has improved nearly 400 percent.
- Perhaps more impressively, revenue has increased from £11 billion in 2006 (from 100 countries) to £17.6 billion in 2013 (from 50 countries).

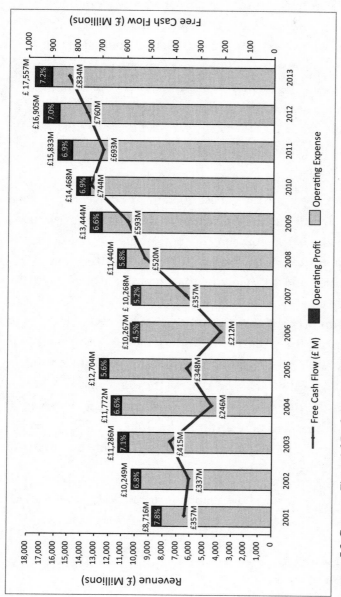

FIGURE 5.2: Compass Financial Performance 2001–2013

Note: Revenue reduction between 2005 and 2006 is because Compass Group sold its roadside and travel catering businesses for a combined £1.82 billion in April 2006. The transaction included the sale of 43 Moto motorway service areas to Australia's Macquarie Bank for an estimated £600m. Compass's Select Service Partners (SSP) travel concessions business was also sold to companies controlled by private equity firm EQT Partners, for an estimated £1.2 billion.

Source: Capital IQ, Compass Group Annual Reports 2006–2013

- **New category or business entry.** When Chiquita expanded into the new business of fruit chips and fruit smoothies, it was leveraging its brand, but the overinvestment required in this new business (consumer packaged goods) led to a critical underinvestment in its core (banana production and distribution). The further you go from your core business, the greater the risk from expansion and the more likely you are to overinvest in it (because "we need to make this work"), often leading to an abdication and underinvestment in the core business.

There are other variants of these expansion models. But each requires a thoughtful analytical vetting. Indeed, one mistake many companies make is to approach this bottom-up (reaching for the expansion opportunity knocking on their door) vs. top-down (taking a systematic and full view of the potential avenues and the suitability of each).

This is ultimately about trade-offs. It is usually not too difficult to come up with a list of options. Whether they are viable options is a different question. So given that we are all prone to the optimism bias, how do we best evaluate and assess these expansion opportunities, and ensure that we are not underestimating the incremental complexity of an adjacency? In brief, here are some key considerations (discussed in length in Chapter 14, "Avoid the Pitfalls of M&A and New Market Entry"):

- Will this expansion shore up our core business, or weaken it?
- Will this adjacency build scale in our business, or create complexity?
- Do we have the capabilities and operating model to execute on this?
- Is the "juice worth the squeeze"? Does the business case reflect the additional complexity costs?

Resisting Siren #3: Repeatable Differentiation (vs. Smash Hit)

No one likes Smash Hits more than Hollywood. But blowing a large production budget in pursuit of them is no guarantee of success. Chris Meledandri, the movie producer and CEO of Illumination Entertainment, learned this lesson the hard way. Early in his career, he oversaw the release of *Titan AE*, an animated science fiction feature that lost $100 million for Twentieth Century Fox,[5] an experience that Meledandri describes as "extremely painful" and that shaped his thinking and approach to movie-making.[6]

"I didn't like having that big financial failure," Meledandri said. "I didn't want to expose myself to those catastrophic results."

His response, according to studio veterans, was notable in the "discipline in selecting projects that can be done at a relatively modest cost—by Hollywood standards—and then providing plenty of oversight to hit that number."[7]

"There are many, many components that come from the years of the experiences that we've had," he says. "It would take a semester at a graduate school to walk through how we [make savings compared to our competitors]."

He has focused on building a broad audience for his movies with kid-friendly humor that also appeals to adults, and as a result has had his fair share of hits, all done at modest budget. The *Ice Age* series grossed $2.8 billion worldwide; *Despicable Me 2* was a billion-dollar movie and the most profitable in Universal's 100-year history.

But he is careful to ensure that no single movie he makes *has* to be a blockbuster, due to his focus on cost containment. In other words, he has orchestrated his business to repeatedly find differentiation and value in the eyes of his customers, while recognizing that it is very difficult to *guarantee* a blockbuster. The Smash Hit, when it comes, is a bonus.

So one approach to increasing the odds of success is lowering the cost of each bet. This is increasingly critical as it is becoming increasingly difficult to pick winners from the perch of an ivory tower, due to the complexity in markets. This dynamic underscores another aspect of improving your odds: experimentation. We discuss the topic at length in Chapter 10. For many organizations, it is not just a matter of embedding new processes and analytical approaches, but a whole shift in mindset.

Says Intuit co-founder and chairman Scott Cook, who has embraced experimentation into his organization: "It's natural for bosses to want to decide. Now we teach our leaders that it's your job to put in the systems that enable your people to run your experiments fast and cheap and to keep making them faster and cheaper. Yield as many of your decisions off to the experiment as possible."

For Jeff Bezos, who has embraced experiments as a means of building Amazon, the process of experimentation is the antidote to the Smash Hit: "What really matters is, companies that don't continue to experiment, companies that don't embrace failure, they eventually get in a desperate position where the only thing they can do is a Hail Mary bet at the very end of their corporate existence."[8]

Is Your Operating Model Fit for Purpose?

Companies pursue Smash Hits partly because that is how they've traditionally competed. Their processes, structures, systems, and incentives—and yes, even mindsets—have all been oriented around this objective. So even with a shift in strategy, companies can struggle unless they adapt their way of operating and their tempo.

Consumer electronics giant Samsung has built a system and culture that is based on fleeting advantage and speed. According to Samsung's chairman Lee Kun-hee: "Today, losses incurred from missed opportunities are much greater than direct losses incurred from commercial trade. . . . When we decide on something we have to do, we have to go all in to seize opportunities, or at the very least, minimize opportunity costs. If we do not bring creative products and services to market faster than others, we will not survive. This is an era when timing is critical and speed is vital."[9]

In *The Samsung Way*, the authors report that "For Samsung, speed is a strategy in and of itself." As such, the business has organized itself to support speed of decision making and speed of execution. For example, accelerated decision making on short-term and day-to-day matters is a management norm inside Samsung. Professional managers have the authority to make decisions on short-term routine matters on the spot.[10]

Also, the business has structured itself to support speedy execution. For example, Samsung "clusters" the location of activities in its value chain to improve knowledge sharing and accelerated problem solving. According to Lee Won-Shik, former EVP of Samsung Electronics: "When we were developing our 1-megabyte DRAM chip, our design director would ask the PA division every morning, 'What changes do you need?' The design team would then make the necessary changes within the day, with the PA team receiving improved mask sets three or four days later. In contrast, our competitors would take up to a week to get this process done." Other techniques used include parallel development (where different internal teams compete to develop the same product), and leapfrog R&D (where the business invests in first-, second-, and third-generation technologies simultaneously.

Resisting Siren #4. Reinvention and Reconfiguration (vs. Castle Walls)

Despite the many history lessons, many companies do whatever they can to protect a legacy source of advantage, even if the opportunities are shifting elsewhere. They hear the Siren call: *The higher the walls, the better!*

The alternative is to build a capability for reinvention—constantly reconfiguring the business in line with market changes. In Chapter 11, "Build, Dismantle, Repeat," we cover some of the cultural practices, processes, and incentives that can tip the scales in your favor. But it is worth noting that while many companies recognize the need for and engage in new innovation, most struggle with the very necessary act of creating space in the business for these innovations to take hold.

Even when people see the need to "dismantle"—to free up the human and financial resources to focus on better opportunities elsewhere—they are often waylaid by the drag of complexity. Complexity creeps in incrementally, but you need to remove it in chunks, and unwinding this complexity requires a holistic approach. For example, many companies hesitate to embrace portfolio optimization because (they argue) such moves hit the top line without impacting the cost structure; indeed, the best approach is frequently to adjust the portfolio and right-size the underlying operating model *at the same time.* We call this idea Concurrent Actions. It is at the root of the work required for Reinvention and Reconfiguration: stubbornly working the many interconnected levers that cut across the product portfolio, your processes, and your assets and structure to release resources in preparation for your next wave of growth.

In our work supporting companies with large-scale portfolio optimizations, we have witnessed firsthand the challenges of this journey. Indeed, many institutional biases undermine the best intentions for corporate renewal:

- **The "value stock" squeezes out the "growth stock."** When a legacy business has been the dominant driver of revenues for a long period of time, diverting resources to new areas of investment carries some friction. But increasingly companies need to maintain what we call "dual realities"—that is the reality of extending cash flows from a legacy business and the reality of nurturing what might completely replace it. It requires some tolerance for ambiguity, but the key is to create options—ensure your business has a mix of growth plays as well as value plays. Ensure that the former doesn't get squeezed out by the latter and recognize that each requires scrutiny around success metrics and investment profiles.[11]

- **The measurable trumps the unmeasurable.** Another bias that undermines a company's ability to transform itself is its focus on the measurable. An old story told to illustrate this observational bias goes thus: A policemen is helping a drunkard who is searching for his lost watch under a street lamp. After a few minutes the policeman stops to ask if the man if he's sure that's where he lost it. No, he replies, he thinks he lost it in the park, *but the light is better here.* This is how many organizations become complex in the first place. As companies introduce more complexity, the benefits of this are local (another sale), but the costs, such as new processes, are distributed across the organization (traditionally hard to measure,[12] hence often treated as nonexistent).

- **The parts overpower the whole.** Functional or business unit (BU) strength can sometimes undermine efforts to refocus the business in new areas and new markets. Strong functional leaders can de facto refuse to engage in such efforts, forcing an executive-level showdown. We have seen it frequently enough for it to make this list. BU leaders are looking to grow their own business. Capital allocation that happens at the BU level vs. the CEO level can lead to overinvestment in declining markets.

The antidote in all these cases is a mix of analytical insight, organizational capability, and bold leadership. From an analytical perspective, it is important to see the business accurately: where are you currently making money, where is there increasing commoditization (a warning sign), where complexity is increasing faster than top-line growth (see Chapter 12, "Know Where You *Really* Make Money"). It is also important to ensure that you have early detection systems for picking up early signs of decline and market shift (see Chapter 11, "Build, Dismantle, Repeat"). It is also critical to consider: Is your operating model fit for purpose? (See Chapter 15, "Transform Your Operating Model"). If you are uncertain, then flip this around and assess the complexity in your business. High complexity usually equals high drag, a potential source of friction for reconfiguration.

Finally, the above may get you to 80 percent of the answer. But the remaining 20 percent resides firmly with bold leadership (see Chapter 7, "Be Bold!"). In fact, in many cases it is close to impossible (or at least very expensive) to get much higher than the 80 percent threshold. Absent bold leadership, the organizational biases tend to exert themselves: the value stock mentality crowds out growth areas, the measurable defeats the unmeasurable, and organizational drift sets in.

You have now met the Sirens (see Figure 5.3). You may have even recognized one or two as being present in your growth strategy or at least lurking nearby. You now have also seen how a number of organizations come up with strategic responses to find new markets without falling victim to the Siren Song. Their stories should serve as inspiration. It's possible to find profitable growth in a complex world.

But in our conversations with business leaders, a common question remains: *What separates those that resist the Sirens—and grow profitably—from those that don't?* The answer to that question—and

#	Siren	Siren Song	Strategy
1	The Expanding Portfolio	"More is better than less." "Whatever the customer asks for." "Let's see what sticks."	**Smart Variety**
2	The Greener Pasture	"We won at home; we will do great over there, too." "This is a natural growth adjacency for us." "Competition is less tough elsewhere."	**The Winnable New Market**
3	The Smash Hit	"A single thing will determine our success." "Bet the farm; this has to succeed." "If we can just find a differentiated product."	**Repeatable Differentiation**
4	The Castle Walls	"We like where we are, it has served us well." "Declining margins are a short-term blip." "Customers want quality, not a low-priced knockoff."	**Reinvention and Reconfiguration**

FIGURE 5.3: Summary of Chapters 4 and 5

the focus of the rest of the book—lies in the mindset and capabilities of leaders and their organizations. Our message is this: you may need to adapt both to today's conditions. We put the components of the needed mindset and the critical capabilities into two separate but mutually supporting categories. The first set, pertaining to clarity of vision, degree of ambition, and boldness, we include under the Explorer's Mindset. The second set, pertaining to self-knowledge, skills, and discipline, we include under the Navigator's Skill Set. You can think of the first as the engine or sail, and the second as the rudder. If you have deficits in one or the other, or both, then the chances of falling victim to the Sirens are increased. We will introduce these critical mindsets and disciplines in the next chapter.

CHAPTER 6

Explorers and Navigators

"Fear and discomfort are an essential part of strategy making."

—ROGER L. MARTIN

With some notable exceptions, few executives would comfortably embrace the title of Explorer.*

For one, the word *exploration* still conjures up romantic notions and legendary figures from the nineteenth century and earlier, which may seem distant from today's everyday realities. Secondly, even a light dusting of these same figures reveals deeply flawed individuals who, while driven to extraordinary achievements, would not today be held up as model citizens. For example, Henry Morton Stanley, of "Dr. Livingstone, I presume" fame, was at one time associated with King Leopold II's brutal Congolese empire,[1] and considered by some to be the inspiration for Marlow, the complex protagonist in Joseph Conrad's *Heart of Darkness*.[2] Indeed, what motivated these individuals was a mixed bag, ranging from the conquistador's search for the "cities of gold" to the more enlightened thirst for knowledge personified by James Cook, who in three epic voyages discovered more of the earth's surface than any other man.[3]

---

* Messrs. Bezos, Branson, and Musk come to mind: each pursuing a space venture (Blue Origin, Virgin Galactic, and SpaceX, respectively).

These are different times today, to be sure, but if you can make the mental leap from one context to another, we think there's no better term for distilling some of the critical qualities at the heart of leadership in a complex world: *willingness to lead despite incomplete information, boldness, determined focus, and adaptability.*

Moreover, we like the term *explorer* as it conveys a certain level of natural risk—one cannot discover new lands without taking chances—thereby putting a bright light on some of the harder truths that can get obscured over time about achieving profitable growth in a large organization. It is not a straightforward process, and there are no guarantees. Rather, it requires an explorer's sense of boldness and ambition, guided by strong navigational skills, to stay off the rocks.

Lack of navigational skills is evident in many of the Sirens stories from Chapter 4. Consider the story of Rubbermaid, where the strategy was clear, as shown by CEO Schmitt's statement, "Our objective is to bury competitors with such a profusion of products that they can't copy us."[4] But what was lacking was an understanding of the impact of proliferation on service levels and cost structure.

Before the discovery of a practical means for determining longitude, successful exploration was frequently a happy accident, the result of good luck, despite great seamanship and the best charts available. The lack of a reliable means of navigation led to many shipwrecks and the loss of life in the process. In fact, when the British government passed the Longitude Act of 1714, laying out a prize for anyone who could come up with a "Practicable and Useful" method for determining longitude at sea, it was largely in response to a disaster in 1707 off the Isles of Scilly in which four homebound British warships under the command of Admiral Sir Cloudesley Shovell became lost in the fog, disoriented, and believed themselves to be off the northwest coast of France. In fact, the ships were sailing just off the Isles of Scilly on the southwest tip of England. The ships crashed and sank, killing 2,000 sailors. It was also a reflection of the current belief that whichever nation could crack the code of determining longitude would control the seas and become the dominant economic global power.[5]

Before John Harrison's clock-based method for determining longitude became commonplace, sailors used crude navigational techniques such as "dead reckoning" to assess longitude. "The captain would throw a log overboard and observe how quickly the ship receded from this temporary guidepost."[6] Not surprisingly, they frequently missed their mark, missing land entirely and spending more time at sea. More time at sea with no fresh fruit meant scurvy, a dreadful and deadly disease caused by vitamin C deficiency. Forced to navigate by latitude alone, most followed well-trafficked routes, or hugged coastlines where they could. The resulting traffic jam left ships vulnerable to piracy.

Piracy, scurvy, shipwrecks: thankfully not issues usually on a CEO's agenda! But these were considered the cost of doing business as a merchant ship in the sixteenth and seventeenth centuries, before better navigational tools changed the game, a parallel with the opportunity companies have today in building new capabilities for finding scale and profitable growth.

The Explorer's Mindset

Scurvy may be long gone, but the challenges facing leaders are no less daunting.

In an interview with the *Guardian* newspaper,[7] Unilever CEO Paul Polman said, "These are very difficult times; it's very uncertain going forward. You get currencies that go up and down 20 percent, you get markets that shift very rapidly. So you need to have people who can feel comfortable dealing with a VUCA world—volatile, uncertain, complex, and ambiguous."

Casey on VUCA

VUCA: the term resonates in corporations, but like many useful lessons for strategy, it originated in the military. It was developed as a framework by the U.S. Army War College in the early 1990s to describe what the world would be like after the Soviet Union's collapse.

In an article for *Fortune* magazine, retired General George W. Casey Jr., formerly commanding general of the multinational force in Iraq and army chief of staff, articulated his thoughts on the topic. He said, "In reality, VUCA has never been more relevant, for the military and for business. I experienced VUCA environments in Bosnia (1996), in Kosovo (2000), and in Iraq (2004-07)." He describes Iraq as the most complex environment he had ever experienced. "The reporting that I received was all over the map—Sadr had been killed! No, he was just wounded. An errant bomb had damaged the mosque! No, it was the hotel next door. The Iraqi Special Forces had arrived! No, they were still on the way."

Extrapolating to business, he said it's critical for leaders to *marshal their energies around highest impact areas*, something that goes hand in hand with clear purpose. "Leaders are human and possess only so much intellectual and emotional energy. To succeed in a VUCA world, we must expend that energy in the areas that produce the highest payoff for our organizations." In addition, he retained an "offensive mindset." He said, "I worked aggressively and opportunistically to gain an advantage. That attitude kept me from being cowed by the complexity and ambiguity of the situation."

Even putting aside the considerable uncertainties in markets, leaders face many new challenges in their day-to-day activities:

1. **Excessive demands on time and focus.** With increased complexity, even the most disciplined leaders and organizations are struggling to find sufficient time and management bandwidth to deal effectively with everything on their plate. Productivity is impaired by the multiple "mental change-overs" of multitasking required on a daily basis.

2. **An overwhelming (nonlinear) increase in data availability, coupled with an increasing need to make decisions on 80 percent (or less) of the information.** As the pace of data creation increases—for example, it is estimated that Walmart collects multiple petabytes[8] of data every hour on its customer transactions[9]—so does the responsibility to make productive use of it. But that requires new strategies and capabilities that are often lacking, creating new management challenges. Moreover, it can lead to a false supposition that all decisions can be *definitively* addressed through detailed analytics. For many strategic decisions, data can help increase the odds, but at some point represents simply hesitation. It is a great paradox that just as the amount of information increases, so does the need to make decisions with an 80 percent confidence level (or lower) as the importance for earlier decisions increases.

3. **Given the above, a greater difficulty separating out truly critical from just important.** A competitor launches a new product category; operational issues arise; a strategy colleague proposes a further expansion overseas; every week detailed reports land on your desk: *Where do you focus your time?* It is not uncommon for leaders to be inundated with information, ideas, and requests. Schedules are frequently

booked up two months in advance. Given this level of absorption by the business, it can be increasingly difficult to retain perspective, to pull up to understand what is truly critical to the business.[10]

These are new dynamics that have significantly complicated the leader's task over the last decade. As a result, some companies are losing sight of the elements that propelled them forward in the beginning: a deep focus on the customer, a compelling vision and offer, and willingness to adapt and learn.

The antidote to these challenges is the right leadership outlook that can help restore focus on serving the customer and finding a source of differentiation. In our work with clients, we have identified five key leadership components that separate those who are able to cut through complexity and find growth from those who tend to drift in its current. We've captured the Explorer's Mindset in the five statements below. Read through them and think about how true they are for your organization.

EXPLORER'S MINDSET

1. Our strategy is bold and reflects our distinctive beliefs.
2. We are ruthlessly focused on a few things.
3. Speed is built into everything we do.
4. We experiment frequently to improve the odds.
5. We easily transition in and *out of* new opportunities, products, and markets and shift around resources correspondingly.

How did you do? If you shared these with colleagues, would there be strong agreement, or would an energetic discussion ensue? What matters is not precision, but rather *frankness* in your assessment of how your organization stacks up against these statements. (A client once told us that they were a "reality-based organization," an aspiration we'd endorse.) If these statements do not describe your current organization, don't worry. In Part III of the book, you'll find ideas and resources to help you close the gap.

The Cultural Determinants of High-Growth Companies

The components of the Explorer's Mindset listed represent a distillation of our collective experience helping clients compete in a complex world. Others are reaching similar conclusions. One such is Professor Charles O' Reilly of Stanford Graduate School of Business. In an August 2014 *Journal of Organizational Behavior*, O'Reilly and his colleagues looked at the impact of culture on corporate growth. Their findings were that corporate cultures that emphasized what they referred to as "adaptability" generally produced revenue growth. According to O'Reilly and his colleagues, "adaptive" cultures are those that encourage:

- Risk-taking
- A willingness to experiment
- Innovation
- Personal initiative
- Fast decision making and execution
- Ability to spot unique opportunities

Also important are the traits they choose to minimize. O'Reilly says, "There's less emphasis on being careful, predictable, avoiding conflict, and making your numbers." He points to Amazon as an example of a long-term adaptive growth culture, characterized by frugality, decentralized decision making, and taking risks outside the core business.

He continues, "If you think about the culture that develops in most large successful firms, you can see how what's required for success in mature businesses is almost the opposite. . . . In these circumstances, managers and systems reward behaviors that while successful in the short term don't encourage the experimentation that's needed for long-term success. The result? We see companies like HP missing new markets."

The Navigator's Skill Set

The second dimension is what we call the Navigator's Skill Set: the set of new capabilities critical to navigating our new complex environment. In some cases, these are skills such as New Market Entry that require some adaptation to account for today's conditions. In other cases, we identify new capabilities (such as Square-Root Costing) to accurately understand where you're making money in your organization. We've captured below the five skills that comprise the Navigator's Skill Set. Once again, read through and consider how close your organization reflects the statements:

NAVIGATOR'S SKILLSET

1. We know where we *really* make money.
2. We are deliberate in how we manage our portfolio.
3. We approach new markets and targets with discipline.
4. Our operating model is fit-for-purpose.
5. We execute efficiently and consistently.

Again, how did you do? Which represent the biggest gaps? In Part IV, we will discuss ways to bolster each of these.

To underscore the importance of these capabilities, consider what happens if an organization has a strong Explorer's Mindset yet is deficient in the Navigator's Skill Set. When Ron Johnson came in as new CEO of JC Penney in the fall of 2011, the move was widely lauded as just what the ailing department store chain needed. Johnson had a stellar track record and was considered one of the most accomplished merchandisers and retailers of his time. In the 1990s, he orchestrated the transformation of Target into a modern retailer.[11] He then went on to collaborate with Steve Jobs on the creation of the Apple Store, introducing defining elements such as the Genius Bar, and in the process building what was to become the company's primary point of connecting with customers, as well as developing Apple into the most profitable retailer in the United States.[12] So when he joined JC Penney, he was viewed as something of a savior. Certainly, the retail chain needed something of a miracle. It had suffered years of underperformance, with a tired, dowdy image and cluttered stores:

> While Johnson spent several months deliberating J.C. Penney's transformation, the executive team toured company stores and warehouses, finding dusty, excess inventory and crowded, outdated sales floors. They also criticized the inefficiency of J.C. Penney's corporate headquarters in Plano: according to one report, during January 2012, a staff of 4,800 watched 5 million YouTube videos during work hours. [Incoming COO Michael] Kramer recalled how he felt about the company's culture when he first joined: "I hated the company culture. It was pathetic."[13]

Just 17 months later, Johnson was fired by the board. He had indeed taken bold action. "Penney's had been run into a ditch when he took it over. But, rather than getting it back on the road, he's essentially set it on fire," said Mark Cohen, a former CEO of Sears Canada.[14] The bold action had alienated its core customers, and shareholders witnessed a catastrophic drop in share price. It is too easy to armchair-diagnose the situation after the fact. But even at the time, many saw his key transformational initiatives as being risky:

> *The new pricing strategy is ambitious—and risky. Customers have been trained by Penney's and others to hold out for massive discounts. In the era of online shopping, few have the inclination to visit a store with a faded brand like J.C. Penney's. Johnson knows all of that and seems to relish the challenge.*[15]

In fact, much of the value he brought to JC Penney would have been enhanced by the disciplines inherent in the Navigator's Skill Set: His focus on instinct and experience was helpful in setting a vision, but leveraging the data on what shoppers wanted would have focused this. His disregard for testing was something he picked up from Steve Jobs, and perhaps an asset in the context of creating a new entity such as the Apple Store, but catastrophic in this case, as he refused to test the impact of a new pricing strategy. His vision for the stores was distinct, but the operating model for the build-out of custom shops was rife with complexity: with unique fixtures and merchandise, with different footprints within thousands of stores, with construction by different contractor teams, the odds were always stacked against this being accomplished in a cost-effective manner. A consideration of scale would have been helpful. And his general lack of feel for JC Penney's core customers was the unintended consequence of a desire by Johnson and the board to broaden the appeal to include a younger demographic, but ended up, as Johnson later admitted, insulting the core customer.[16]

Identify Your Starting Point

Thus far we have shared 10 statements. The degree to which you recognize your organization in them—or do not—may indicate the degree to which you are vulnerable to the Sirens, and will start to illuminate the shifts required, either in mindset or capability, in order to find growth in a complex world. This is summarized on the two-by-two chart in Figure 6.1, the *Explorer-Navigator Matrix*. Every CEO, COO, and corporate leader needs to determine their starting point, where their company sits in the matrix. If you are still not sure, here are profiles for each quadrant:

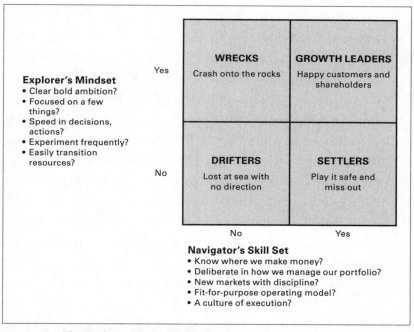

FIGURE 6.1: The Explorer-Navigator Matrix

* **Drifters.** These companies lack both the bold leadership of Explorers and the solid executional strengths of Navigators. Because they lack clear strategic direction, Drifters are stuck with lackluster operational and innovation capabilities. They therefore drift in the marketplace and suffer market share loss and profit erosion. This year doesn't look much different

for them than last year. These companies are often defined by slow decision making, organizational inertia, and silos, as individual leaders vie for fiefdoms in different parts of the business. How quickly they decline will depend on the strengths and speed of their competition. If your business is drifting, then you will need to embark on a journey that pulls on elements described in both Parts III and IV, defining your level of ambition and focus, and shoring up capabilities to execute on this.

- **Settlers.** These organizations lack the boldness of Explorers and so rely completely on their Navigation skills. They function efficiently but are late to the party. With many strong operational and financial capabilities, these companies may even describe their strategy as that of a "fast follower." But that can lead to a tendency to diffuse energy over too many initiatives, become reactive and avoid making true strategic trade-offs. As life cycles shorten, Settlers become more vulnerable. If you fall into this category, the opportunity is in injecting true strategic direction and focus to marshal resources to a point of market leadership (as discussed in Part III).

- **Wrecks.** This is what happens to Explorers who lack Navigator skills! Often energized by a bold strategy (and one frequently driven by individual conviction), companies in this quadrant are nonetheless vulnerable to giant missteps and may crash on the rocks. Absent organizational discipline and a focus on the drivers of customer value, these organizations may convert boldness to ill-fated acquisitions, market expansions, or discontinuous strategies. If your business is trending this way, then you will gain enormous value from adding the disciplines described in Part IV: in essence, ensuring that your current levels of ambition and energy yield outcomes that *your* customers actually value, that they will pay for, and that you can deliver.

• **Growth Leaders.** Companies in this quadrant combine the strengths of Explorers and Navigators. They focus resources on areas where there is a good chance of winning and creating scale in their businesses. Growth Leaders have a clear and bold strategy that stretches the business and, in so doing, provides a sense of mission and urgency. These organizations are characterized by coherence and deliberateness. They have a culture of execution, discipline in market expansion, and an informed view of how and where they make money.

Become a Growth Leader—Again!

As you consider which quadrant best describes your current situation—and assuming you're among the many who can relate to Drifters, Settlers, or Wrecks—you may wonder, *How did we get here?*

The fact is, many organizations are launched on the back of innovative products that addressed customers' needs in new and different ways, or similarly disrupted the markets, and yielded great financial success. *In other words, most began as Growth Leaders, albeit at a much smaller revenue base, before the quest for growth ultimately undermined that which made them successful in the first place.* This is helpful to understand as a motivator, as the goal is much more around rediscovering something that once defined you, rather than finding greatness for the first time.

When a company loses focus—often in the pursuit of growth and scale—it tends to drift. Corporate leaders, who previously were primarily focused on serving the customers, now find their calendars brimful with meetings on operational issues, firefighting, and people issues. It's a central irony that a lot of the challenges we are highlighting in this book arise in the name of serving the customer (more choice, more options, and so on), yet *one of the biggest side-effects is often a loss of customer focus.*

Therefore, in order to regain status as a Growth Leader, it is the leader's job in particular to recapture and embody the qualities that underpin the Explorer's Mindset—boldness, focus, speed, experimentation, and reinvention—as doing so will return the business to an external customer focus. It is critical to assess frankly your organizational capabilities (Navigator's Skill Set), as absent an accurate audit, a business is likely to fall further prey to the Sirens.

The rest of this book is designed to help you reinvigorate the mindset and skill set required to close your gaps, as a counterpoint to the slow atrophy and internal focus that can creep into large businesses over time. We wish you fair winds and following seas!

The Sirens as Lighthouses vs. Lures

Another way to triangulate your starting point is to understand where specific Sirens lie in wait. If you look at your organization and believe it shows signs of falling victim to the Castle Walls siren, it may tell you that you're a Settler, with need to focus on the Explorer's mindset. Hence it can help inform, or triangulate, your starting position.

To add some further clarity to this process, we want to add a further distinction to the Sirens we described in Chapter 4. Each Siren puts out a specific allure, and how an organization reacts to this can be either aggressive or passive. (See Figure 6.2.) For example, let's take the Expanding Portfolio. An aggressive manifestation of this is when an organization throws a lot at the wall to see what sticks. It's the build-it-and-they-will-come approach to product innovation. A more passive manifestation is simply reacting to whatever customers ask for.

The end result is product proliferation in either case, but whether it's the former or the latter is important as it reveals specific traits and weaknesses.

#	Siren	Siren Song	Response to the Siren		The Frequent Reality
			Aggressive (A)	Passive (P)	
1	The Expanding Portfolio	"More is better than less"	Throw a lot at the wall to see what sticks	Whatever customers ask for, we'll provide	Confused customers and increased complexity and costs
2	The Greener Pasture	"We will do great over there"	Winning at home means we'll win in new markets	Other markets must be easier than this one	Erosion of core business through lack of focus; misadventures in non-core
3	The Smash Hit	"A singular thing will determine our success"	Bet the farm, as this has to succeed	Roll the dice in hopes of one success	Rapid commoditization and flat-footed organization
4	The Castle Walls	"We like where we are; it served us in the past"	Re-invest in our core competence	See declining margins as short-term blip	Decline in share and margins; bias to inaction and inward-looking focus

FIGURE 6.2: Aggressive and Passive Responses to the Sirens

The classification by quadrant is below. If you have identified
Sirens, use this two-by-two to triangulate your assessment as
to which quadrant you're starting from.

WRECKS Expanding Portfolio (A) Smash Hit (A) Greener Pasture (A)	**GROWTH LEADERS**
DRIFTERS Expanding Portfolio (P) Smash Hit (P) Greener Pasture (P) Castle Walls (P)	**SETTLERS** Castle Walls (A)

 # CALL TO ACTION

Assess Your Strategy and Set a Course

Opportunity:

You have now met the Sirens, and seen how some organizations adapt their strategies and build organizational capabilities to resist the Siren Song and achieve profitable growth. What dangers do you see? Which Sirens do you see as potentially steering you off track? The first step is to assess your strategy to ensure your business is not in danger of being lured in by a Siren Song.

Key questions for discussion:

- Which Siren(s) is your business susceptible to?
- What are the implications for your business if you fall prey to the Siren(s)?
- How can you adapt your current path to resist the Siren Song?

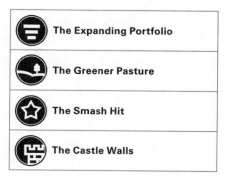

Areas to investigate:

- Assess your strategy to identify which, if any, Sirens are present.
- Assess what it would take to navigate to a better outcome, e.g., Smart Variety vs. the Expanding Portfolio.
- Based on initial review of the Explorer's Mindset and Navigator's Skill Set, assess whether you most closely resemble a Growth Leader, a Drifter, a Settler, or a Wreck.[1]
- Based on this, identify priorities for further analysis and improvement.

#	Siren	Siren Song	Strategy
1	The Expanding Portfolio	"More is better than less." "Whatever the customer asks for." "Let's see what sticks."	Smart Variety
2	The Greener Pasture	"We won at home; we will do great over there, too." "This is a natural growth adjacency for us." "Competition is less tough elsewhere."	The Winnable New Market
3	The Smash Hit	"A single thing will determine our success." "Bet the farm; this has to succeed." "If we can just find a differentiated product."	Repeatable Differentiation
4	The Castle Walls	"We like where we are, it has served us well." "Declining margins are a short-term blip." "Customers want quality, not a low-priced knockoff."	Reinvention and Reconfiguration

Note: the purpose here is to identify opportunities for improvement, not lower morale! To that end, it is often helpful to take a more granular view of the business and ask, which parts of the business are Growth Leaders, and which parts are veering toward Drifters, Settlers, etc.?

PART III

The Explorer's Mindset

CHAPTER 7

Be Bold!

"The rewards in business go to the man who does something with an idea."

— **WILLIAM BENTON, PUBLISHER,
BUSINESSMAN, AND POLITICIAN**

There is no substitute in this world for boldness.

The world we enjoy was certainly built by the bold—whether Martin Luther, Martin Luther King Jr., or Sergey Brin.

Creation, at its core, is an act of boldness; and growth, at its core, is an act of creation. The dictionary defines boldness as "courageousness, and daring"—and to create where there was nothing before, often in the face of the unknown, doubt, or skepticism, is indeed an act of courage, and one of daring. But for our readers, perhaps an even more useful definition for boldness is *belief put into action*. This is the core of growth, as all growth depends on both belief and action—an idea and an activity.

Consider entrepreneurship. Entrepreneurs are driven by a certain view of the world, a belief about the future, *and* they take action based on that belief. Putting belief into action is the essence of entrepreneurship. Entrepreneurship therefore is fundamentally an act of boldness. This is much more than saying that to be an entrepreneur you must be bold, that you must be courageous and daring. This is certainly true, but it is much more than that.

As entrepreneurs ourselves, we have thought long and hard about what *entrepreneurial* really means. As founders of a business, for example, we have never had a prospective employee tell us that he or she doesn't want to work in an entrepreneurial company! Everyone we talk to, it seems, wants to work in an entrepreneurial company, but what does that really mean?[1]

The word *entrepreneurial* may mean a myriad of things to different people, but in our experience we have concluded that *the single word that best describes entrepreneurship is boldness*, and boldness—the willingness to put action behind belief—is what most separates entrepreneurs from most people. Take away either the *belief* or the *action*, and there is no entrepreneur.

But as most of our readers are likely business executives of major corporations, and may not see themselves as "entrepreneurs," why our focus here on entrepreneurship?

Entrepreneurship Isn't Just for Startups Anymore

In the Age of Complexity, with the loss of the primacy of scale and ever-accelerating rates of change, growth increasingly requires that companies be entrepreneurial *whatever their size or market position.*

This wasn't always the case. Before the Age of Complexity, smaller companies, sure, had to be entrepreneurial, but large, established companies not so much. In the Industrial Age, economies of scale afforded larger companies competitive and cost advantages over smaller ones, creating significant barriers to new entrants. With more to lose and less to gain, rather than putting action, and necessarily risk, behind belief, large companies tended to focus on avoiding risk. Indeed, it made sense for large companies to avoid rocking the boat too much.

But that isn't the world today. Your boat is likely already being rocked whether by you or someone else, so it might as well be by you. No longer do larger companies necessarily have the advantage—that is a relic of that brief period of time we called the Industrial Age. The key distinction today isn't between small and large companies, but between entrepreneurial and nonentrepreneurial companies.

Hence, to grow in the Age of Complexity you must be entrepreneurial and not just managerial. You must put a belief about the future—often a contrarian, unique belief—into action.

Elon Musk, for example, is probably at the far end of the boldness spectrum. He has pursued bold ventures in rockets (SpaceX), electric cars (Tesla), and power generation (SolarCity). He recounts that when he started these ventures, he thought the probability of success was less than 50 percent. "But I also thought these were things that needed to get done. So even if the money was lost, it was still worth trying." Indeed it *was* almost lost. Musk recalls: "Between 2007 and 2009, I was in a world of hurt. Everything was going wrong. In 2008, we had the third sequential failure of the Falcon 1 rocket, Tesla couldn't raise financing because of the financial market meltdown, and Morgan Stanley couldn't honor the deal they had with SolarCity, since they were running out of money as well. There was a time when it looked like all three companies could fail."[2]

They didn't. Things worked out for Musk as the financial markets rebounded.

But nonetheless, Musk's lesson from this experience is instructive, as counterintuitive as it is to those trained to weigh risks, cut losses, or keep emergency funds on hand: "Don't leave any dollars in reserve, you can always feed yourself, but don't leave money on the table."

We will all have to adopt more bold thinking if we are going to find a path to differentiation and scale in today's complex world. To bring this home, here are a few key lessons for bringing more boldness into your organization.

Entrepreneur or Small Business Owner?

It was a beautiful spring day in Newport Beach, California, and Andrei was catching up with a friend who had cofounded a successful commercial real estate capital company about 14 years earlier.

Andrei's friend described himself not as an entrepreneur but as a small business owner. What is the difference? The friend explained: "An entrepreneur creates something new and builds a business around that to bring it to the world"—think Steve Jobs, Bill Gates, or Elon Musk.

"A small business owner, on the other hand, is just that, the owner of a small business." Think of your local dry cleaner, the Chinese restaurant down the road, or the printing company around the corner. Another taxi company may be a small business. Uber is an entrepreneurial venture.

Small business owners typically replicate something that exists today. Certainly, they take risks, may put everything on the line, and typically work exceedingly hard. They fight for each mile on a generally level playing field and for meager returns. Entrepreneurs, on the other hand, create something new, founded upon a belief about the world and the future. If successful, they can capture disproportionate profits and launch explosive growth.

As owners of a small business ourselves, we use this differentiation as a litmus test: Are we really entrepreneurs or just small business owners? Do we bring something new to the world, or are we just another boutique management consulting firm with the same frameworks, approaches, and analytics trying to get our piece of the pie? The first path has much more to offer—for ourselves, our clients, and our world—while the second in many ways is much harder and less rewarding. We challenge ourselves to be the former, and look to our beliefs about complexity, the future of the world, and our truly unique methodologies and analytical tools to be what separates us as entrepreneurs from just being another boutique consulting firm.

We urge you to challenge yourself and your organization to become more entrepreneurial. Is your company just another business, fighting for a little bigger piece of the pie and consigning yourself to mediocre profits and growth? Or are you an entrepreneurial company with a unique belief about the future, bringing something new to the world, whether product, service, or business model?

Lesson #1: Articulate a Unique Belief, Then Act on It

In his book *From Zero to One*, PayPal cofounder Peter Thiel[3] poses the question, "*What important truth do very few people agree with you on?*"[4]

It is just such a "first principle" question that can cut through a lot of noise on the topic of differentiation. If your organization is not unique in what it collectively believes—about customers, about how to serve them, about the direction of technology and the market—you'll find yourself competing with many others in a zero sum game, with the prospect of meager returns, and likely adding more complexity than scale.

What to do instead? A plaque in Amazon headquarters famously reads: "There's so much stuff that has yet to be invented. There's so much new that's going to happen. People don't have any idea yet how impactful the Internet is going to be and that this is still Day 1 in such a big way." At the 2013 shareholder meeting, Amazon CEO Jeff Bezos updated this belief: "In fact, I believe that the alarm clock hasn't even gone off yet," he said. "We're still asleep in our beds, far from having even pressed the snooze button."

This unique statement of belief has fueled Amazon's long-term focus, even at the expense of short-term profitability. It is a belief that has Amazon spending billions of dollars developing the India market, which they see as a trillion-dollar opportunity. And why they are doing so at breakneck speed: Amazon was slower to go after China, losing ground to Alibaba. In India, Bezos challenged his team to go in with guns blazing. "He challenged us to think like cowboys, not like computer scientists," said Amit Agarwal, who heads Amazon India. "We needed to move very fast."[5]

Similar unique beliefs are reflected in the mission statements of many of the companies that are shaping our world: "Our vision is to be earth's most customer centric company; to build a place where people can come to find and discover anything they might want to buy online" (Amazon). Or SpaceX, which is seeking to "enable human life on Mars." To borrow a phrase from a great statesman,[6] if your mission is modest, then you'll likely have lots to be modest about!

Consider what you truly and uniquely believe as an organization that differentiates you from the crowd, and put resources behind this belief.

Don't Be One of the "Pseudo" Bold

Don't mistake doing many things for being bold. It may feel bold—"Look at how many things we are doing"—but it is actually the antithesis of real boldness. Rather, pseudo boldness seeks comfort in numbers: so many strategic initiatives (i.e., I'm not really sure any one of them will add enough value), so many overlapping decision makers (i.e., I don't know whose judgment I trust), or much shared responsibility (i.e., I don't want to choose who I will rely on, including myself). Pseudo boldness reflects a lack of conviction or willingness to place a bet.

True boldness, on the other hand, cuts through all this. The truly bold are driven by a belief that makes it very clear to them where to focus, whose judgment to trust, and on whom to rely. They have a clarity of vision and purpose that focuses action and resources.

Lesson #2: Communicate Passion, Optimism, and Purpose

In their book *Bold*, authors Peter H. Diamandis and Steven Kotler profile a number of billionaires. What is striking is the number of mental strategies they have in common, including passion and purpose and rationally optimistic thinking.[7]

Communicating passion and purpose is critical, as the path is frequently difficult and long, and without this fueling the journey, it is easy to lose steam.

"The usual life cycle of starting a company begins with a lot of optimism and enthusiasm," says Elon Musk, speaking to Diamandis and Kotler. "This lasts for about six months, and then reality sets in. That's when you learn a lot of your assumptions were false, and that the finish line is much further away than you thought. It's during this period that most companies die rather than scale up."

This underscores Lesson #1, as it is difficult to have purpose without a unique belief. Our worldview shapes our actions; if we are the only ones with a specific belief, it is much easier to rally behind the notion that *only we can reshape things*. Without it, we are just one of many.

Another common element among billionaires is a high degree of optimism—again, a source of fuel for the journey. This may not be as simple as it seems. Another theme from PayPal cofounder Thiel is that there are cultural differences in how people believe in this notion. In *Zero to One*, he introduces a framework (see Figure 7.1). According to Thiel, the United States has always been an optimistic country, while China and Europe on the other hand have been more pessimistic in outlook. More interesting though is the other dimension, between definite and indefinite. Definite means you believe

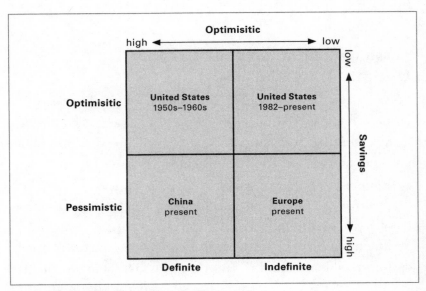

FIGURE 7.1: Thiel's *Definite Optimist* Framework
Source: *Zero to One*, by Peter Thiel

that your actions matter; you expect the future to take a definite form, therefore what you do makes a difference. If you expect an indefinite future, you see it ruled by randomness, therefore your actions don't shape the future.

In Thiel's view, Europe tends toward indefinite pessimists—the future is bad, and you can't change it. China is also pessimistic, but definite, meaning that the future tends toward bad, but you can impact that, so work hard. Saving and investment rates reflect these dynamics.

America before around 1970 was characterized by definite optimism: *A brighter future awaits us, and through our efforts we can achieve it.* But since 1970 America has migrated to a different type of optimism, indefinite optimism—I expect the future to be rosy, regardless of what I do today. Says Thiel: "To an indefinite optimist, the future will be better, but he doesn't know how exactly, so he won't make any specific plans."

By contrast, entrepreneurs by nature are definite optimists. They believe in a better future and that their actions matter. This is required mindset for competing in the Age of Complexity. Here again is Elon Musk: "I didn't go into the rocket business, the car business, or the solar business thinking this is a great opportunity. I just thought, in order to make a difference, something needed to be done. I wanted to have an impact."[8]

Lesson #3: Don't Waste Time with Reasonable Goals

"The reasonable man adapts himself to the world; the unreasonable one persists in trying to adapt the world to himself. Therefore all progress depends on the unreasonable man."[9]

This quote from George Bernard Shaw gets to the heart of leadership. A reasonable man accepts the world around him, argues for reasonable goals, and points out that "we cannot ask people to do more than they're capable of."

An unreasonable man questions the world around him; and for a company looking to grow and upset the established order of things, there's no more powerful a question than: *How do we get to 10x improvement?*

If you're the insurgent, incremental improvement won't get you anywhere. You can't just challenge yourself to do 10 or 20 *percent* better. That by definition means you are accepting the same set of conditions and constraints as all the incumbent competitors, but just trying to do it a little bit better, which, given your relative lack of resources, is unlikely.

To get to 10x better, you need to reject the incumbent conditions and constraints. You need to commit to using your creativity and new technology to run a completely different race than the current set of competitors are running.

Truthfully, no one really expects a company to achieve 10x improvement. GoogleX's Astro Teller says, "Even if you think you're going to go ten times bigger, reality will eat into your 10x. It always does. There will be things that will be more expensive, some that are slower; others that you didn't think were competitive will become competitive. If you shoot for 10x, you might only be at 2x by the time you're done. But 2x is still amazing."[10]

Still, there are some who think that "unreasonable goals" could put too much stress on employees with difficult-to-attain goals. Not true. There is increasing evidence to the contrary. Psychologists Gary Latham and Edwin Locke found setting bold goals increased performance and productivity by 25 percent:

> *We found that if you want the largest increase in motivation and productivity, then big goals lead to the best outcomes. Big goals significantly outperform small goals,*

medium-sized goals, and vague goals. It comes down to attention and persistence—which are two of the most important factors in determining performance. Big goals help focus attention, and they make us more persistent. The result is we're much more effective when we work, and much more willing to get up and try again when we fail.[11]

"What? Governor?!"

Earlier in his career Andrei worked for self-made billionaire Andy Beal, first at Beal Aerospace Technologies, a private rocket venture, and later at Beal Bank, both based in Texas.

Beal is a classic American success story. Son of a mechanical engineer, as a teenager he began fixing and reselling televisions. Then, at just 19 he began buying, renovating, and reselling real estate, buying his first house for just $6,500. While a college student at Baylor University in Texas, he purchased an apartment building for just $217,500, renovating and selling it three years later for more than $1 million. Eventually, he started Beal Bank, and grew it into the most profitable bank in the United States, with an annual return on equity of over 50 percent over a five-year period. Then he used his wealth on ambitious ventures such as Beal Aerospace Technologies, one of the earliest private rocket ventures. With net worth of over $12 billion, he ranks #38 on Forbes's list of wealthiest Americans.

Many years ago, while Andrei was director of strategic operations at Beal Bank, Beal asked Andrei about what he aimed to do in life. Andrei mentioned possibly exploring politics. Beal responded enthusiastically, "That's great, Andrei. What will you do?"

Andrei responded: "Maybe I could get a spot on my local city council. It's a good place to begin to learn the ropes and pay my dues."

Beal looked dumbfounded. His enthusiasm instantly evaporated. "What about Governor?!" he exclaimed.

"You don't just start as governor of Texas, Andy."

"Why not, Bush did!"

To Andy, the reasonable thing was to run for governor, and the unreasonable thing was to run for city council. Andrei later reflected: "Although it seemed crazy to me at the time, and while my political thoughts have long since faded, Andy's response on this and his clarity and audacious boldness on other occasions have stuck with me, and his wisdom, as embodied in his boldness, is proven out in his accomplishments. Indeed, Andy's example—to be bold, to dream big, to put yourself out there—in part led me to found this firm with Stephen Wilson several years later."

Note: Andy is among other Texas entrepreneurs that have had significant impact on both of us, including Michael George, founder of George Group Consulting, for whom we both worked and where we both met.

Large Companies Can Be Bold

It may be tempting to think that boldness in business is the domain of the insurgent—and in particular the startup—not the incumbent. *The startup has less to lose, so it can afford to dream big.*

In fact, *given the right leadership*, all the advantages are with the large companies. While it is true that incumbents are often more vulnerable to the Sirens (including Castle Walls that can prevent bold action), those are avoidable mental traps. More to the point, large companies have greater resources that can be harnessed to good effect, including deep relationships with lots of customers. Indeed, many industries are being reshaped by giants such as Amazon, Google, and SpaceX.

It's not just these relative newcomers that are demonstrating boldness among the large. GE has a 124-year history and more than 300,000 employees. That's a large ship to turn. Surely if it can be bold, so can the rest of us.

Beginning five years ago, GE began a transformation, with CEO Jeff Immelt leading the way, moving from a traditional industrial conglomerate known for refrigerators and jet engines to a software-centric company. Specifically, it is looking to be at the center of the Industrial Internet—the Internet of Things applied to industry and machines (its bold belief). There is more to do, but already the business reported $6 billion in software orders in 2015 and is looking to be at $15 billion by 2020—a top 10 software company (more than 2x gains already).[12]

Says Immelt: "Digital is transforming industry whether we're ready or not. Just like you've seen the consumer internet, there's an industrial internet, and it's going to be a game-changer for business. The principle is harnessing data and turning it into productivity. Think of a jet engine: when one flies from DC to Chicago in the U.S., that engine is going to create a terabyte of data. If we can improve the installed base of GE engines globally by 1% that saves airline customers around $3 billion."[13]

Most importantly, the company is putting these beliefs into action with a series of dramatic changes: It is moving its headquarters from suburban Connecticut to an urban center. It has sold off its finance and appliance divisions. It has hired thousands of software developers, created its own operating system, and developed apps that it says it will sell to other manufacturers as part of the Industrial Internet. Finally, it has reengineered its culture, dropping elements such as forced ranking in performance reviews that the company was famous for under CEO Jack Welch and adopting a "culture of simplification": fewer layers, fewer processes, fewer decision points.

And while it may be too soon to tell how well this will pay off, if a firm of GE's size and tradition can pivot to a new direction, then the answer to the question above is clear. Large *can* be bold! Moreover, it epitomizes belief put into action: belief that GE's future is as a digital industrial company, and action in the radical reshaping of the business including a significant shedding of assets such as GE Capital.

Certainly, boldness in business has always been important, and critically so. As we asserted at the beginning of this chapter, the Industrial Age was created by the bold—the Explorers, if you will, who had the vision, took the risk, applied capital, and drove companies and industries to amazing new heights. But the beginning of the Industrial Age was different than the end, and the mindset that launched the industrial revolution, and built the companies we have all heard of, was different than the mindset that predominated large companies at the end of the Industrial Age, and even today.

In the first half of the industrial age, economies of scale benefited the bold, creating a virtuous cycle of growth and profitability. By the second half of the industrial age, however, large companies did not have to be as daring. They did not have to continue exploring to reap the fruits of scale and the competitive advantages it afforded. Their primary tasks became managing risk and keeping a good thing going. Sure, there was innovation coming from larger firms, but it tended toward steady and staid—think Detroit in the 1970s.

Smaller companies, on the other hand, had to take the risks, be entrepreneurial, and put action behind belief to compete with the large firm's scale advantages. They had to have enough entrepreneurship to overcome the scale advantages of larger firms.

Now in the Age of Complexity, these dynamics have changed. Large companies are discovering that the complexity they've added to stay large is a burden, not an advantage—steady and staid is leaving them in the dust. Complexity has leveled the playing field. Entrepreneurship is now required from all companies. What we are saying is this, that boldness in business is more important today than at any time since the industrial revolution, as today it is not just small companies but all companies that must be bold!

CHAPTER 8

Simplify

> *"Can I make one suggestion to you my friend? Just sim-*
> *plify. There is just too much going on here—you're evil,*
> *you're asthmatic, you're a robot, and what is the cape for?*
> *Are we going to the opera?"*
>
> **—PHARAOH KAHMUNRAH TO DARTH VADER,**
> ***NIGHT AT THE MUSEUM 2***

Without focus, your bold agenda will likely die on the vine. The chairman of a major multinational corporation bemoaned to us that the amount of complexity in the business had grown to such a level that its leadership had lost the ability to drive bold new strategies through the organization. Essentially, they could no longer "steer the ship" (his words). That's an awful position to be in if you're compet-ing on a level playing field without discernible strategic advantage.

As we will discuss in Chapter 16, "Master Execution in a Complex World," complexity can undermine a company's ability to execute. Ironically, the prescribed cure for complexity in many companies is the addition of *more* management systems, initiatives, and priori-ties, which can be worse than the disease.* Without the ability to

---

* Greg McKeown in his book *Essentialism: The Disciplined Pursuit of Less* points out that when the word *priority* came into the English language in the 1400s it was sin-gular. It meant the very first thing. Only in the 1900s did the term become one we could pluralize to *priorities*. "Illogically, we reasoned that by changing the word we could bend reality. Somehow we would now be able to have multiple 'first' things."

execute, your bold agenda will go nowhere. Indeed, if we are defining entrepreneurship as *putting belief into action,* one could make the case that the most challenging part for big companies is the latter part of that phrase—getting things done!

In Part IV we discuss some skill sets and capabilities that can help you simplify. But it all starts with a specific leadership mindset—a Simplification Doctrine, which reflects a belief in the power of focus and simplification as a key lever toward achieving profitable growth. Without this, there is little impetus to attempt the hard work of simplification, and no last line of defense against the complexity that will inexorably attempt to creep into your business.

The right leadership mindset of course is just a starting point; it's insufficient without the accompanying strategies and capabilities. But it is the anchor for the rest of the business. If the CEO is not *ruthlessly focused on a few things* (Explorer's Mindset), then there is little chance of focus surviving at lower levels of the organization. Moreover, while in theory everyone reading this is nodding along with the intrinsic value of focus and simplification, in practice it frequently manifests as somewhat of a contrarian, radical mindset, and one that upsets the natural order of things (generally a trait of Explorers).

When Steve Jobs returned to Apple in 1997, after being previously ousted as CEO in 1985, the first thing he did was radically simplify the business. Steve Jobs's biographer, Walter Isaacson, writing in *Harvard Business Review,* described the scene of his return:

> *After a few weeks of product review sessions, he'd finally had enough. "Stop!" he shouted. "This is crazy." He grabbed a Magic Marker, padded in his bare feet to a whiteboard, and drew a two-by-two grid. "Here's what we need," he declared. Atop the two columns, he wrote*

"Consumer" and "Pro." He labeled the two rows "Desktop" and "Portable." Their job, he told his team members, was to focus on four great products, one for each quadrant. All other products should be canceled. There was a stunned silence.

This simplification is what saved Apple. In retrospect it makes all the sense in the world. At the time, it felt radical. "Deciding what not to do is as important as deciding what to do," Jobs told Isaacson, "That's true for companies, and it's true for products."

The Simplification Doctrine

For Steve Jobs, this was a doctrine forged through the diverse influences on his life, including his love of the Zen gardens in Kyoto and the appreciation for simplicity he gained while working at Atari. Atari games came with no manual, and the only instructions for its Star Trek game were "1. Insert quarter. 2. Avoid Klingons."[1] For the rest of us, we will need to forge our own such doctrines based on our personal experience, having seen what works and what doesn't, but in any case it should reflect the following realizations, beliefs, and convictions:

- **People generally like to make things more complex, not simpler.** It's natural to make things more complex, to add a feature, a capability, or your own spin on something. According to Isaacson, "Jobs would grab a phone at a meeting and rant (correctly) that nobody could possible figure out how to navigate half the features." Indeed, "Any intelligent fool can make something bigger, more complex" whereas "it takes a touch of genius—and a lot of courage to move in the opposite direction."[2] It is important to recognize this as a starting point, as only then does the necessity of the Simplification Doctrine become apparent, as a critical counterpoint to human nature.

- **People sometimes do embrace simplification, but not in their own backyard.** Anyone who has been involved in a portfolio rationalization project understands this. Even when people accept the benefits of streamlined portfolio, they want the other person to be the one trimming his portion of the product line. Every product or project it seems is someone's "baby," and therefore the process of simplification can surface unusual levels of resistance and emotion.

- **Simplification is never simple, and takes hard work and imagination to accomplish.** Complexity is a system issue and therefore requires a holistic approach to unwind it, often requiring "concurrent actions"—coordinated sets of initiatives across the operating model, the portfolio, and your processes—to release benefits. Furthermore, an information asymmetry frequently exists. For example, it is very easy to point to the incremental revenues that will come from adding an additional product variant, but much harder to quantify how customers will respond to a simpler portfolio. This is not to discourage but rather set the right context: simplification is not simple, and if you expect it to be, it can be a discouraging journey.

- **But the destination is worth it—simplification can differentiate a product, a product range, a customer experience, or even a business.** We discuss the specific virtues of simplifying and tackling complexity elsewhere in this book. For many growth leaders this is the keystone to their management philosophy. Isaacson described how Steve Jobs, in looking for industries or categories ripe for disruption, would always ask who was making products more complicated than they should be.

* **The bottom line is that it befalls leadership to take on this task, even if it generates resistance.** Left unchecked, people add complexity; and complexity is hard to take out, but doing so can generate transformative results for a business. It can also be transformative for leaders, as Thiel, speaking on the advantages of smaller companies, points out that "even more important than nimbleness, small size affords *space to think*" [emphasis ours]. Leading an organization to resist its natural tendencies requires real leadership, and in this case with uncompromising demands for simplicity and focus. Resistance to such demands often says more about the natural headwinds than those fighting against them.

Why the Simplification Doctrine Is Critical

To understand why it is important to anchor on this set of beliefs, it is helpful to look at a few examples of how the Simplification Doctrine can make a difference.

One such example we hinted at above is the launching and sustaining of a company's simplification efforts. "Complexity is killing us," is a common refrain from executives we encounter, who point to symptoms of the underlying issue. But for many, launching an effort to simplify in response to these symptoms is at least partly an act of faith.

While the Navigator Skill Set can arm you with rational underpinnings for your simplification agenda, leadership must still be prepared to overcome the natural challenges recognized by the Simplification Doctrine. A Simplification Doctrine, personally held, therefore helps leaders steel themselves in preparation for overcoming expected points of resistance, as people love to add things but fight the notion of taking them away.

Of course, a good executive is used to quickly discerning the top issues, despite partial data or dissenting opinion. For many, the need to address complexity in the business is self-evident, but without a belief in the transformative value, and moreover the feasibility, of simplification, the CEO agenda can easily be diluted with less demanding and also ultimately less rewarding objectives.

Indeed, the right mindset is critical is in protecting key strategic priorities against a nonstop barrage of daily demands. A key risk for executives is that their vision for the business gets substantially degraded. Strategic direction and priorities become swamped by a multitude of functional priorities, incremental initiatives, and well-intended activity. Companies get lost in many small bets versus a few meaningful bold ones. The onus becomes focus on continuity, defense of existing positions, and spreading the wealth evenly across multiple opportunities (which underscores the problem with capital allocation happening at the business unit level or lower, resulting in being an inch deep and a mile wide). Incrementalism is a sort of corporate kryptonite, robbing the organization of its capital, focus, and power to take bold action.

It is important, in today's world, for leaders to ensure that the strategic planning process is anchored around identifying the big opportunities—those that you want to take advantage of—and an assessment of what it would take to get there. It is not budget setting (budget setting is important, but it is not strategy) and certainly not a mechanical inflation from the year before.[3] It is about laying down some broad-stroke priorities; these are your strategic nonnegotiables. Your nurturing of these is one of the most critical aspects of leadership in the Age of Complexity. By identifying, articulating, and reinforcing these parameters—*a bold direction built on different beliefs than the rest of the market*—you will guard against your strategy devolving into incrementalism.

These priorities should be centered on two key decisions: which markets to serve, and how to win in each market. The first, where to play, is focused on which products and services do we offer, to which customers, in which markets or regions. The second, how to win, should be focused on ensuring that you have the right operating model, channels to market, and the right pricing for each customer segment. *Everything else is secondary!* Granted, there is a lot that goes into making these decisions, but anything that doesn't support making them is less important than what does. Certainly, one needs to be cognizant of how the complexity of the offering impacts service levels and other related dynamics. But unless you are clear on these strategic anchor points, it is likely that the business will soon be swamped by a myriad of lower-level strategies, some of which may inadvertently be competing with each other.

Finally, the right mindset can elevate the interests of both customers and shareholders in leadership's decisions regarding *what the business should be, and what it shouldn't be.* One could view the increasing influence of activist hedge funds through divestitures in this light. *Simplify and focus* was the key message from investor Nelson Peltz to PepsiCo's CEO Indra Nooyi in a long campaign to split its beverage and snacks units. For Peltz, CEO and founding partner of New York–based investment firm Trian Partners, the issue was clear, as reported in *The Economist* ("Let My Fritos Go."). The business had "lost its entrepreneurial spirit" and was "shifting to a plodding, 'big company' mentality."[4] By splitting up the company, it would allow for both halves to regain their competitive edge.

The core issue was complexity. Along with diversification comes complexity—and PepsiCo had much of both. The key question was whether the inadvertent costs of PepsiCo's enormous complexity (across its products, processes, and organization) had grown to the point that they outweighed the synergies that came with it. Synergies are clearer, if not always realized. The costs of complexity are more diffused and difficult to quantify, but no less real. The same *Economist* article went on: "Whatever synergies there may be from packaging pretzels and bottling cola under the same corporate roof are undone by bureaucracy and extra costs"—a perfect description of how complexity inadvertently destroys value. The article goes on to make the point that the share prices of focused companies like Hershey's, L'Oréal, and Coca-Cola are a higher multiple of earnings than those of diversified PepsiCo and Procter & Gamble.*

In the end, something of a truce emerged: Peltz backed off in exchange for an additional board seat, a platform to exert ongoing pressure on costs and efficiency. Nonetheless the topic of splitting the company is unlikely to go away, at PepsiCo or indeed within any combined businesses where complexity eats away at efficiencies.

Nooyi clearly believes that the synergies of a combined business outweigh the costs of complexity. Time will tell. But one can argue the point that as CEO, it is her responsibility to understand the impacts of complexity and the right mindset to separate out the Winnable Market from the Greener Pastures Siren. Not only does this help hone the core business—by eliminating distractions—but it also protects against ill-advised acquisitions and business ventures that will impede the ability to compete.

---

* There are clearly many great conglomerates, such as Berkshire Hathaway and Koch Industries, to name but two. These do well based on some specific expertise: the former in identifying undervalued companies and the latter in its acquisition and operating model efficiency. There are others, but this small population comprises the exceptions. Many, if not most, are bloated organizations that do many things okay vs. a few things very well. Indeed, some well-regarded conglomerates such as GE are focusing on areas where they think they can compete more effectively, such as the Industrial Internet, and divesting the rest.

The Great Divestment

We believe we are seeing the beginning of what we will call the Great Divestment.

Back in the 1990s, we saw a surge in mergers and acquisitions. Companies that were on the left-hand side of the Complexity Curve could take on more variety. As companies continued to move to the right of the curve, they began to feel the unintended impacts and costs from all the complexity. It was not surprising that during the late 1990s and 2000s we saw a trend of "One-(insert company)" initiatives that sought to finally integrate all the various acquisitions. There was One-Conagra, One-Vodaphone,[5] One-Pfizer.[6] These were often ill-fated attempts to remove complexity through standardizing systems, processes, and functions, typically falling under their own weight.

In recent years, we have observed a new trend. Large companies that were previously acquiring and merging have reversed course and begun spinning off business units just a matter of years later. The main reason for these splits is to allow each part to become more focused and compete more effectively.

- In 2001 HP joined with Compaq in a highly publicized $25 billion merger, and in 2008 HP acquired EDS for $14 billion. But then in 2015 the massive HP split into HP Inc. (selling printers and PCs) and Hewlett Packard Enterprise (selling servers, software, storage, networking, and associated services).
- In 2000 AOL was worth $200 billion and purchased TimeWarner for $147 billion. In 2009 when the companies reversed course with a split, AOL was only worth

approximately 1 percent of its premerger value and Time-Warner was valued at well less than half of what AOL had purchased it for nine years earlier.

- In 2002 eBay acquired PayPal for $1.5 billion. eBay sold the deal as a synergy—eBay would encourage buyers and sellers on eBay to utilize the PayPal service. Yet, just 13 years later in 2015 the two businesses parted in an effort to "create sustainable, long-term value for stockholders and deliver great opportunities and experiences for customers worldwide."[7]

- After a wave of acquisitions and increases in product offerings that started as early as 1985, consumer goods manufacturer Sara Lee started to reverse the trend beginning in 2006 by divesting its European meats and branded apparel businesses. In 2011, Sara Lee split one final time into Hillshire Brands to include its North American operations while its international beverage and bakery businesses fell under D.E. Master Blenders 1753. The split allowed the two new companies to focus on their core businesses. The results were positive for both sides of the split. Hillshire brands was acquired by Tyson Foods in 2014 for $7.7 billion, and D.E. Master Blenders 1753 merged with Mondelez International in 2015.

Warren Buffett summed up the case of mistaken mergers and acquisitions best when he said, "Whenever a company makes a deal, I go to the store and I buy a congratulations card and I buy a sympathy card. And then five years later I decide which one to send."

It was said long ago that the army that fights on all sides loses. This is no less true in business and no less true today. You must achieve economies of *density*, not just scale. Spreading your resources and actions across too many things dilutes your density. Many may recognize this, but it takes leadership to avoid the temptation of fighting on all fronts to put resources behind the one critical battle that is imperative to win. Simplification flows from the top down, not the bottom up. It takes the right mindset, a keystone for simplification, to unlock the potential of focused deployment of resources against a specific goal, which is not only *more effective*, but also *faster*—a critical enabler for growth in a complex environment and the topic of the next chapter.

CHAPTER 9

Accelerate

"Capitalism has always had its skates on."

Or so claimed the *Economist* in a 2016 article on the pace of business.[1] More than 25 years earlier, George Stalk Jr. and Thomas M. Hout of the Boston Consulting Group had lauded the benefits of speed in new product development and production with their book, *Competing Against Time* (reportedly a favorite of Apple boss Tim Cook). Today, the notion of speed is bandied around corporate offices as the key to competitive success: "We are putting a premium on speed and competitiveness versus perfection," wrote GE chief Jeff Immelt in his 2014 letter to shareholders. Certainly it frequently *feels* like the world is accelerating: the 2016 *Economist* article pointed to the shortening technology adoption lag between rich and poor countries as an example of this.

At the same time, organizations seem to be slowing down. In the summer of 2015, for example, we were invited to address CEOs and CFOs of the Australian units of several multinational organizations headquartered in North America or Europe. The key issue they shared with us was one of speed, particularly the speed of decision making as the local country unit sought approval from HQ for key initiatives focused on Australia customers. Said one exasperated CEO, "Decisions take months!"

The comments from these Australian executives, many of whom worked for aggressive, market-leading organizations, sparked some underlying questions: *If these companies, which understand the value of speed, struggle nonetheless to move at pace amidst today's complexity, does that mean that traditional strategies for speed are insufficient? And given the origin of the comments—geographic units of large multinationals—is the core issue an organizational one?*

So perhaps it's time to do more than issue a decree to *just go faster* and instead rethink speed at a more granular level—where it matters—and consider whether our traditional strategies and structures for achieving speed are still applicable in a complex environment.

In this chapter, we'll explore the truth behind the perception of ever-increasing speed in business and present strategies for how you can accelerate your organization even in the face of increasing complexity.

Reality: Markets Are Getting Faster

Let's pressure-test the notion that business is speeding up.

First, let's look externally to the operating rhythms of markets and customers. The data suggests that corporate life cycles are indeed accelerating. According to one study of the S&P 500, the average tenure for a firm has dropped from 61 years in 1958 to just 18 years in 2012.[2] This shortening reflects new sources of competition: new players from neighboring industries, entrants from overseas, and VC-funded players who are now maturing into full competitors.

It also reflects new sets of winners and losers within the existing arena of competition, driven by shorter product life cycles, changing customer tastes, and accelerating technology. The consumer electronics industry, with perhaps the fastest "industry clockspeed," is the epitome of this as devices can go from market-dominant to has-been in the space of months. True, industry clockspeeds vary. Consumer electronics and cosmetics run fast,[3] a dynamic that mandates more rapid new product development. Pharmaceuticals and automobiles are medium clockspeed industries. Slower industries include aircraft, petrochemicals, and steel.

But the question for each organization is: within your clockspeed class, *is the pace getting faster*? In a study of product life cycles in the automobile industry, for example (a medium clockspeed industry), we see that lifespans have shortened by close to 50 percent in certain vehicle categories such as city cars (Figure 9.1).

Segments	1970–1983	1984–1993	1994–2006
A (city cars)	14.7	10.3	8.0
B (compact)	9.5	8.9	7.2
C (medium)	10.5	9.5	8.6
D (upper medium)	9.0	9.0	8.0
E (large)	12.0	10.9	10.2
Average	10.6	9.7	8.4

FIGURE 9.1: Automobiles Product Life Cycle Duration
Data set from top European brands: Alfa Romeo, Audi, BMW, Citroen, Fiat, Ford, Lancia, Mercedes, Opel Peugeot, Renault, Toyota, Volkswagen.
Source: Giuseppe Volpato and Andrea Stocchetti, *Managing Product Life-Cycle in the Auto Industry: Evaluating Carmakers Effectiveness*, Ca' Foscari University, June 2008

Equally important from the standpoint of revenue capture is that the shape of a product's life cycle curve is changing (Figure 9.2). The traditional view of a product's life cycle presumed a period of ramp-up, peak sales, followed by *gradual* decline that represented an extended period of significant revenue. But data suggests that the growing intensity of competition and customer expectations are causing a far more abrupt ending to product life spans. No longer will there be a long tail that can be relied on for significant revenue.

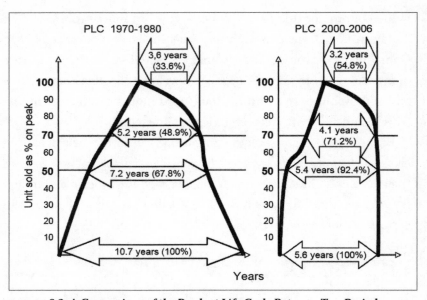

FIGURE 9.2: A Comparison of the Product Life Cycle Between Two Periods

Source: Giuseppe Volpato and Andrea Stocchetti, *Managing Product Life-Cycle in the Auto Industry: Evaluating Carmakers Effectiveness*, Ca' Foscari University, June 2008

The implication is that, with life cycle compression, a greater share of revenues (and margin) in many businesses is coming from products and services introduced in the last few years. This need for "replacement margin" puts an even greater stress on innovation and rapid product development.

Complication: Complexity Is Making Us Slower

Shortening product life spans, frequently driven by startups and focused players, are sobering because many large companies are simultaneously getting slower in a number of important ways. A few years back, for example, three securities analysts and a venture capitalist noted that the number of new drugs approved per dollar spent on R&D drops by half every nine years (Figure 9.3). This

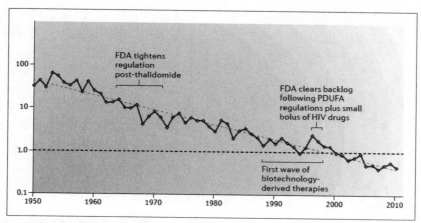

FIGURE 9.3: Number of Drugs per Billion US$ R&D Spending
(Inflation-adjusted)

Source: Jack W. Scannell, Alex Blanckley, Helen Boldon, and Brian Warrington, "Diagnosing the Decline in Pharmaceutical R&D Efficiency," *Nature Reviews: Drug Discovery*, March 2012

analysis, which became known as Eroom's Law, highlighted a significant challenge for the pharmaceutical industry.*

The authors highlighted a number of potential root causes, including:

- An ever-growing back catalog of successful approved medicines, which raises the bar on new drug discovery and increases the complexity in development (the "better than the Beatles" problem)†

---

* Eroom is Moore backward. Gordon Moore, the co-founder of Intel, predicted that "The number of transistors incorporated in a chip will approximately double every 24 months." The prediction proved accurate and was used in the semiconductor industry to guide long-term planning and strategy.

† Yesterday's blockbuster drugs are now generic, deterring R&D in some areas, and reducing the economic value of new drugs. This crowding is similar, the authors suggest, to a scenario under which "any new song had to be better than the Beatles, if the entire Beatles catalogue was available for free, and if people did not get bored with old Beatles records."

- More-cautious regulators
- A "throw money at it" tendency, adding human resources and overinvesting in R&D (which we would usually see as a precursor to organizational complexity)
- An overreliance on basic research in screening methods in generating new molecules (which have yet to pay off)

The result is more regulation, more participants in the process, more technology, more organizational steps—in sum, more organizational complexity and opportunities for delay.

It is instructive by comparison to look back at conditions in the 1950s and 1960s when cycle times were remarkably short. During that time, regulations were less rigorous, which led to much faster drug approvals. The first antidepressant, imipramine, for example, completed its preclinical development and *three* clinical cycles within just five to six years. In comparison, by 2005–2006, the clinical development for a new drug was typically more than nine years.

Outside pharma, we see similar dynamics. In one of our recent studies, we found that despite impressive growth, 7 out of the top 10 largest banks in the United States (which by inference have some of the most complex banking operations) have worse efficiency than average-sized banks. Andy Beal, CEO of Beal Bank (the most profitable bank in the United States) commented: "Regulators and government officials should . . . take notice. Complexity dramatically increases costs and risk of failure. It is like a cancer that eats away at efficiency and profitability."[4]

Across industries, we hear our clients comment on what we might call the Great Deceleration: *Our internal bureaucracy is stifling innovation and impeding execution. Our customers are expecting faster response times yet we are getting slower.*

An Important Measure of Speed: Margin Replacement Ratio

When these dynamics coincide—accelerating product life cycles and slower product development timelines—companies have an acute issue to deal with: the commoditization of significant portions of their business overtaking their ability to generate new sources of advantage. We call this the *margin replacement ratio*:

$$\frac{\text{Product Life Span}}{\text{Product Development Lead Time}}$$

For example, if your industry saw a similar compression in life cycle as the auto data featured in this chapter—from 10.7 to 5.6 years—and at the same time saw a deceleration in the pace of new product lead time, (e.g., from 3 years to 6 years) the ratios would look like this:

$$\text{From } \frac{10.7}{3} \text{ or } 3.6$$

Any decline, but in particular a shift to a ratio less than 1, should be an alarm bell for an organization. Think of this ratio as similar to a carbon monoxide detector. Organizational inertia typically precedes declines in market advantage. However, given that market shifts, commoditization trends, and generally industry life span changes do not happen overnight, and generally don't announce themselves, they can go undetected. A decline in the margin replacement ratio over time is a signal

to an organization to make some strategic and structural shifts
before crises hit.*

Speed in a Complex Environment

For answers, it is never a poor choice to look to the military—in
this case, how Joint Special Operations Command (JSOC), under
the leadership of General Stanley McChrystal, initially struggled
in the battle with Al Qaeda in Iraq and Afghanistan before finding a more successful path under a different structure. According
to McChrystal, JSOC struggled in the early days to make a dent
against the enemy, despite its superior expertise and resources. The
culprit? The military's bureaucratic organizational structure that
was unable to keep up with the complex and dynamic conditions
on the ground.

"With the advent of Al Qaeda and developments in technology,
everything changed," said McChrystal. There was no centralized
enemy; Al Qaeda and other groups were amorphous, constantly
shifting networks that could move quickly, strike ruthlessly, and
then vanish back into the local population. Meanwhile, the U.S.-led
forces were trying to operate in a bureaucracy where information
slowly climbed the chain of command and decisions trickled down.
As McChrystal put it, "Command-and-control hierarchy just wasn't
working for us. To defeat an enemy like Al Qaeda in Iraq (AQI), we

---

* One word of caution: a common response in the face of a declining margin replacement ratio is to pursue multiple product development projects in parallel. When
done in a deliberate manner, that can be an effective response. Samsung, for
example, pursues "leapfrog" R&D, developing first-, second-, and third-generation
technologies simultaneously. But it does so on a foundation of an operating model
designed specifically to support this strategy. Otherwise, such an approach would
yield organizational complexity, delayed release dates, and cost overruns.

had to beat them at their own game—the phrase *it takes a network to defeat a network* became our mantra."[5]

JSOC pivoted, and replaced an emphasis on efficiency and risk-mitigation with a focus on adaptability and responsiveness. McChrystal emphasizes that these shifts were, at heart, about liberating the natural pace and adaptability of individual teams from a sluggish infrastructure. He writes, "The defining attributes of AQI's network—fluid adaptability and strong lateral bonds—had remarkable similarities with the traits that made our individual teams perform incredibly well. We just needed to reshape the superstructure that bound those teams together to look more like the bonds within those teams."[6]

The switch allowed the forces under JSOC command to increase their performance twentyfold—going from 15 to 300 operations a month—with minimal increases in manpower and resources. Along the way, they also achieved notable wins, such as locating and killing terrorist leader al-Zarqawi.

The specifics of the situation may be unique, but the lessons and strategies are broadly applicable for any organization that is competing in a complex environment. McChrystal himself sees plenty of analogies outside the military: "Sclerotic organizations inhibit everything from foreign-aid delivery to health-care performance to global governance, costing billions of dollars and millions of lives every year." Traditionally, companies would look at "leaning out" processes to remove non-value-add time and become faster; or they would deploy teams to assess ways to improve the overall efficiency and speed of their business. But these approaches flounder in the face of increased complexity, with startups acting as insurgents, and with conditions changing overnight. In less volatile surroundings, focusing your efforts primarily around improving the efficiency of your operations makes a lot of sense. But in a fast-changing environment, different elements become important. Adaptability and responsiveness outweigh efficiency.

The key lesson for companies: *a Taylorist[7] efficiency-focused approach to achieving speed is incompatible with—and indeed may be at odds with—achieving speed in a complex world.*

Three Keys to Speed and Overcoming Organizational and Process Complexity

JSOC's experiences and similar experiences from many other organizations point to three key conclusions about how to accelerate in a complex environment.

1. Keep Teams Small If You Want Them Fast

JSOC teams were connected as a network, but the individual teams of Delta Force and SEAL Team Six remained small. There are many great examples of how small teams can outpace larger ones. Toward the end of World War II, the U.S. Army Air Corps asked Clarence "Kelly" Johnson to create America's first jet fighter to counter the new jets of the Luftwaffe. The goal: a prototype in 180 days!

Such a timeline sounds farfetched by today's aerospace development standards. But in fact Johnson achieved this with 37 days to spare. How? For one he persuaded his Lockheed bosses to let him create a top-secret department that sidestepped the corporate bureaucracy. He also handpicked a very small team. In fact one of his "rules of management" was: "The number of people having any connection with the project must be restricted in an almost vicious manner. *Use a small number of good people* (10 percent to 25 percent compared to the so-called normal systems)"[8] [emphasis ours].

More recently, the Apple engineer who led the development of the iPhone software shared that the team responsible was "shockingly small."[9] Jeff Bezos of Amazon seems to embrace the same concept in his Two Pizza Rule: for teams to be effective, he said, they should be limited in size, small enough to be fed with two pizzas. Large teams tend to generate complexity in communications and coordination, and can drive down individual contribution.

We have seen this in our own work. At one European industrial machining client, we found that for every additional engineer added to an order, the result was an additional delay of several days, cumulating in a significant impact on overall delivery time.

A Lesson in Speed: Fashioning a Glasshole in 90 minutes

"Glasshole (noun): an individual who behaves inappropriately while using the Google Glass interface"

If you're going to prototype a product, do it fast. In *How Google Works*, Eric Schmidt reported that the team working on Google Glass built the first prototype in just 90 minutes. "It was quite crude, but served a powerful purpose: Don't tell me, show me." But when the product launched, it was met with a barrage of concerns, primarily regarding privacy and intellectual property.

Google Glass is a headset that you wear like eyeglasses with Internet availability. What created controversy was its capability to video and record surreptitiously, with the backlash leading to the rise of the term *Glasshole*. (Google prefers the term *Glass Explorer*.)

The product ultimately was withdrawn from the market as a consumer device. Google commented: "We're continuing to build for the future, and you'll start to see future versions of Glass when they're ready. (For now, no peeking.)" Google describes the experience as an "open beta" experiment. Others call it a flop. Are there are any lessons?

"When a new technology first emerges there's a friction caused by the clunkiness of the technology not quite being sophisticated enough and society not being used to the idea." So says Tim Brown, CEO of design consultancy IDEO. But, he says, "Over time, those two things get closer and closer together. Eventually that friction goes away and the technology is accepted. He sees a bright future for the product as this gap closes.

A different perspective is that Google failed to develop a compelling use case; that it was technology in search of purpose. Instead of focusing on prototyping the *product*, had Google spent more time prototyping the *concept*, the argument goes, it would have quickly uncovered many of the barriers, both psychosocial and regulatory, to the rapid acceptance of the product. In fact, many are seeing some very clear uses *in nonconsumer areas*, for instance in healthcare, law enforcement, and manufacturing.

In the meantime, for intrepid Glass Explorers, Google released a guide on how not to be a Glasshole, which included the advice, *Don't be creepy or rude.*

2. Less (Multitasking) Is More!

Another key to organizational speed is to strip away the burden of multitasking. For one client, a public-sector organization, this required an understanding of the workload and how projects were currently structured. In this situation, productivity had declined, specialists with key skills were rarely available and projects invariably slid beyond expected scopes, budgets, and timelines. The organization's hypothesis was that the team was creaking under the weight of work and operating near capacity. In fact, this turned out *not* to be the case! There was plenty of capacity for all the project work. But most people were working on multiple projects. Critical specialists were allocated (formally and informally) across many more. Critically, for every one 'full-time-equivalent' (FTE) of effort a project required, it was, on average, split across five contributors (and in many cases as high as 10 or more contributors). With resources spread, and given the nature of the projects—highly variable, "creative" project work—the interdependency and waiting time compounded exponentially.

The organization reversed this by dedicating fewer individuals more fully to fewer projects at a time, while introducing a utilization "buffer" of at least 30 percent. By reducing individuals' work variation and enforcing buffer time, the organization stripped back the queueing time that had become engrained and relieved the overhead "tax" that proliferated with each additional project. (See Figure 9.4.)

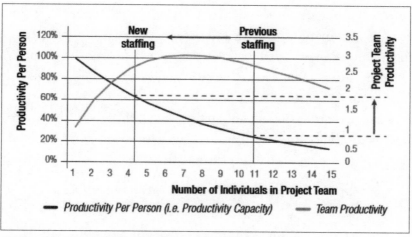

FIGURE 9.4: Improving Productivity by Focusing Resources

Overall, by reorganizing the same work under a more focused model, even allowing for the resource buffer on all work, the organization became 10 percent "overstaffed"; excess capacity that was immediately transferred via staff reallocation.

3. Transform Your Decision Making

One of JSOC's key lessons was that in a fast-changing environment, adaptability and responsiveness take precedence over the traditional military focus on efficiency and risk mitigation. To achieve these goals, JSOC made two changes in its approach to decision making that were previously anathema in the military:

- **Liberal sharing of information**, which McChrystal refers to as "radical transparency"
- **Decentralization of authority**, which enables quick decisions at the local level

The rationale for radical transparency was simple. Bureaucracy is great at compartmentalizing information and sharing it only on a need-to-know basis. But by 2004 in JSOC it was impossible to foresee which elements of the organization would need to know a given piece of information. So instead of trying to control information, the organization changed course to share it as broadly as possible, including status updates, intelligence, and strategic developments. Their motto became: "Share until it hurts, then share some more."[10]

This unprecedented level of sharing required a very deliberate shift in thinking. It was uncomfortable cutting across traditional silos, but it brought with it unexpected benefits:

> *Now interestingly enough as we did this and sped up. . . .*
> *We got much, much faster, [and] because we got faster, we*
> *got better in getting intelligence and it was harder for the*
> *enemy to react. So not only did our speed go up dramati-*
> *cally . . . but our success rate actually went up. Now that*
> *was unpredictable to me.*[11]

Radical transparency was also an enabler of the second principle: pushing decisions down to the local level. McChrystal recalls that by the time he got to be a senior leader at the height of the war in Iraq, he was making very few decisions. He saw that as the way it should be, because, if he was making decisions that someone else could make—someone else closer to the action—then that would be a mistake.[12]

Distributed decision making is an increasing reality for many organizations. Your team on the front line are the fastest responders and frequently provide more accurate information around opportunities to serve customers.

Consumer goods company Reckitt Benckiser has built an enviable top- and bottom-line record through its strategy of acquiring unique assets with market-leading positions. To enable that, decision-making speed is a priority, enabled through a decentralized organization.

Said CEO Rakesh Kapoor, "In our markets, speed matters. However, as organizations grow they inevitably become more complex, which makes them rigid and slower to respond. We must constantly battle against this, so our culture and business can thrive. We announced Project Supercharge at the start of 2015. It is our program to ensure we have a simpler, more agile organization, which focuses our efforts on our consumers and our retail customers. Supercharge is already delivering real benefits."[13]

We make one point of caution. Yes, it's good to have decisions made closer to the action. But without some form of guidance—whether that be culture, norms, or decision rules—you may end up creating a lot more complexity. In this regard, the military has an advantage in terms of the high levels of training and rules of deployment; in the corporate world, we need to get equally adept at creating rules of thumb that can help guide distributed decision making.

Here's an example: Compass Group, the contract foodservice and facilities management company, did just that creating its Management and Performance framework (MAP), which boiled down what matters in business performance to five key areas (two revenue-related and three cost-focused). For example, MAP1 guides the conversation about markets, meaning where the company will play and why (which sectors and clients) and how these will impact the business. MAP3 focuses on the need to manage the cost of food.

Compass has been successful in executing its strategy, not because its strategy is clever or secret, but because it has trained more than 10,000 of its employees throughout the organization to understand it deeply. This enables everyone to understand the drivers of the business, which is critical as management and decision making have become far more local.

Triage Your Decisions

Another big factor shaping decision-making speed is the mistake of treating all decisions equally, what Amazon's Jeff Bezos calls ""one-size-fits-all" decision making. In his 2015 Letter to Shareholders, he explains that "some decisions are consequential and irreversible or nearly irreversible." They are one-way doors, in his words. But most decisions are much simpler. "They are changeable, reversible . . . two-way doors."

Bezos observed that in large organizations, most decisions are treated like the one-way doors—with great deliberation and seriousness because the consequences cannot be easily reversed. The consequences, he wrote, were "slowness, unthoughtful risk aversion, failure to experiment sufficiently, and consequently diminished invention."

We see this dynamic frequently in large companies. One leader told us of his company's culture: "Things move so slowly around here. Everything has to be gold-plated. So the quality is great, but this means we take forever getting anything accomplished."

Do not let your organization fall into this trap! Be clear about which decisions truly are "one-way doors" and therefore require appropriate deliberation, and which ones are reversible, where the onus should be on speed and experimentation.

Becoming Satisfied with "Roughly Right": How to Embrace Ambiguity

The temptation to lead as a chess master, controlling each move of the organization, must give way to an approach as a gardener, enabling rather than directing. A gardening approach to leadership is anything but passive. The leader acts as an "Eyes-On, Hands-Off" enabler who creates and maintains an ecosystem in which the organization operates.[14]

We live in a far more ambiguous world than our predecessors. Once you accept that, sharing information and pushing down decisions become far easier, and your operating rhythm accelerates.

Ironically, decision delay seems particularly acute now that we have oriented toward Big Data and advanced analytics, which would seem to promise more granularity, not greater ambiguity. Unfortunately, despite—or perhaps because of—all the mountains of data now available to us, determining growth strategy and execution is still largely more about leveraging many different sources of insight than it is a detailed analytical exercise. Nimble organizations are satisfied with quickly making a *roughly right* decision and see little value in using up time to pursue precision.

It is comforting to think that by adding more "process" to decision making we are taking all risks out of new strategic initiatives or that we are effectively guaranteeing their success. But, as Roger L. Martin points out in the article "The Big Lie of Strategic Planning," "Given that strategy is primarily about revenue rather than cost, perfection is an impossible standard. At its very best, therefore, strategy shortens the odds of a company's bets."[15] Having a highly detailed and complex process just adds significant delay to critical decisions—which is time that comes with a significant opportunity cost. Chairman Lee of Samsung has said that missed opportunities pose a greater threat than direct losses.

He writes: "Short of misusing company funds, we have to be ready to do whatever it takes. When we decide on something we have to do, we have to go all in to seize opportunities, or at the very least, minimize opportunity costs. If we do not bring creative products and services to market faster than others, we will not survive. This is an era when timing is critical and speed is vital."[16]

The challenge for leadership is recognizing where additional data is useful, and where it will fail to add insight (due to the high number of unknowns) or will cost more in lost opportunity compared to the advantages of acting quickly. To act quickly, leaders have to be willing to embrace ambiguity over precision. The mental switch isn't easy. Strategic planning is daunting, and people try to make it less so by treating it as a problem that can be solved with lots of information.

As Martin states in his article, this is a great way to cope with fear of the unknown but "a truly terrible way to make strategy." Good strategy for the nimble is the result of a simple rough-and-ready process of thinking through what it would take to achieve what the organization wants to accomplish, and then assessing whether it's in a position to realistically achieve those goals. The goal of strategic planning isn't so much to anticipate and plan for all potential roadblocks, but to optimize the chances of success.

Culture, complexity, strategy, and structure: many elements combine to slow down decision making, activity, and results. This is happening at the moment in history when customer expectations around speed and service are rising through the roof. Organizations cannot rely on what worked before, but need to set in motion specific approaches to inject speed in a newly complex environment (think *steer* vs. *drift**). One such—a focus on increased experimentation—is the focus of our next chapter.

---

* As in: "Does a ship sail to its destination no better than a log drifts nowhither? . . . And there you have our difference: to be in hell is to drift: to be in heaven is to steer." George Bernard Shaw, Man and Superman, Act III.

CHAPTER 10

Improve the Odds

"There are two ways to get fired from Harrah's: stealing from the company, or failing to include a proper control group in your business experiment."[1]

—GARY LOVEMAN, HARRAH'S ENTERTAINMENT CEO

The very first Siren we discussed in Chapter 4 was the Expanding Portfolio. This Siren may be one of the most attractive because it promises success while staying close to home. It is the potent combination of two thoughts that creates the pull: (1) most new products fail, and (2) a slightly different version of a successful existing product is likely to sell at least something.

These statements ignore the fact that incremental line extensions may also cannibalize existing sales and such moves are unlikely to launch you into another echelon of growth. But the thought of "some" success while staying inside a protected harbor is a powerful allure.

Boldness, as we've discussed, is the antidote to this. But betting the farm is rarely a good strategy in business or at the casino, as it limits your time at the table. So the real question you should be asking is, *How can I improve the odds of discovering rich new sources of growth?*

The answer lies in a mindset and accompanying set of behaviors that can help bridge the gap from yesterday's more linear world to today's world in which a high degree of interconnectedness makes predicting winners incredibly difficult. It boils down to three behaviors:

1. Cast a wider net for sources of growth.
2. Focus on inventing new business models, not just products and services.
3. Use experimentation to rapidly find more winners.

Element #1: Cast a Wider Net for Sources of Growth

In an environment where there is relative stability and predictability, continuing to tap the same sources for new ideas may well suffice. As captured in Figure 10.1, companies may look inside their industry, using classic stage-gate new product development processes and gathering intelligence about what competitors are doing. They also look outside, exploring adjacent industries or acquisitions where there may be synergy.

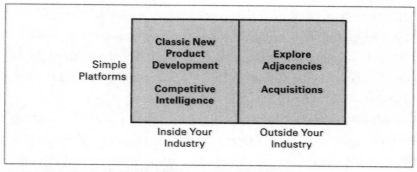

FIGURE 10.1: Sources of Growth Ideas (Stable Environment)

All of these traditional approaches still play an important role, particularly in high-dollar capital projects, where the outcomes are more predictable at the outset and where risk-management is critical. Under these circumstances, a stage-gate process manages risks and ensures that what emerges is a functioning solution.

However, the complexity of today's market is challenging the relative value of traditional approaches, the linear structures or "simple platforms" that have traditionally generated new growth ideas. We are entering what Google's lead economist Hal Varian calls a period of *combinatorial innovation*:

> *If you look historically, you'll find periods in history where there would be the availability of different component parts that innovators could combine or recombine to create new inventions. In the 1800s, it was interchangeable parts. In 1920, it was electronics. In the 1970s, it was integrated circuits. Now what we see is a period where you have Internet components, where you have software, protocols, languages, and capabilities to combine these component parts in ways that create totally new innovations.*[2]

The opportunity for combinatorial innovation is open to all industries, not just computing. Clearly the advances in computing power, in combination with the technology of your industry, offer tantalizing opportunities if you allow them to propagate. Once upon a time, a company needed to be well established before it could gain access to economical large-scale computing power. Now the playing field has been leveled with operations like Amazon Web Services, which reportedly adds—every day!—physical server capacity equivalent to the amount needed to support Amazon.com when it was a $7 billion annual revenue company, scale that enables startups to access computing power on demand. Such shifts in landscape mean that many existing businesses are vulnerable to disruption. Think of Square in the payment processing industry, Uber in transportation, and Netflix in entertainment content development and distribution. In a combinatorial world, two trends emerge:

- Completely new competitors appear, potentially posing existential threats.
- The innovation that spurs step-change growth is more likely to come from outside your traditional competitor set than from within it.

To increase your odds of finding new sources of growth, therefore, you need to cast a wider net in your search for new ideas. Challenge yourself: Does innovation only come from the NPD process or from the engineer working on the front line? From asking customers through interviews and surveys or from watching how they actually use your product? From within your industry or from outside?

Even within your industry, there are ways to tap into new ideas you might otherwise have overlooked. And there are relatively simple things you can do to reach beyond your own boundaries. These methods are summarized in the top of Figure 10.2 and discussed below.

Architect the Culture

Frequently seen as ethereal rather than something that be engineered, culture is often approached passively instead of proactively. Culture isn't neutral, you are on one side of the fence or the other, and it isn't ethereal. While culture involves values and beliefs, it is difficult to measure those. A more practical definition of culture, one that can be more directly measured, is that culture is the collection of organizational practices, norms, and behaviors that define one group as distinct from another.

Culture fits right between personality and human nature, as shown in Figure 10.3. Personality is specific to the individual, and is both innate and learned. Human nature, on the other hand, is

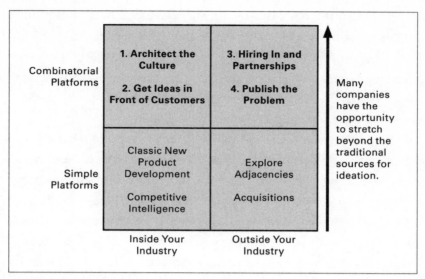

FIGURE 10.2: Sources of Growth Ideas (Complex Environment)

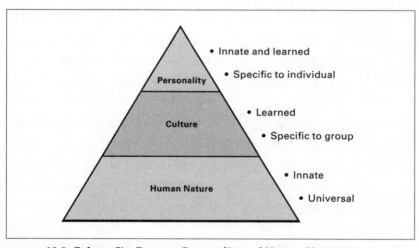

FIGURE 10.3: Culture Sits Between Personality and Human Nature

Source: Hofstede, Hofstede, and Minkov, *Cultures and Organizations: Software of the Mind*, third ed., 2010

universal and innate. Culture differs from both personality and human nature in that it's entirely learned and specific to a group. That group is your company. The very best organizations in every industry are very deliberate about their culture. They take an active role in managing their culture to keep it healthy, and they design and build their desired culture into the company.

A key test for your culture "blueprint" is to assess *to what degree do the organizational practices and behaviors support or erode tapping new sources of growth*—that is, will your current culture help or hinder your efforts in the top two quadrants in Figure 10.2?

Google's Eric Schmidt describes an early experience that illustrates the power of culture to drive innovation. In May 2002, Larry Page discovered that many ads that popped up on a Google search were completely unrelated to the search theme. Instead of calling the person responsible or convening a meeting, he printed out the pages of poor-quality results, highlighted the offending ads, and posted the pages on a bulletin board. He then "wrote THESE ADS SUCK in big letters across the top. Then he went home."

A group of engineers (none of whom were even on the ads team) saw Page's note, agreed with his succinct analysis of the ads, and went to work on the issue over the weekend. By the following Monday, they sent out an e-mail that "included a detailed analysis of why the problem was occurring, described the solution, included a link to a prototype implementation of the solution the five had coded over the weekend, and provided sample results that demonstrated how the new prototype was an improvement over the then-current system."[3] The gist of their insight—that ads should be placed based on relevancy—became the basis for Google's AdWords, a multibillion-dollar business.

To begin architecting culture, leaders need to understand how to change behaviors. What we believe drives how we behave, but it is very hard to move culture by first focusing on changing beliefs in order to drive behaviors. But it is possible to do the reverse: focus on consequences (which can be positive or negative) to drive behaviors, which ultimately start to change beliefs. Action begets belief more than the other way around.

Get Ideas in Front of Customers

Software developers have embraced Agile development practices because of hard-earned lessons: customers are notoriously unreliable at telling you what they *think* they would like, and the best way to get useful information is to put an actual product in their hands to see what they *actually* like.

While rapid customer engagement has now become a fixture of software development, it is equally important in other areas. Luckily, it is increasingly feasible as rapid prototyping tools such as 3D printing (or "additive manufacturing") gain prominence. This approach has come a long way from its roots, and today, can handle materials ranging from titanium to human cartilage."[4]

Don't think that rapid prototyping is restricted to physical products, either. With a little bit of creativity (and perhaps some software support), you can create mock experiences where customers can see what new services would be like.

In both cases, the basic technique involves offering different configurations of a product or service to different sets of customers in order to gather feedback on preferences. This both reduces risk in the new product launch and accelerates the time to market.

Hire In and Partner

Says Rita Gunter McGrath in *The End of Competitive Advantage*: "In a situation replete with complexity and unpredictability, one never knows where the next important idea will emerge. If the senior team is very homogenous, it limits the amount of mental territory that they can cover."

If new ideas are more likely to appear outside your industry than within it, then you need to find ways to bring novel ideas into your company. You can do that by increasing the diversity in the background and experience of the people you hire or by partnering with companies who have creative or technological resources that your organization lacks.

For example, much was made of Apple's hires in preparation for the launch of the Apple Watch. The CEO of fashion house Yves Saint Laurent joined Apple in 2013, and Apple stores have been seeking retail candidates with *"a fashion or luxury background."*[5] But even before then, with the appointment of Angela Ahrendts from fashion retailer Burberry to head Apple Retail, the signals were clear that Apple saw an impending fusion of fashion and technology with the advent of wearable technology, and was gearing up.

If companies think of themselves as an island rather than part of an ecosystem (through partnerships whether formal or informal), it can be very hard to drive innovation and new ideas. John Geraci clarified the issue when he described his experience as director of new products at the *New York Times* from 2013 to 2015. His job was to lead a team in the creation, launch, and development of a new, revenue-driving product that would help restore growth to the company's bottom line. In a 2016 *Harvard Business Review* article, Geraci wrote that "it was big, heady stuff" but also "a resounding failure."[6]

In Geraci's first year, the NYT focused on finding entrepreneurial employees, bringing in the right DNA. In the second year, when it became apparent that the new products were not going to hit their targets, the paper shifted its focus and created a special executive board that was supposed to implement a venture capitalist mindset to evaluate new initiatives. But this too didn't work. Why? Because there wasn't enough infusion of outside thinking. Geraci describes the NYT as an "organism" with a "wholly internal engine." For example, NYT employees stay in for lunch and meetings because their "network is inside the building."

Geraci says this internally focused business model worked for our predecessors. "But in today's world, it doesn't. Companies with the organism mindset are too slow to adapt to survive in the modern world. The world around them changes, recombines, evolves, and they are stuck with their same old DNA, their same old problems, their same old (failed) attempts at solutions."

The alternative is what he calls an ecosystem mindset, where organizations realize they are part of a wider ecosystem. He has seen this mindset in almost all startups but no larger companies. The goal, then, is to make better connections with your ecosystem. How? Geraci's advice: "Open the doors. Let the light stream in. Get out of the building. Interact. Not just the strategy team, not just the CEO, but everyone. *The new value is not inside, it's* out there, *at the edges of the network*" [emphasis ours].

Publish the Problem

In a period of combinatorial innovation, you are accepting that new ideas for old problems may come from unexpected places. But that only happens when people know what the problem is you're trying to solve. In the words attributed to Sun Microsystems cofounder Bill Joy, "No matter who you are, most of the smartest people work for someone else." Two external options involve leveraging the crowd:

- **Crowdsourcing** means publishing a description of the problem in forums available to a large number of people. This technique gives you the chance to tap into a vast network of talent and ideas, but is most applicable for consumer products since that by definition is the makeup of the crowd. However, the underlying notion of crowdsourcing—sharing your problems with strangers—remains uncomfortable for most managers. In a *Harvard Business Review* article on the topic, the author commented that "Pushing problems out to a vast group of strangers seems risky and even unnatural, particularly to organizations built on internal innovation." Which is why "Despite a growing list of success stories, only a few companies use crowds effectively—or much at all."[7]

- **Crowd contests**—where you offer an incentive or prize for the best option submitted for solving a challenge—are a different beast than crowdsourcing. They tend to attract well-funded teams that can afford to pursue moon-shot ideas. They actually have a long history (e.g., the Longitude Prize, as discussed in Chapter 6). But today's technology means that crowd contests are both viable and often the preferred option,[8] particularly for issues where you don't know which approach or technology will offer the best solution. And while not suited for every challenge, and bringing with it its own management challenges, the crowd that competes in a contest brings a quantity and diversity of minds that simply cannot be matched internally.

Element #2: Invent New Business Models, Not Just Products or Services

In the past decade, companies have focused so much on improving their ability to churn out new products and services that it can be disconcerting to think that sources of new growth lie elsewhere. Many companies see continual product introduction as a key driver of business success, and some, such as 3M, make it a priority and key metric. (3M tracks this through its New Product Vitality Index, which measures the percentage of revenue in any one year coming from products created in the last five years; 3M NPVI tops 30 percent.)[9]

All this activity, however, perhaps obscures the fact that launching exciting new products is rarely enough to sustain margins, especially since the price advantage of new products is quickly eroded by copycats. Apple is probably the best-known example of the alternative. The company continues to build momentum, despite the rapid general commoditization of smartphone features because Apple didn't just invent a new suite of products, it invented a new business model. This disruptive business model has changed, among other things, how music is sold and consumed (for example, single tracks vs. entire albums), how photos are taken, and how people connect with the world.

A disruptive business model is simply an integrated set of processes and resources to create value for a customer in new and unique ways. Clayton Christensen suggests this means focusing on areas where barriers prevented people from getting particular jobs done—insufficient wealth, access, skill, or time—and there is higher potential for such disruption in industries "where companies focus on products or customer segments, which leads them to refine existing products more and more, increasing commoditization over time."[10]

Looking at new business models is a much-discussed but underutilized lever for innovation, and one that can open up new growth opportunities. In a recent survey, "breakthrough innovators" were nearly twice as likely to innovate new business models as other "strong" innovators.[11]

Zipcar is an example of a disruptive business model, pioneering the concept of car sharing. The company, leveraging phone-enabled technology for reservations and digital keycard systems to unlock cars, solved a specific challenge for the untapped market of young urban consumers: access to automobiles without the headaches and cost of ownership. Zipcar's approach offers a counterpoint to the traditional rental car companies—focusing on different customers (young urbanites or "Zipsters" versus business travelers), leveraging technology for convenience (access to cars via iPhones and key-cards versus rental car counters), offering more granular units of consumption (you can rent by the hour versus 24-hour increments), and with different inventory (Toyota Prius and MINI Cooper versus Chevrolet Malibu and Toyota Corolla). Ultimately it changed the rental car industry. Avis acquired Zipcar in 2013 and rivals Enterprise and Hertz are following similar strategies.

Taking Advantage of the Sharing Economy

Zipcar is a player in what has become known as the *sharing economy.* Others include Airbnb (accommodation) and Uber (transportation). Enabled by new technology, the sharing economy presents opportunities for disruptive business models for some and existential threats for others.

"For companies in a growing number of industries, it's no longer sufficient if you leverage digital technologies to rationalize and optimize your internal production," says NYU professor Arun Sundararajan. "If your business relies on a model of consumption that is inefficient for your consumers, chances are that there's already a new sharing economy marketplace that is looking to streamline it for them."[12]

Element #3: Use Experimentation to More Rapidly Find Winners

According to Harrah's CEO Gary Loveman, there exists a "romantic appreciation for instinct."

He said, "What I found in our industry was that *the institutionalization of instinct was a source of many of its problems*" [emphasis ours].[13] In other words, gut instinct is not a very effective guide to portfolio expansion opportunities in the Age of Complexity.

The best way to correct instinctual bias is through testing and experimentation. If the "romantic appreciation" endures, it does so more as a source of comfort than a source of utility. The sea of combinatorial possibilities is so vast that predicting the big winners in advance is close to impossible. Thus if we accept the notion that a greater portion of future revenues will come from new rather than incumbent businesses, and recognize that we are prone to viewing new businesses with rose-tinted glasses (that is, unreliably), then it is critical to inject data and testing into the mix. Don't just look in the mirror, step on the scale. That means building a system for learning and testing: an experimentation machine.

Becoming an Experimentation Machine

Intuit co-founder and chairman Scott Cook sees experimentation less as a choice than as a requirement in order to adapt to the new environment. Cook tells how he always assumed that as a company grew, the quality of decision making would improve. But at Intuit, he says, he noticed it wasn't improving. He began to worry: "Are some of the things we're doing unknowable? Is it not possible to predict consumer behavior?"

His personal epiphany about testing came in response to studying and comparing Toyota, Yahoo, and Google. He discovered, for example, that Toyota operates as a "massive series of experiments" throughout the organizational hierarchy. He also talked to Yahoo employees, who told him that Google beat them by running 3,000 to 5,000 experiments a year, trying new things "at a ferocious rate." The Yahoo-ians told him, "They just outran us. We tried management . . . but we didn't have that experimentation engine."

This led Cook to make Intuit into a "testing" culture. Testing cultures have a number of benefits:

- You can make better decisions because you're looking at real consumers and real outcomes, not just theory.
- It neutralizes hierarchy, which means that you enable your most junior people to test their best ideas, and provides a means to avoid having majority rule crush creativity.
- You get surprised more often. As Cook writes, "You only get a surprise when you are trying something and the result is different than you expected, so the sooner you run the experiment, the sooner you are likely to find a surprise, and the surprise is the market speaking to you, telling you something you didn't know. Several of our businesses here came out of surprises."

Experimentation vs. Market Research

We talked earlier in this chapter about the need to get actual products or services into the hands of customers in order to get useful feedback. This same principle is true when deciding *what* products or services to offer. Cook gives an example of the supremacy of experimentation over market research for this purpose.

He says that Intuit noticed that 60 percent of new prospects approached the company on the very day they needed payroll checks cut. But traditionally, it would take several days to set up an account so that checks could be processed. Then an engineer had an idea: What if Intuit could cut paychecks right away and do the payroll setup afterward?

Cook details how Intuit did a first pass at market research by asking the opinion of 20 payroll customers whether they would use this option, and none said they would do it. But Intuit didn't stop there. At the behest of *The Lean Startup* author Eric Ries, the business set up an actual experiment: offering the option, even though it didn't actually have the functionality yet. Ries told Cook: "If they pick the paychecks first, setup second, we say, 'So sorry, we haven't built it yet,' and give them a $100 gift certificate."

Cook said: "When [we] didn't ask an opinion [but] just watched behavior, 58 percent clicked on 'I want to cut the checks first.'" So the company built that functionality. Now, says Cook, the payroll division is "going to have their fastest customer growth in ten years because of an experiment."

Bart Becht, who ran multinational consumer goods company Reckitt Benckiser for many years, believed in using testing to nurture ideas where people demonstrated ownership and excitement, even if the idea went against the grain.

As an example, he cited a huge internal debate over the merits of a product called Air Wick Freshmatic, which automatically releases freshener into the air on a schedule. The idea originated when one of the Korean brand managers saw a new kind of dispenser in stores there and believed it held some promise for Reckitt Benckiser. So he brought the idea to a meeting at headquarters. According to Becht there was strong disagreement over whether and where (meaning in what markets) such a product could work. The argument against the idea was that it was a completely new type of product for the company and would require new manufacturing facilities.

However, two people saw potential and were willing to fight for it, which was sufficient for Becht to approve testing (on a small scale). Testing launched in the United Kingdom, was a huge hit, and by the end of the year the product was in more than 30 countries.

All of which is to say that the first prerequisite for building an experimentation machine inside your business is an *experimentation mindset*: a recognition that senior management doesn't have a monopoly on good ideas, that it is increasingly hard to predict customer behavior, and that testing can both be a source of surprises and a correction to bias.

To do this right, here are some key factors to consider:

- **Know when you're experimenting and when you're not.**
  If you mistake an experiment for a business launch, you may invest too much or go too long before pulling the plug. In *The Science of Success*, Charles Koch, CEO of Koch Industries, writes that its businesses have certainly suffered "when we forgot we were experimenting and made bets as if we knew what we were doing." He describes the company's decision in the early 1970s to plunge heavily into the trading of petroleum and tankers. It was an experiment, but the company didn't treat it that way. The result? "When the Arab oil cutback hit in 1973 and 1974, we were caught with positions beyond our capability to handle, leaving us with large losses. That was certainly a great learning experience, but I'm not sure I could stand that much learning again."

- **Use the experiment to improve your "assumption-to-knowledge" ratio.** Academics Rita Gunther McGrath and Ian MacMillan make the point in their book *Discovery-Driven Growth* that confirmation bias can undermine new businesses, saying it "leads people to embrace new information that reinforces (confirms) their existing assumptions and to reject information that challenges them. Not so bad in an existing business, where your initial assumptions have a good shot at being on the right track, but dangerous in a new business where you're not yet clear on what you are doing."

The way we think and make assessments is much more likely to be rooted in the dynamics of our incumbent businesses, while our future depends upon an accurate assessment of the new. If we are trying to improve our assumption-to-knowledge ratio, it is important before we start to state our assumptions. When organizations don't state their assumptions in advance, they run into two problems: assumptions become converted into facts in people's minds, and organizations don't learn as much as they could.

- **Set up metrics to help constantly refine your experimentation capabilities.** Think of it as a key metric for the Age of Complexity: the number of "at bats" you have, the number of times you get to test, tinker, and engage with customers. As Amazon's Jeff Bezos believes, if you double the number of experiments, you double your chances of discovering new innovations. Google's Schmidt is even more specific: "Our goal is to have more at-bats per unit of time and effort than anyone else in the world." Part of the rationale for this is that while experimentation is more likely to get you to new customer-relevant ideas faster than ivory tower planning, the odds are still low. That is, you need to do a lot of experiments. Therefore it becomes a numbers game. Which is why companies like Google, Intuit, and Amazon talk in terms of efficiency metrics and work to improve the processes and systems of testing in terms of speed, cost, and rate of learning.
- **Suspend what's not working.** Tied to "at bats" but worthy of focus in its own right, the Achilles heel of many experiments is that they linger too long. Everybody loves to start things, but nobody likes to stop things. We become disinterested and disconnected from things that aren't working. Corporate incentives tend to discourage the declaration of failures. Or, we remain overly optimistic that, given a bit more time and

another round of funding, this experiment or venture will turn around. The failure to stop what isn't working has to change. As evidence: One of Steve Jobs' first actions when he rejoined Apple in 1997 was to kill the Newton, an early personal digital assistant. He writes that by shutting it down, he freed up engineers who could then work on new mobile devices.[14]

How to Experiment like a Genius

Perhaps no one understood that testing is a numbers game better than Thomas Edison. It is said that in inventing the first commercially practical incandescent light bulb, Edison experimented with more than 1,600 materials (including coconut fiber, fishing line, and even human hair), filling more than 40,000 pages of notes before coming upon carbonized bamboo as workable filament.[15]

Understandably, it was Edison who later said, "Genius is one percent inspiration and 99 percent perspiration." He also said, "I have not failed 10,000 times—I've successfully found 10,000 ways that will not work." Clearly, failure, and learning from failure, is part of the innovation process.

To experiment like a genius, ask yourself these questions:

How efficient are your efforts at finding successes? Edison's trying so many materials for the filament meant he was more likely to find a workable one. The more he tried, the more likely he was to succeed.

How willing and fast are you to declare something a failure? Edison viewed failure as learning. He didn't resist declaring something a failure, and when something failed, Edison quickly learned from it, and then moved on. Today, we too often see organizations reluctant to declare something a failure, and as a result "zombie" efforts hobble on, consuming precious resources.

How much do you learn from each failure event? Edison kept things simple, helping him learn a lot from each failure. But today, process and organizational complexity impede capturing, retaining, and sharing learning.

The side benefit of developing this discipline is the spotlight it puts on the differences between operating the current business and developing the new business, and as a result a more realistic view emerges of what it will take to succeed with the new business.

Making Yourself Less Vulnerable to Attack

Two key challenges define ideation and innovation in today's world. This chapter has been about the first challenge: improving the odds of finding the next big idea. This requires new mindsets and structures so you can quickly and easily find and take advantage of the ideas *no matter where they originate*. This focus, by definition, anchors organizations in the reality of customer feedback and helps ward off internal bias. It leads you toward an experimentation mindset, which usually creates greater clarity of vision. Companies operating with a focus on discovery and experimentation "realize sooner that their core positions are facing the threat of erosion," say McGrath and MacMillan.[16]

The other key challenge—making sufficient room in an organization for new ideas and dismantling the old—is the focus of our next chapter.

CHAPTER 11

Build, Dismantle, Repeat

"I give the talkies six months more."

—CHARLIE CHAPLIN, 1931*

A defining critical characteristic for leaders in the Age of Complexity is being able to guide their organizations through the inevitable waves of change. *Do new things, and stop doing the things you've always done.* Sounds simple, but it's surprisingly hard to do. The business that can do both at the same time is a rare beast. The dynamic has a name: *creative destruction,* a term coined by Austrian-American economist Joseph Schumpeter to describe the transient nature of competitive advantage. This cycle, as we've argued in this book, is accelerating.

---

* *The Jazz Singer,* the first talking picture, was released four years earlier in 1927, and its success launched a wave of productions in the new format. Despite this trend, Chaplin's *City Lights,* a silent picture and reputedly his favorite, was released in 1931 and was nonetheless a commercial and critical success. One journalist wrote, "Nobody in the world but Charlie Chaplin could have done it. He is the only person that has that peculiar something called 'audience appeal' in sufficient quality to defy the popular penchant for movies that talk." It is notable that while Chaplin vehemently resisted the notion that "talkies" were here to stay, he was alone among silent movie stars to find success in the new format. His critique was that it was a narrowing versus expanding art form. He wrote in the *Times* (as reported in *The New Yorker*) that "The silent picture, first of all, is a universal means of expression. Talking pictures necessarily have a limited field, they are held down to the particular tongues of particular races."

Some companies respond to creative destruction by hunkering down behind Castle Walls. They've fallen victim to Siren #4. They like being where they are and don't want anything to change.

Companies may invest heavily in innovation ("adding the new") or in operational excellence ("optimizing the current state"). But the required counterpart ("taking out the old"), in the form of complexity reduction, tends to be neglected. Why? There are many possible reasons:

- The drag of complexity isn't quantified—companies don't know how much it is really costing them to "continue the old."
- All their attention is on the "new" because it is more interesting than the old.
- The impacts of complexity affect an entire system; the costs therefore don't fall onto any one person's lap.
- Established businesses are often power centers, which can create a preservation bias.

Also, creative destruction has rarely been practiced as a management discipline. While most executives have heard of creative destruction, few have grappled with the practical changes required in mindset and practices in order to surf these waves of transient advantage. What makes sense at the intellectual level can feel very different when you're living inside it.

The story of how Andy Grove and Gordon Moore shepherded Intel out of a dying market (memory chips) and into a new market (microprocessors) is well known. But the arduous process by which they *stopped doing the things they'd always done* is worth reflecting upon. In fact, even armed with the correct insight about the future of the market, Grove and his team met resistance in the form of Intel's "religious dogmas,"[1] both of which centered on the importance of memory chips as the backbone of their organization. And

Grove himself—known as a bold, decisive leader—admits he was emotionally conflicted about the nature of the change:

> *To be completely honest about it, as I started to discuss the possibility of getting out of the memory chip business with some of my associates, I had a hard time getting the words out of my mouth without equivocation. It was just too difficult a thing to say. Intel equaled memories in all of our minds. How could we give up our identity? How could we exist as a company that was not in the memory business? It was close to being inconceivable.*[2]

Even if you are not called upon to execute such bet-the-company pivots, it is likely you will find yourself required to exit out of certain markets and businesses and redeploy resources to areas of higher value.

Of course, it doesn't have to be a wrenching, traumatic experience. Certainly, this is sometimes the necessary medicine when there is a sudden unexpected market shift, or a new competitor makes a surprise entry. But in a transient-advantage world, the onus should be on building capabilities for *ongoing weeding and pruning*, versus bringing in the bulldozers and earthmovers. In fact, there is evidence that top-performing growth companies tend to do just that. Academic Rita Gunther McGrath recalls that her research assistants, in gathering data on these top-performing companies, found very little evidence of sudden, wrenching exits. Instead, they "seemed to have a knack for integrating their old technologies into new waves."

So to help you achieve this, we'll introduce four strategies in this chapter that can help you embrace creative destruction:

- Make space through ongoing vigorous pruning.
- Anchor on customer needs, not assets.

- Rethink your business definition.
- Give new ideas room to thrive.

Make Space Through Ongoing Vigorous Pruning

If companies build a capability for ongoing pruning of their portfolio and a constant monitoring of their market position, they can avoid having to make traumatic exits from a market or segment. But it requires discipline and accurate insights into where value is being created in their business—often a critical gap.

For example, consider one of our clients, "ToolCo," a major professional tool manufacturer, which had gone through several SKU rationalization exercises in the past. Its efforts targeted removal of the bottom 5 percent of low-volume products, disturbing normal operations, and did *not* achieve the desired cost reduction benefits because the company did not understand the sources of its profitability.

Our analysis showed that 99 percent of ToolCo's sales came from just 35 percent of its SKUs, and that most of the low-volume SKUs were unprofitable at the gross margin level. Furthermore, ToolCo's growth plans required a significant increase in manufacturing capacity and a significant investment in CAPEX.

From our complexity analysis, we saw that ToolCo's low-volume products were consistently undercosted, as high-volume products were disproportionately absorbing the majority of overhead costs. A deeper pruning of its portfolio allowed ToolCo to concentrate its manufacturing in fewer production lines with higher utilization, increasing plant and staff productivity. Plant CAPEX for machinery and floor space was also avoided by redeploying underutilized assets to make room for growth.

The benefits: a 45 percent increase in capacity with minimal investment, and 15 percent EBITDA lift, at just one of its manufacturing plants, with similar results elsewhere in its business. The results of its subsequent changes are shown in Figure 11.1.

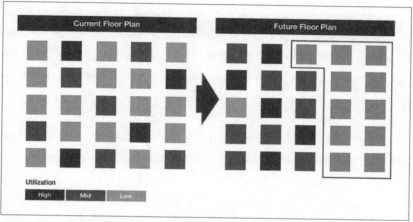

FIGURE 11.1: Pruning for Growth. By removing the majority of the low-volume, undercosted products, ToolCo created the capability to grow its other products (or new products) by 45 percent through asset redeployment and floor space utilization of the manufacturing cells.

Anchor on Customers, Not Assets

The word *assets* has a positive connotation. In a previous age, asset accumulation was a competitive advantage, available to only the biggest companies. Having lots of physical assets presented an insurmountable barrier to entry for any new entrant trying to compete against you. You'll recall the example of Samuel Insull, who established Chicago Edison's fortunes by building larger power stations than anyone else and then acquiring competitors to gain further economies of scale.

But in the Age of Complexity, assets can act as anchors, inhibiting change or contorting the future opportunity to fit the current asset footprint. The accumulation of assets can also create an environment where we are more likely to make strategic mistakes. Leaders get trapped in the mindset of a former age, and see assets as a differentiator, as something their organization has that others don't, and therefore an "advantage." As a result, they may extend a bias toward strategies that leverage existing assets.

As we have discussed earlier in this book, companies are now able to get access to assets *without* ownership: for example, on-demand computing through Amazon Web Services, or on-demand manufacturing through network orchestration. Access without ownership enables a faster, more flexible response to market conditions, as the time it would take to shed assets injects delay in decision making and execution. To illustrate the point, consider the time, effort, and deliberation involved in selling and moving to a new house, not a small undertaking. Now compare that to the task of switching hotels.

It is difficult to imagine now, but when now-defunct Blockbuster launched its own DVD-by-mail service in 2004, many saw the news as the beginning of the end for then-rival Netflix.

"Blockbuster's move poses a potentially serious threat to Netflix," wrote the *Wall Street Journal*.[3] Though Netflix was originally viewed as a niche business—Blockbuster passed on snapping it up for $50 million in 2000—the DVD-by-mail model grew to represent a threat to the Blockbuster's business. Netflix had pioneered the business model, but Blockbuster enjoyed many advantages. It had a bigger brand and 5,500 locations. Netflix had grown its business to 1.5 million subscribers, but that was dwarfed by Blockbuster's 48 million accounts.[4] So when Blockbuster announced it was getting into the DVD-by-mail game, many assumed it would crush the upstart Netflix.

As we all know, things didn't quite work out that way. Just six years later, Blockbuster filed for bankruptcy, and by 2014 its remaining U.S. stores were shuttered. Netflix meanwhile has gone on to become a $6.7 billion video streaming giant. (See Figure 11.2.)

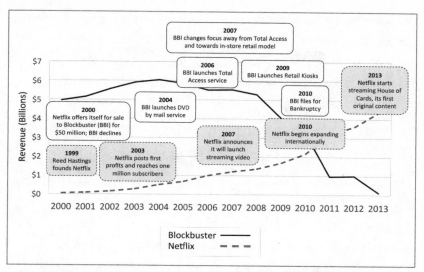

FIGURE 11.2: The Changing Fortunes of Blockbuster and Netflix

What happened in those intervening years? Blockbuster was led first by John Antioco (CEO from 1997 to 2007) and then Jim Keyes (CEO from 2007 to 2011). Both were well regarded in retail circles as effective leaders with strong track records. And the business was alert to the impending dawn of video-on-demand. Antioco came to recognize the threat from DVD-by-mail and streaming and launched an integrated program called Total Access (also doing away with the troublesome late fees!). But another way of looking at the issue is that Netflix had one business to focus on (video distribution), and Blockbuster had two (video distribution and retail). At one point, video distribution happened via Blockbuster's retail stores. When that stopped being the case, the retailer essentially had two separate businesses on its hands, with arguably limited synergy.

According to Vijay Govindarajan, a professor at Dartmouth's Tuck School of Business: "Blockbuster's cardinal sin . . . was maintaining its commitment to a vast retail network, even when that was no longer the way movie renters wanted to shop."[5]

In other words, Blockbuster made strategic decisions based on the assets it had (the retail stores) rather than customer needs.

Give Customers a Reason to Visit

Compounding Blockbuster's problem was that it missed the retail basics.

If your business definition is retail, then the question is how best to attract your core customers with a compelling offer—building loyalty and trust over time—and delivering it in an efficient way with an attractive in-store experience. These are the retail basics. If your business is video distribution, then stores become irrelevant in a digital age.

Jim Keyes approached Blockbuster's business as a retailer. The former 7-Eleven CEO focused on upping the value of every basket, including convenience store type arrays such as candy, snacks, and other impulse buys. *But he hadn't addressed the core issue of giving customers a reason to visit.*

Also, despite being a pure retail operation, the business had done little to build trust with customers. Even though Antioco did away with its punitive late fees—the bane of customers and the original spark for Reed Hastings to found Netflix—once Keyes took the reins, he brought back those fees, arguing that the business couldn't afford to lose the $200 million profit contribution.

So as a retailer, the basics were missing. What became apparent was, when it was no longer *necessary* to go to Blockbuster to rent a movie, people simply stopped coming.

Rethink Your Business Definition

Were there strategic options that would have improved Blockbuster's chances?

As access to digital TV shows and films is becoming ubiquitous, it is notable how Amazon and Netflix are producing their own proprietary content as a source of differentiation—a not unthinkable path for Blockbuster had it moved away from its store network to a streaming-only strategy.

Of course, it's very easy to judge after the fact. As we've said in this book, strategies are inexact. But the clearer your view of the situation—and the more you're aware of the types of traps before you—the better your chances of getting it right. Certainly if Blockbuster had defined its business around the notion of *movie experts* versus retail or video distribution, it might have come up with different strategies.

Business definition underpins successful strategy. It can not only lead to a more nimble strategic response, but also significantly reduce the sense of trauma that comes with change.

Consider the case of Eastman Kodak, an American icon that filed bankruptcy in 2012 in the wake of the rise of digital cameras and built-in smartphone cameras. At the same time, its chief competitor, Fujifilm, diversified and grew despite the migration to digital technologies. The difference in outcomes can be traced to their adaptability.

Both companies saw that change was coming. Larry Matteson, a former Kodak executive, recalls writing a report in 1979 detailing how different parts of the market would switch from film to digital, starting with government reconnaissance, then professional photography, and finally the mass market, all by 2010 (as reported in the *Economist*).[6]

Interestingly, there was a vast difference in how the two firms digested that information. At Kodak, there was "complete and utter denial," according to one source.[7] Steven Sasson, the Kodak engineer who invented the first digital camera in the 1970s, remembers management's dismay at his feat: *"My prototype was big as a toaster, but the technical people loved it. But it was filmless photography, so management's reaction was, 'that's cute—but don't tell anyone about it.'"*[8]

From a margin perspective, the reaction was rational: film was the cash cow, and the longer you could extend its run, the better. But the end of the run was also predictable.

Both firms eventually awoke to the threat. Kodak decided to stick close to home, betting its future on digital imaging (which was more challenging from a profit perspective, and further challenged with the advent of smartphones). Fujifilm, in contrast, took a different path. It adjusted to a new business definition based on its existing pockets of expertise—such as nanotechnology, photosensitive materials, and chemicals—rather than specific products. For example, the company discovered it could exploit its chemical expertise for other markets such as drugs, LCD displays, and cosmetics. (Its knowledge of collagen, which keeps photos from fading due to its antioxidant qualities, was a springboard for an anti-aging-skincare product line called Astalift.)

That is not to say that Fujifilm's transition was painless. "Both Fujifilm and Kodak knew the digital age was surging towards us," said Fujifilm CEO Shigetaka Komori. "The question was, what to do about it." Indeed, as part of the restructuring, Fujifilm shut plants and announced layoffs. All told, the restructuring led to the loss of 10,000 jobs and a total charge of ¥350 billion ($3.3 billion).

"The most decisive factor was how drastically we were able to transform our businesses when digitalization occurred," Komori said.[9] When the boat is sinking, he said, no one complains too loudly. Nonetheless, by stretching its business definition away from imaging, Fujifilm was able to map out a path forward that was economically viable while leveraging its existing capabilities.

Give New Ideas Room to Thrive

Disengaging from legacy lines of business is only half the battle. You need new ideas. Ironically, it is not uncommon for emerging businesses to be crowded out by parts of the business that have historically provided the lion's share of revenue, or to be yanked before they have had a chance to find their feet.

In this regard, startups have a big advantage over larger firms. In the latter, if a new venture is not a hit out of the gate, there is a lot of pressure to abandon the project or let it linger and just move on. Startups, on the other hand, *have* to succeed, and if the first iteration doesn't work, their natural instinct is to reinvent and reconfigure until something works. You'll hear many refer to this as a *pivot*. This is in stark contrast to many large corporations.

Entrepreneurs are not focused on avoiding the stigma of failure; they are focused on making their business work. To that end, it is not uncommon for startups to spend a lot of time going down blind alleys before finally finding the path to success. Yelp began life as an automated system for e-mailing recommendation requests to friends, a proposition that fell flat. Only when the site allowed users to post reviews about local businesses—an idea that seemed like an interesting feature but hardly a growth engine—did things take off.

In *The Lean Startup*, Eric Ries discusses what he calls an "overriding challenge" in developing a successful product: "deciding when to pivot and when to persevere." Many very valuable ideas, businesses, and products have only found their way after: (1) a *pivot*, which may include switching to a different customer segment, application, channel, etc., and (2) *perseverance* in spite of a significant setback.

Microsoft experienced this firsthand with its much criticized— then much praised—Surface tablet. It developed its first versions of the Surface tablet in total secrecy using conventional product design and development methodology. It was an interesting concept that failed due to poor execution, both on product features and requirements and technical aspects of product development. The result: a $900 million write-down!

A *CNNMoney* article explained that "Microsoft didn't want to tip off its competitors, so it holed the team away in a secret lab and even gave it a meaningless codename, 'WDS.' Customers were never asked for feedback—and it showed."[10] Secrecy kept Microsoft from continually engaging with its customers to ensure refinement of the broad convergence concepts that everyone found so appealing. "It was ginormous, essentially eliminating any advantage of being a tablet." Microsoft has since turned its development methodology completely around and moved to a rapid prototyping model that allows continuous customer engagement during product development. The result, the Surface Pro 3, has been a big success.

"When you look at that writedown and that moment, it was, of course, humbling," said Panos Panay, head of surface computing. "But Microsoft has been so amazing and not once wavering on its commitment to making amazing products. Not once."

Microsoft has the resources to stand behind Surface, but nonetheless its continued doubling down on the product until the company got it right is noteworthy. (That's nonetheless an expensive way to get it right! Did Microsoft forget the lesson from Chapter 10—know when you're experimenting and when you're not?) Start-ups don't have a billion dollars to burn. Ries suggests reframing the term *runway*, a term entrepreneurs use to describe the time they have remaining to achieve success before they run out of money. He says:

> *The true measure of runway is how many pivots a startup has left: the number of opportunities it has to make a fundamental change to its business strategy. Measuring runway through the lens of pivots rather than that of time*

suggests another way to extend that runway: get to each pivot faster.

What are the implications for large multinational businesses? A primary lesson is that even the best ideas don't come out of the box perfect. They need nurturing and a lot of testing and reworking until they become hits. So don't let an initial setback define the ultimate success or failure of a new growth initiative.

Second, ensure that pivots are part of your vocabulary and that of your business. Big companies are naturally burdened with less agility than startups (more layers of decision making, more budgetary controls, more voices in the room). Like a giant ship, they have a slow turn radius. But just as premature abandonment is nonproductive, so too is blind perseverance—automatic pilot that carries you off the edge of the cliff despite the emergence of new information that suggests a course correction is needed. Pivots are part of the discovery process. A good question to ask, therefore, at the beginning of the project is, how many pivots can we afford? That way the topic is at least on the table.*

---

* **Pivot, Persevere—Kill?** In Chapter 10, in discussing how experiments can help develop new growth opportunities, we recommend that you "suspend what's not working." But here we are suggesting that you give good ideas a chance, through pivots and persevering. How to reconcile the two? It is not always a straightforward answer. But a couple of principles can help: (1) *Know when you are experimenting and when you are not.* If it's the latter, then that implies that you have already developed some market or technical insight that you are betting on, which may warrant continued investment; (2) *Be clear about your organizational constraints and capacity, and how many bets you can support.* Steve Jobs implies that he might have tried to salvage the Newton if Apple wasn't in such dire straits. The biggest resource constraint is likely your best people. You'll have to pick your bets. So if this is outside the future focus of the business, then it may warrant suspension. These are hard choices, but lack of focus will delay development and dilute efforts.

Evaluating Your Vulnerability

In the examples given in this chapter, none of the changes were like a thunderbolt from a clear blue sky. Blockbuster saw Netflix on the horizon; Kodak and Fujifilm were both aware of the technology changes and what they could mean for their existing businesses. Of course, that is not always the case. A number of businesses, including music distribution and satellite navigation devices, have been upended in rather rapid and dramatic fashion by the arrival of smartphones. But many times, the changes come gradually, or as Andy Grove puts it, "instead of coming in with a bang, approach on little cat feet."[11]

The key is, does your organization have the right mindset to observe the changes and subsequently take action?

Frequently, what stops organizations from doing just that are the mental models that deafen them to these subtle changes, or discourage them from taking action. High Castle Walls! So how susceptible are you to ignoring a grave threat?

Consider to what degree the following statements describe the business. The more your business thinking sounds like this, the more vulnerable you are:[12]

- **We do resource allocation by business unit, and usually start with last year's number and adjust accordingly.**
  Resource allocation is one of the best ways as a leader to ensure your business is moving in sync with the market, and to control expansions and manage exits. That is why it is usually a mistake to decentralize resource allocation—as few managers will ask for less budget each year.[13] The money becomes hostage to the business unit instead of being smartly reallocated to growth areas. It also underscores the need to do zero-based resource allocation (starting with a clean sheet of paper) versus making it a purely budgetary

process (which often starts with last year's budget, followed by a negotiation for a percentage increase).

* **Before we pursue new opportunities, we ensure that they won't cannibalize key products or key areas of existing business.** It is understandable to be concerned about new competition for your top-selling products and services— even if the competition comes from your own organization. But either you cannibalize your product line, or someone else will. When Amazon launched Marketplace—where third parties could offer used books in direct competition with Amazon's own listing—there were immediate protests from publishers saying it would undermine sales of new books and from inside Amazon itself, where category managers were now doubly challenged in meeting sales numbers. But Bezos saw this as offering more choices for customers. "Jeff was super clear from the beginning," said Neil Roseman (a former VP of engineering at Amazon, quoted in *The Everything Store*). "If somebody else can sell it cheaper than us, we should let them and figure out how they are able to do it."[14]

* **Our channel partners are our top priority; we won't pursue anything that creates channel conflict.** Channel conflict has always been a creeping issue for companies working through intermediaries to consumers (such as consumer goods companies distributing through retailers). The challenge: how to keep these intermediaries happy while being attentive to the end consumer, who now has many direct options and unprecedented access to price comparison given the rise of e-commerce and aggressive competitors like Amazon. The activity of "managing" channel conflict represents a source of delay and inefficiency that upstart competitors can exploit with sharp, direct appeals to your consumers.

- **At the end of the day, what matters is incremental revenue.** An incremental sale can be good or bad: bad if it creates more complexity and the costs outweigh the revenue; bad if it's at odds with long-term customer value. When Jim Keyes reintroduced late fees at Blockbuster, he cited the significant profit contribution it represented. But it was one more nail in Blockbuster's coffin.
- **Our sense of history and corporate legacy strongly influences our strategic decisions.** A sense of pride in the accomplishments and legacy of a business is intrinsically a positive, unless it hinders our ability to match the pace of change in the market or takes us further from what customers want. At the end of the day, customers didn't care about Kodak's legacy, only Kodak did.

If the above statements reflect your organization, then your risk is high. Raise the red flag about these practices. Be vigilant to how they may disguise or downplay disruptive threats.

Your New Starting Point: Plan for a World of Fleeting Advantage

In *The End of Competitive Advantage*, McGrath writes that within companies that master the cycle of Build, Dismantle, Repeat, "Exits are seen as intelligent and failures as potential harbingers of useful insight." Moreover, she says, companies develop a rhythm for moving from one area to another, in line with a life cycle. This contrasts with the vast majority of organizations that possess a "presumption of stability," which she says creates all the wrong reflexes:

> *It allows for inertia and power to build up along the lines of an existing business model. It allows people to fall into routines and habits of mind. It creates the conditions for*

turf wars and organizational rigidity. It inhibits inno-
vation. It tends to foster the denial reaction rather than
proactive design of a strategic next step. And yet "change
management" is seen as an other-than-normal activity,
requiring special attention, training and resources.[15]

In the Age of Complexity, this orientation has to be switched 180 degrees. Presume that you will always have only a *transient advantage* with whatever you create. Switch the questions that you're asking as a leader. Instead of "How will we deal with the unexpected?" ask "What can we do so we are always ready for the unexpected?" Instead of "how can we conserve our assets?" or "How can we avoid trauma?" ask, "How can we be positioned to reconfigure easily?"

The bottom line is that markets outperform companies for a very simple reason: *they do not yearn for stability and continuity.* They are unencumbered by a sense of history, existing relationships, or fear of cannibalizing themselves, elements that can make companies vulnerable to disruption. So, what's a leader to do? Put the assumption of discontinuity at the center of your strategy-making process, watch out for Castle Walls, and orient your processes and decision making to the reality of transient advantage.

CALL TO ACTION

Assess Your Explorer's Mindset

Opportunity:

We have defined the key components of the Explorer's Mindset—the mental models that frame how companies approach the pursuit of growth and tend to govern subsequent behaviors. In other words, your culture. Assessing how well your organization reflects the Explorer's Mindset can reveal potential areas of opportunity and is the first step to building a more assertive growth culture.

Key questions for discussion:

Explorer's Mindset	Discussion Questions
Our strategy is bold and reflects our distinctive beliefs.	• What is our "unique belief," and how does it shape our strategy? • What *unreasonable* goals should our business embrace?
We are ruthlessly focused on a few things.	• As leaders, do we share a simplification doctrine? • How focused are we on a few key strategic priorities?
Speed is built into everything we do.	• How would our margin replacement ratio compare to competitors'? • Are we structured for adaptability and responsiveness, or efficiency?
We experiment frequently to improve the odds.	• How far and wide do we look for sources of growth? • How well, how quickly, and how often do we experiment?
We easily transition in and out of new opportunities.	• Are we oriented toward transience or continuity? • What practices and beliefs hold us back? (Fear of cannibalizing existing products, channel conflicts, etc.)

Areas to investigate:

- Based on your discussion, and additional review and analysis, plot where you sit on the Explorer's Mindset axis (see figure).
- Estimate where competitors may be positioned relative to you.
- Identify key areas of focus for targeted improvement.

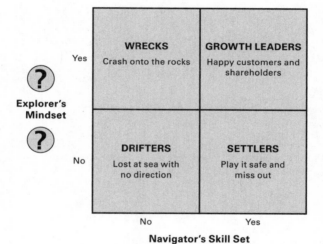

PART IV

The Navigator's Skill Set

CHAPTER 12

Know Where You *Really* Make Money

"If a blind man leads a blind man, both will fall into a pit."
—MATTHEW 15:13-14

Most companies do not truly know where or how they make money!

This may be a shocking statement, but upon reflection it should ring true. If your company is like many others, you know your overall costs, but you do not know your costs at a more granular and actionable level. You know how much overall profit you make, but you do not have a clear picture of your profitability by product or by customer. And like others, you probably have a strong belief that many things your company does, sells, or provides are in reality much more costly, and therefore less profitable, than your figures show.

And if this is the case, then the converse is also true—that some of what your company does is actually much *less costly*, and therefore much *more profitable*, than you may realize. We call these products, customers, segments, activities, and so on your *islands of profit* in your sea of costs.* But with all the cross-subsidizations

---

* Referring back to the Whale Curve introduced in Chapter 2 and covered in more depth in our first book, *Waging War on Complexity Cost*, the islands of profit are the 20 to 30 percent of products that in many companies generate over 300 percent of profits; and the sea of costs are the remaining 70 to 80 percent of products that destroy 200 percent or more of profits.

that typically exist in most companies today, the picture for most is opaque at best, with the islands and sea blending together behind a fog bank.

Many executives have confided in us that they don't truly believe the standard cost and profit figures their accounting or finance departments provide. They know that massive cross-subsidizations mask the true cost and profit of their products, customers, market segments, and activities. They have strong suspicions that particular products, customers, and regions are much more costly than the organization realizes. But the organization continues to manage its business, almost as a matter of faith, based on standard cost and profit figures, as it knows nothing else. The business is navigating choppier waters in an ever thickening fog bank.

This needn't be the case. What would it mean if you could lift the fog and gain a clear view of your real cost and profit at the product, customer, and segment level? What would it mean if you really knew where you make, and lose, money?

In this chapter we discuss three steps toward navigating your profit trajectory:

1. Understanding where you make and lose money today (i.e., knowing your complexity-adjusted operating profit by product, customer, region, and so on)
2. Understanding how your profitability by product, customer, region, and so on can be expected to change if or as volume changes (i.e., knowing your profit scaling curves)
3. Understanding how greater or lesser levels of complexity can change your profit scaling curves (i.e., knowing how to shift your scaling curves)

What's at Stake?

Navigation starts with knowing where you are, and growing in the Age of Complexity starts with knowing where you are making money and where you are not. Without a clearer and more granular view of real cost and profit than traditional costing methodologies and the vast majority of accounting and finance departments can provide, companies are as the blind leading the blind. Consider the implications:

- Undertaking product rationalization efforts without knowing how much profit each product actually generates
- Setting prices without knowing the real costs of your products and services
- Advancing new products without understanding the likely full cost implications of those decisions, nor their impact on the profitability of other products
- Making decisions around resource investments without really knowing the likely full costs and therefore returns of those decisions—including underinvesting in the real drivers and creators of profit
- Making acquisitions based on synergies that not only are not achieved but were never really there for the taking
- Basing business plans on economies of scale that never materialize

Our premise here is this: in the Age of Complexity (1) most companies do not know, at an actionable level, where they really make money, and (2) without knowing where you make money you cannot reliably navigate to profitable growth.

Of course, once you know where you are—meaning where you make money—you must decide where to go. But unless you know this, nothing else matters. So this is where development of your navigation skills begin.

Beware Standard Cost and Profit

A theme in this book is that complexity has changed the game, rendering traditional approaches outmoded and more dangerous to rely upon. Chief among these is traditional product costing, commonly referred to as "standard cost." (Next but not far behind is a common misplaced reliance on contribution margin, which we will get to later.)

Standard costs are full of cost allocations, but *allocations based upon the outmoded fixed-variable cost paradigm of the Industrial Age*—such as spreading overhead costs across a portfolio of products in proportion to each product's sales. By not recognizing the impact of complexity costs, standard costing is left rife with cross-subsidizations. Further, as complexity has grown, the difference between standard cost/profit figures and the true cost/profit has only increased, and to untenable levels for many companies.

Borrowing some terms from Lean, all costs are either value-add (VA) or non-value-add (NVA). For example, the raw materials in a product are likely VA. So too is the time involved in the actual machining of a part—or perhaps the time to manufacture it at a gross production rate on a production line. But items such as set-ups or changeovers, indirect labor, losses and inefficiencies, the cost to transport, store, and handle inventory and WIP, and manufacturing overhead overall, not to mention corporate overhead, are by definition NVA. Standard costing tends to deal generally well with VA costs, which are more tangible and easier to measure and assign, but does not deal well with the ever increasing NVA costs, which are more difficult to assign to a specific product.*

---

* Remember, complexity costs tend to grow exponentially with the level of complexity. And while complexity costs and NVA costs are not necessarily the same, complexity is what drives NVA costs to be so large. At a practical level, where NVA costs are large, we can then treat them as complexity costs. For more information on how complexity drives NVA costs, see our first book, *Waging War on Complexity Costs*.

Consider how we typically develop our standard cost figures: We may know the actual cost of something, such as we pay a supplier $2.65 per pound of copper, for example, and since Product A contains, say, two pounds of copper we put $5.30 toward the unit cost of Product A, and continue to other materials and other cost categories. This part is rather straightforward.

Increasingly, however, the costs that we put to a product are allocations of shared resources and costs—indirect costs and overheads—where the portion of the resource consumed by a specific product is much less clear or tangible than, say, the measurement of two pounds of copper. Although these costs are less tangible at a product or customer level, they are no less real, and without better methods for costing, and left with only the outmoded fixed-variable cost paradigm, we force ourselves to convert such costs into unit costs that are much easier to deal with. The result: we tend to "peanut butter" spread these costs, spreading them in proportion to volume (whether by revenue, units, weight, or so forth).

With no other approach, we treat all products as equal consumers of such overhead, other shared costs, and many inefficiencies, even though that is rarely the case. For example, we worked with a major brewer that for years had produced only a very small number of high-volume beers at its largest brewery. With essentially just two products, its namesake brand and the light version of the same, it was very easy to develop a production schedule. Then, with the growth of craft beers and the resulting growth in the number of the brewer's products, and its packaging variety as well, the production schedule became a complex science at the brewery, necessitating creation of a production scheduling department. The cost of this department rolled up into manufacturing overhead, which was then allocated along with the rest of manufacturing overhead to individual products in proportion to their volume produced. The result was that the vast majority of the production scheduling cost was being borne by the two high-volume legacy products that had been relatively easy to schedule on their own, and not by the many lower-volume craft products that had necessitated creating the production scheduling department in the first place.

Granted, your standard costing may already account for some differences between your products and services in generating NVA costs. Perhaps you already account for one product requiring more setup time than another, or some products running slower or having higher scrap on your line, or some services being more time consuming to provide, but you likely don't account for the fact that with all the variety of products, raw materials, WIP, and finished goods, your facility is larger and more sprawling, increasing travel time all around. You likely don't account for the fact that some products (and costumers, segments, etc.) consume much more overhead, engineering, customer service and support, and other shared and overhead resources per unit than do other products.

However, it is likely that we don't need to convince you that your standard cost figures increasingly don't reflect reality. Based on our experience, we are confident that at some level you already believe this. Executives know this in their bones. In fact, for years many intrepid executives have tried to tackle this issue, attempting to sort through this complex costing mess, almost to the point that they have given up. But don't give up just yet.

ABC Falls Short

Activity-based costing (ABC) was to be the panacea for our costing ills. Developing in the 1970s and 1980s in the manufacturing sector, and defined in 1987 by Robert Kaplan and William Bruns in their book *Accounting and Management: A Field Study Perspective*, ABC initially sought to account for the indirect and overhead costs left out of traditional cost accounting, and later to correct for the growing cross-subsidizations involved in standard costing to more correctly allocate indirect costs to specific products.

However, ABC grew too cumbersome. While well intentioned and in several applications even useful, ABC was not able to keep pace with the growing complexity of our world. In application, *ABC began to fail under its own weight, falling prey to the complexity it was meant to address.*

We consider ABC a "bottom-up" approach. It involves identifying all indirect activities and assigning the cost of each activity to all products (or customers) based on the actual consumption by each. This worked well when the level of complexity—the variety of activities and products—was, although material, still low. It worked as a method of complexity costing when the level of complexity was still not that high. It was a temporary solution. With greater complexity there became ever more and smaller-volume activities to identify, and many more products to assign cost to. As complexity grew, the level of effort required to apply ABC grew exponentially, and ABC initiatives became enormous, cumbersome, and resource intensive projects that strained under their own weight.

Further, ABC is a very static exercise, yet the more complex a system is the more dynamic it tends to be. After counting all the "beans" and assigning costs to all products and/or services, and adding everything up, the resulting answer only reflects the organization as it was when it was counted. Once processes or the product/service portfolio is changed—often in response to the results of the ABC study—one would have to count all over again to see the new cost picture. And in a complex system, things are highly intertwined—impacting one area tends to affect a myriad of other areas.

However informative, such efforts in today's complex world become so unwieldly and impractical that executives often simply abandon them or never want to repeat them. Indeed, we have met many a battle-scared senior executive that never wants to go through an ABC effort again.

But ABC's being an impracticable solution for today's costing crisis does not mean that the need for and value from knowing where you really make money has abated. Rather, it is as important as ever. We just needed different tools.

Square Root Costing

Square Root Costing (SRC) is the most exciting development in the world of costing in many years. It is a practical methodology for correcting the cross-subsidizations that have plagued standard costing, and is far faster, much less cumbersome, and significantly less resource intensive than ABC. SRC can accomplish this because it is the only costing methodology based on an accurate under-standing of complexity costs. It isn't constrained to the outmoded fixed-variable cost paradigm. It recognizes complexity costs as a category of costs on their own with their own unique dynamics, rather than force-fitting them into buckets as either variable costs or fixed costs, neither of which they are. In short, it is a costing methodology suited for today's complex world.

SRC is easier and faster since it is not a bottom-up "count the beans" approach like ABC. Rather, it is a top-down, allocation-driven costing approach, as is standard costing, but importantly with a broader menu of allocations methods than standard costing.

Many of our clients, using SRC, have quickly gained a much clearer view of their true product and customer profitability, blow-ing away the fog obscuring their islands of profit and exposing a sea of costs. These companies have used SRC to inform product and service portfolio optimization efforts and product strategies; develop new product costing models and business rules for product management, including minimum efficient volumes for products, product families, brands, regions, and so on; and broadly, to inform strategic decisions.

Invariably, *they find that their small-volume products, services, customers, regions, and activities are more costly and less profitable than reflected in their standard cost,* often much more so. This does not necessarily mean that these products and services are unprofitable, as the price point may be sufficiently high to cover the costs, but they are almost always not as profitable as they had appeared.

The reason is simple: complexity is the opposite of scale. Remember, as we described in Chapter 3, complexity breaks up scale, and profitability is driven more by economies of density (revenue divided by complexity) than economies of scale (simply revenue). Larger-volume products deliver relatively more scale, and relatively less complexity (i.e., are more dense); whereas smaller-volume products deliver relatively more complexity, for relatively less scale (i.e., are less dense).

Figure 12.1 shows complexity-adjusted operating margins by product segment for one of our clients, a major beverage company. Product Segment C includes the company's major legacy brands. While it still comprised the majority of the company's sales volume, overall sales in this market segment were flat and price points had been slowly declining, which had created pressure to find new and growing market segments.

Segment D represented a new and growing market opportunity, which consisted of specialty products with much higher price points; hence this was where the excitement, and investment, was. Understandably, the company's standard cost figures showed operating margins in Segment D, at 26 percent, to be much higher than that of Segment C, at just 14 percent.[1] With its specialty products and much higher price point, it seemed to reason that the exciting new specialty segment (D) should be more profitable than the old, staid legacy (C).

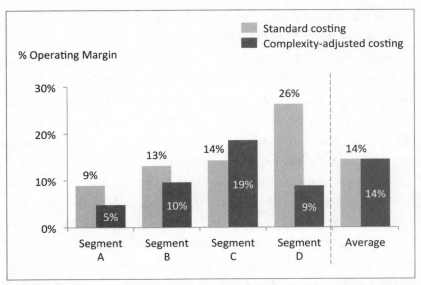

FIGURE 12.1: Complexity-Adjusted Operating Margin vs. Standard Operating Margin for a Major Beverage Company

But these standard cost figures did not account for all the complexity and associated costs that were incurred in order to aggressively compete in and develop and deliver the specialty products making up Segment D. Adjusting for the real costs of this complexity showed not just that the legacy segment was subsidizing the specialty segment, but that the legacy segment was still the most profitable, at 19 percent operating margin, versus the specialty segment's much more accurate figure of 9 percent operating margin.[2] The cost of all of the unrestrained product proliferation incurred in going after the specialty more than consumed the potential value afforded by the high price points.

However, given the flat to declining legacy segment, and higher price point and growth in the specialty segment, the answer was not to shift away from Segment D, but rather to pursue that segment in a more methodical, disciplined, and purposeful manner, moving away from a "throw it at the wall and see what sticks" approach to product development to a more disciplined product management approach with business rules for minimum effective density, specific targets for product volumes, and culling of unsuccessful products.

Gross Profit or Operating Profit?

Standard cost and profit figures typically only go down to the gross profit level. The rationale for this is that it is too difficult to assign selling, general, and administrative expenses (SG&A) and corporate overheads to specific products, or that such costs are too removed from a product and simply should not be tied to specific products. But this is both a shortcoming and a fallacy, often resulting in unprofitable companies full of profitable products and services.

We are emphatic in our belief that product profitability should be assessed all the way down to the operating profit level; and our experience helping transform companies has only solidified our resolve on this point. Complexity is often the largest driver of overinflated SG&A and corporate overheads, and disconnecting these costs from the complexity in your business both gives them a pass and obscures your islands of profit and your sea of costs.

A similar fallacy is an overreliance on contribution margin. Managing a business by contribution margin assumes that all other costs are fixed, and therefore won't change based on the decisions you are making. But we have seen that overhead costs are particularly prone to hidden complexity costs and where we see complexity costs to be most insidious.

Tactical decisions may be informed by contribution margin, but strategic decisions should be informed by operating margin. Tactical decisions are ones where resource allocation decisions are already made, or fixed, such as whether to accept an order for an existing product. Strategic decisions are ones that involve or impact resource allocations, such as what products to bring to market, what customers to serve, what countries or regions to enter. Strategic decisions must be made with a full view of their impact on operating margin and profit. To do otherwise is to blind oneself, adding more complexity, misbelieving other costs to be fixed, only to be later surprised with burgeoning SG&A and corporate overheads.

Looking Under the Hood of SRC

How does SRC work? SRC is a top-down allocation methodology based on a fuller understanding of cost in today's complex world. In Chapter 2 we introduced the three types of cost: variable costs, fixed costs, and complexity costs. These costs vary proportionally with volume, are independent of volume, or grow exponentially with complexity, respectively; and each of these costs dominated the Preindustrial Age, the Industrial Age, and the Age of Complexity, respectively. It is important to understand the dynamics behind each of these costs, so first a little review:

- **Variable costs.** Traditional variable costs are simply proportional to some measure of volume (whether tons, gallons, dollars, hours, etc.). If you double the volume, from say two pounds of copper to four, you double the cost. This relationship is shown as a straight line in Figure 12.2a1, where the unit cost (for example, $2.65 per pound of copper) determines the slope of the line. The unit cost is independent of volume, meaning that it doesn't change over the range of volumes. Therefore, the unit cost is constant, as shown in Figure 12.2a2.

- **Fixed costs.** Fixed costs are almost the opposite of variable costs. With fixed costs, it is the total cost, and not the unit cost, that is constant over volume (see Figure 12.2b1). Another way to say this is that cost is independent of volume. For example, most design, engineering, product development, and registration costs for a product are independent of the volume sold of the product. Some quality costs also fall into this category. For example, if one must perform a quality check on an ingredient tank each day, regardless of how much of the ingredient is added or used from the tank, then the cost of that quality check is independent of the volume of the ingredient used. Importantly, if the total cost is independent of volume, then the cost per unit is highly dependent on volume, and drops rapidly as the fixed cost is spread over more units (see Figure 12.2b2).

These descriptions capture the essence of standard costing. When allocating costs, we treat costs as either fixed or variable, and since fixed is rather extreme, when in doubt we usually allocate costs as variable costs, meaning we peanut butter spread those costs in such a way that we treat all products, customers, and so on as equal generators of those costs, masking real differences between products (and customers, etc.) in generating those costs and creating cross-subsidizations in the process.

However, a significant and growing portion of costs—the large majority of NVA and complexity costs—fit neither variable nor fixed cost categories. These costs tend to go up with volume, but not proportionally with it.[3] Also, their cost per unit tends to drop

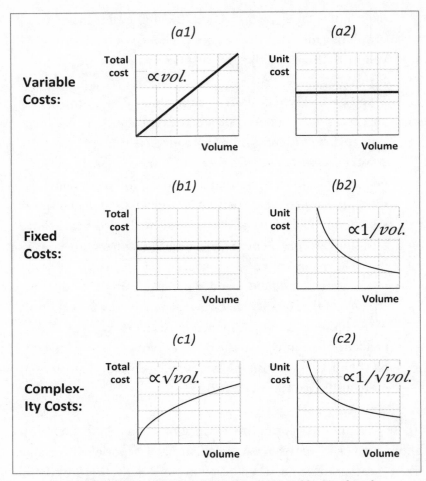

FIGURE 12.2: Relationship of Cost with Volume, for Variable, Fixed, and Complexity Costs

with volume, but not as steeply as that of truly fixed costs. In our work and research we have discovered and categorized this third category of cost:

- **Complexity costs.** Complexity costs tend to follow a square root of volume relationship, meaning that the cost is proportional to the square root of the volume; and since unit cost is simply cost divided by volume, the cost per unit is proportional to the inverse square-root of the volume (see Figures 12.2c1 and 12.2c2).[4]

Why Square Root of Volume?

We did not invent the square root of volume relationship, we discovered it. Years ago we had built several virtual plants—mathematical models representing the real physical plants to optimize things like production scheduling, plant loading, and capacity planning—in support of our work for a pharmaceutical company. In running the models, we began to notice patterns in the data. We then experimented with the plant models, flexing different variables one at a time (such as product setup times, product demands, and inventory holding costs) to see their impact. What we stumbled upon was an ever growing list of costs that were not proportional with volume (i.e., demand), or independent with volume, but varied exactly with the square root of volume.

For example, we found that in a make-to-stock production environment, with an array of products (each with different customer demand but otherwise the same, meaning the same setup time, run speed, yield, etc.), and an optimal production schedule, average cycle stock inventory levels by product were proportional to the square root of each product volume. For example, if Product A had 4x the demand of Product B, then Product A had 2x the average cycle stock inventory.

We also found that the total time spent on setup per product also varied with the square root of volume. So we began to look further, and found other relationships that we should have noticed sooner, such as safety stock varying with the square root of volume.

Further, by dividing by volume, inventory level and setup times per unit of volume varied by the inverse square root of volume. So for example if Product A had 4x the volume of Product B, then the inventory per unit of Product A was half that of Product B. Again we found other such relationships as well, such as the coefficient of variation (COV), meaning that a product with 4x the volume should have one-half the COV.

You have noticed that we have said all else being equal. Rarely is all else equal. But things like run speeds, yields, setup times, and so on vary by factors of two, three, or perhaps tens. But volumes can vary by thousands! For complexity costs, volume (i.e., density) is the dominant driver of cost differences between products—or customers, regions, and so on. By understanding these relationships and introducing them into its costing methodology, SRC can quickly and significantly improve the accuracy of costing figures. In our experience, the square root of volume relationships in SRC correct for approximately 75 percent of cross-subsidizations taking place. In practice, we often find other items to fix more manually to address perhaps another 10 to 15 percent of the cross-subsidizations. At this point we have sufficient clarity to inform business decisions, and going further just passes a point of diminishing returns.

This is a very powerful relationship to understand and take into account in costing. Mathematically, it may look as if complexity costs are just in between the other two methods, so perhaps even without it things would "average out" and come to a good enough answer. However, in practice, this is anything but the case. For costs above gross margin, we tend to mistreat complexity costs as variable costs, yet below gross margin we tend to treat complexity costs as fixed costs. This has two insidious and compounding effects.

First, for costs above the gross margin line—essentially cost of goods sold (COGS)—we tend to mistreat complexity costs as variable costs, peanut butter spreading these costs, with the result that we "undercost" small-volume, less-dense products, customers, activities, and so on. By undercosting small-volume things, we undercost complexity, making complexity appear less costly in our figures, and therefore making organizations more tolerable of taking on more complexity. We pointed out in our first book that the costs of complexity are often hidden, which is in part due to treating complexity costs as traditional variable costs. But while these costs may be hidden, they are still very real. By taking on more complexity, we take on more hidden costs, which we subsidize from our islands of profit, making those islands appear a bit smaller and less profitable than they truly are.

Second, below gross margin—essentially SG&A—we tend to mistreat complexity costs as fixed costs, suggesting that as we add more complexity and revenue, those fixed costs will not grow. But we know from experience that this so often fails to be the case. By mistreating complexity costs below gross margin as fixed costs, we overestimate our potential for fixed-cost leverage, meaning we overestimate the promise of economies of scale (we have seen many a business plan based on economies of scale that the business never realized). By overestimating the promise of economies of scale, your organization is more willing to take on complexity—since it doesn't anticipate the complexity costs that come along with it.

In both cases, by mistreating complexity costs as either variable costs *or* fixed costs, you will underestimate the cost of complexity; and by underestimating its cost, you leave yourself more tolerable and accepting of taking on more complexity, adding hidden costs, obscuring your islands of profit, and eroding the very economies of scale you may be expecting to realize.

By correctly treating complexity costs, SRC presents a clear picture—showing the costs as they truly are, removing the fog bank obscuring your islands of profit and sea of costs, and presents a realistic view of your potential to leverage your real fixed costs and gain scale economies. It is to this last point we turn next, as once you know where you are, you must decide where to go. As you grow your business, how will your costs and profit grow? Will they grow at the same pace, leaving you larger but no more profitable than you are today, or like half of all companies will your costs grow faster than your profits, leaving you larger but less profitable than you are today?

Minimum Efficient Volume?

Managing complexity often comes down to establishing business rules informed by the cost of complexity.

Standard costing tends to undercost small-volume products—leaving larger products (or customers, regions, etc.) to subsidize smaller ones. In correcting for this, SRC tends to shift costs to smaller-volume products. This begs the question, how much more costly are small-volume products than large-volume products, and what is the minimum efficient scale for a product, product family, brand, and so on?

Of course this depends on your particular company, industry, and product portfolio. Figure 12.3 shows a comparison between the complexity-adjusted conversion cost and standard conversion costs by product for an industrial manufacturing company. In this case, small-volume products were as much as six times more costly to produce than their standard cost figures had shown. Also, below annual volume of 10,000 units, the unit price began to rise dramatically. This suggests a minimum efficient volume of 10,000 units per year. Of course, this doesn't mean that products with less than this amount should be eliminated, but does mean that those products have not, or haven't yet, reached an efficient volume threshold.

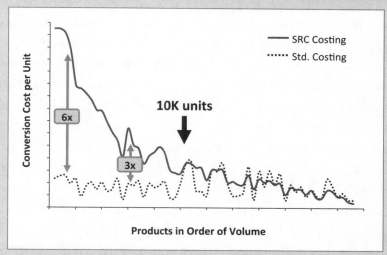

FIGURE 12.3: Comparison of SRC and Standard Costing Conversion Costs per Unit by Product for an Industrial Manufacturer

Return of Scaling Curves

Scaling curves simply show how some measure, for example a company's cost or profit, can be expected to change as revenue grows. A cost scaling curve shows how costs will grow with volume. A profit scaling curve shows how your profit or profitability will change with volume. In the Industrial Age scaling curves were straightforward though important. For example, if a company had $2 million in revenue, and $2 million in costs, half of which were variable and the other half fixed, it would have zero profit. But if it could double its revenue to $4 million (assuming pricing remained the same), it would also double its variable costs to $2 million, yet its fixed costs would remain $1 million, yielding $1 million in profit. The company's profitability would grow from zero percent of $2 million in revenue to 25 percent of $4 million in revenue. Economies of scale indeed.

Although it is much more complex today, companies still need to manage their scaling curves. But despite the need, most companies do not have a clear view at all on how their costs and profit are set to change with scale—and those that believe they do are often disappointed when expected economies of scale fail to materialize. Traditional costing methods are unable to provide scaling curves for several reasons: the errors inherent in standard cost and standard profit figures would be exacerbated and make scaling curves derived from such figures even more unreliable; standard cost approaches typically don't include SG&A, which must be a key part of any meaningful cost curves for managing corporate profit trajectory; and ABC is too cumbersome and not set up for translating its results to a range of volumes. However, because SRC is still an allocation methodology, it is very easy to develop scaling curves—much as it was very easy to develop scaling curves from standard cost figures in the Industrial Age.[5]

Figure 12.4 shows such scaling curves for a variety of products offered by an industrial supply company. All of these products (A through G) had showed positive operating margin based on standard costing. However SRC showed that only two of them (products

A and C) were actually operating margin positive. But the scaling curves revealed much more. They showed products B and D to be subscale, meaning that with sufficient growth they could become operating margin positive, to more than 30 percent and 20 percent, respectively. Product E, with enough growth, would only become marginally profitable. Scaling curves also show how much sales for an unprofitable product (or product family, product line, brand, or customer) would have to increase to become profitable.

On the other hand, products G and F were intrinsically unprofitable, meaning that they would remain unprofitable at any reasonable volume. Whereas the company explored opportunities to grow products B, D, and E, the answer for products F and G was to look for opportunities to transform or eliminate these products.

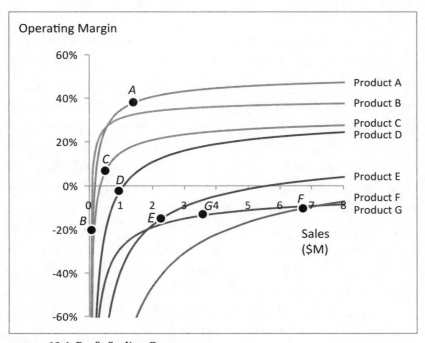

FIGURE 12.4: Profit Scaling Curves

Profit scaling curves can be drawn for any revenue-producing item or groups of items. They can be drawn for products, product families, product categories, market segments, customers, countries, and regions. Clearly, understanding your profit scaling across these many dimensions adds tremendous clarity as you chart a course for profitable growth. The next step is to understand how complexity—adding or removing complexity—changes the shapes of these curves.

Shifting the Curve

If we were to consolidate several products into one product, retaining the same total revenue, we would reduce complexity for the same revenue, and increase density. By reducing complexity, we would gain economies of density, increasing the profitability of the associated revenue.

Removing complexity—for example, pruning a product line—shifts the associated profit scaling curve upward. Conversely, adding complexity shifts the associated profit scaling curve downward (see Figure 12.5). Often, we are adding products—i.e., complexity—to increase sales and revenue. We see ourselves marching along and upward on the profit scaling curve, expecting to enjoy not just more revenue but also greater profitability. But as we add complexity, the curve sinks, and as this cycle continues we find ourselves running up a sinking curve. If we can run up the curve faster than it sinks, then we will increase profitability. On the other hand, if we sink the curve faster than we run up it, we will reduce profitability. This leads us back to our earlier rule of thumb—introduced in Chapter 3—that if we add revenue faster than complexity, we will tend to become more profitable; whereas if we add complexity faster than revenue we will tend to become less profitable.

The real opportunity lies in marching *up* a rising curve; in decreasing overall complexity while increasing revenue, with dramatic increase in density and profitability. How do we do this? This takes us to our next chapter.

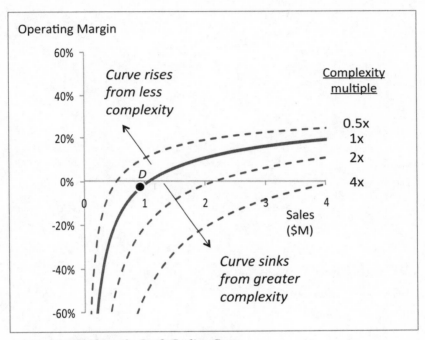

FIGURE 12.5: **Shifting the Profit Scaling Curve**

CHAPTER 13

Reignite Your Core Brands

"Your competition might actually . . . believe that in fact, treating this customer as if she's the only person in the world is worth it. We don't become mediocre all at once, and we rarely do it on purpose. Getting bigger is supposed to make us more effective and efficient. Alas, the way to get there isn't by doing what you used to do, but less well."[1]

—SETH GODIN

Knowing where you make money today is a very good first step. It's a scorecard of sorts, indicating the areas of activity for which customers are willing to pay. It can help refocus the organization on the things that it, alone, can do better than others. Frequently, it highlights the residual value of the central brands, products, and services that helped establish the company in the first place—your "core brands" as we'll refer to them henceforth—and exposes how prior product proliferation programs may have flooded the business with complexity. This complexity is a drag on the business, and a drag on growth, and thoughtful portfolio optimization can provide significant lift. But to really reignite growth in your core brands— a critical skill set in the Age of Complexity—requires additional actions around portfolio segmentation, marketing, innovation, and your operating model.

In this chapter we will focus on how you can free up your core brands from this drag of complexity and mine them for growth and value creation.

The consumer packaged goods (CPG) industry—the focus of this chapter for illustrative purposes—is one that succumbed to the Expanding Portfolio Siren *en masse*, only to refocus in recent years on the value of core brands. That was essentially the thinking that led P&G to shed more than half of its brands, amidst sluggish sales increases, as part of an effort to refocus the business for growth and profitability. A. G. Lafley came out of retirement in 2013 for a stint to take up the CEO spot once again and spearhead the refocusing of the portfolio. At the time of his return, the portfolio ranged from batteries to pet food, detergent, electric razors, deodorants, toothbrushes, and toilet paper.

Framing up his criteria for divestiture, Lafley was quoted as saying: "I'm not interested in size at all. I'm interested in whether we are the preferred choice of shoppers."[2]

His actions, however, yielded significant scale benefits for the consumer goods giant. Despite unloading some significant businesses—its animal foods brands to Mars, its Duracell batteries unit to Berkshire Hathaway, and a collection of 43 beauty businesses to Coty—the remaining brands generated 90 percent of P&G's $83 billion in annual sales (predivestment) and over 95 percent of its profit. Put another way: the 50 percent of its brands P&G unloaded—each with its own dedicated team, financial overhead, share of corporate resources, and drain on management time—generated only 10 percent of its revenues and 5 percent of its profit. The products P&G kept had things in common: they were defined by product technology that made a consumer difference, and they were daily use items.

CFO Jon Moeller explained P&G's new approach as focusing on "core brands and businesses that create the strongest customer preference and the best balance of growth and value creation."

As a growth enabler, the value of returning to the core is twofold: the focus it engenders and the investments it enables by "reclaiming" margin that was otherwise lost to peripheral activities and products and repurposing toward higher-return areas.

For P&G, this has also required a reorganization of its R&D function, shifting power to product category leaders who are closer to the market, and focusing on breakthrough technologies that can have real impact on people's lives. In the past, the business had been absorbed with cosmetic upgrades, as opposed to game-changing innovations.

"We were doing a lot that wasn't adding value for the consumer," said CTO Kathy Fish, "and even worse, that was making it hard for the consumer to shop our shelves."[3] The business is now making investments in support of its core brands and launching new products.

Overall, management expects that with the new portfolio organic growth rate will increase by one percent, and with two percentage points of higher profitability.[4] The strategy is showing early results. To date, the actions have yielded significant cost benefits: P&G recently announced plans to reduce costs by $10 billion between 2017 and 2021, which comes on top of $7 billion it eliminated between 2012 and 2016.[5]

And in its second quarter 2017 results, the first quarter to see the impacts from the brand divestments, its organic sales (a closely watched metric that excludes the impact of foreign exchange, acquisitions and divestitures) rose by 2 percent, higher than expectations, with an upwardly revised sales outlook for the year.[6]

P&G's story is far from unique. We see a common story across the industry. In the pursuit of growth, CPG companies have launched waves of SKU extensions and incremental innovations. Hershey, for example, enjoyed consistently strong growth for many years on the back of product proliferation—up to a point.

"After years of growth and success, we had hit a difficult period," said J. P. Bilbrey, then-president of Hershey North America.[7] "Senior management was not aligned in how we were going to compete—and our results weren't as good as we would have liked them to be."

Hershey's team investigated and found three root issues:

- The company's key retailers and competitors had entered a phase of significant consolidation that was changing influence within the category.
- Consumers were not responding to all the new flavor varieties.
- Hershey's focus on growth through pack type variation was driving complexity, not growth, while its competitors were focusing on brands.

The business, in other words, was operating in push-mode. It had not responded to retailers' growing need for lower inventories, better use of shelf space, and less product and packaging complexity. Instead, the marketing push was to add more and more pack types and flavor proliferations for its classic brands. To turn the situation around, the business shifted from a supply-driven approach to a demand-driven approach, getting to the heart of customer tastes and expectations.

The key takeaway is that the default strategy of simply launching more SKUs and line extensions is insufficient for growth in the Age of Complexity, and is ultimately damaging to what made the company great in the first place. Acknowledging this reality, and the value of reigniting the core, is a critical first step.

Assess Your Growth Drivers and Align for "Core" Growth

Of course, this is easier said than done. According to ConAgra Foods CEO Sean Connolly, it requires "unlearning" some old ways of doing things (Figure 13.1).

"We are clear-eyed that our success will require us to break a number of bad habits, and we are making meaningful progress," said Connolly on the second quarter 2017 earnings call. "We are moving from a focus on volume at any cost to a focus on value creation. From a reliance on trade driven push tools to a reliance on stronger brands, stronger innovation, and consumer pull. We're shifting away from SKU proliferation to optimizing our SKUs with a focus on sustainable returns. And we're continuing to make strides in our approach to A&P [advertising & promotion], which is now more focused, consistent, and tied to ROIs."

From	→	To
Focus on **volume**	→	Focus on **value creation**
Reliance on **trade/push**	→	Reliance on brand **strength/pull**
SKU **proliferation**	→	SKU **optimization**
Erratic A&P support	→	**Focused/consistent** A&P support

FIGURE 13.1: ConAgra Is Changing Key Approaches to Drive Profitable Growth

As is typically the case, stopping old habits is harder than starting new practices. They are engrained in a company's operating model, incentive, and culture. ConAgra was unusually forthright in its enunciation of the issues. Without a clear rebuke to what is not working, it's very hard to architect a future. Connelly achieved this through a three-month period of analysis to get to an up-to-date fact base, and declaring an openness to major change.

Many times the impetus for such an effort is a significant decline in the core, as was the case with Chiquita (as described in Chapter 4). But it can also come from the recognition of profit concentration. Earlier in the book we shared the Whale Curve, and the notion that for most companies 20 to 30 percent of products or services drive 300 percent of profitability. This is both a profit *and* growth issue—consider all the resources tied up in the 70 to 80 percent of products that are unprofitable, and how they could be better deployed to higher-growth areas. This dynamic illustrates just how widespread the opportunity is for reigniting the core. It also suggests how hard it is to liberate these "islands of profit in a sea of cost." To do so requires changing not only the portfolio, but also the supporting processes and quite frequently a company's operating model. This is why it is critical up front to get alignment across the executive team and assess, through a period of analysis, the state of your growth drivers and the value opportunity of focusing and reinvigorating the core.

For P&G, the trigger for their efforts was the recognition that complexity had grown unchecked, resulting in tremendous profit concentration and lower than desired growth. It came from the insight that "simplifying and improving productivity frees up resources for innovation and expansion that ultimately drive profitable growth,"[8] as new P&G CEO David Taylor explained. For Nestlé, with approximately 2,000 brands globally, it was the recognition that its 34 "billionaire brands" constituted 83 percent of its profits with growth of 5.2 percent versus 1.9 percent for the rest of the business.[9]

For another CPG company, a client of ours, we found that despite all the investment, energy, and attention spent on new growth areas, the bulk of the profits still came from its legacy core brand (this was masked by the massive cross-subsidizations that had to be removed to see this picture clearly). Figure 13.2 shows that this company's core brand (Brand A) accounted for 12 percent of SKUs, 27 percent of revenue, but 50 percent of operating profits.

These numbers give a glimpse of the opportunity. Up front, you should also be asking:

- What is the current state, and perception, of our core brands? What competitive threats exist for each?

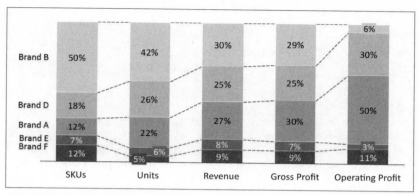

FIGURE 13.2: Legacy Core Brand (Brand A) Subsidizing Other Brands

* Do we have clear category/brand roles within our portfolio to guide decision making?
* What are the customer, operational, and financial impacts of the complexity in our portfolio?
* To what degree are we diluting our marketing spend—and effectiveness—across too many brands and products?
* How do our innovation efforts support or decay the core? Do we understand how our consumers use our products?
* How do we upgrade our operating model fit-for-purpose to reach today's consumers?

As a whole, the answers to these questions will inform the rationale of a "reignite the core" strategy. *How* to do this is the focus of the rest of the chapter, but recognize that this is a significant effort and a transformation journey. The elements of that journey will vary but will likely resemble Figure 13.3.

Define Your Portfolio Strategy

One of the big gaps we see in many organizations is a lack of effective portfolio strategy and segmentation: a failure to identify what

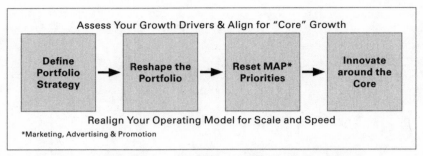

FIGURE 13.3: The Building Blocks for Reigniting Growth in Your Core

roles particular products or segments play in the portfolio. Many times correcting this starts with identifying the jobs that products do for customers, and what value they provide for the business—cash generation, or a beachhead into a new market. This lack of clear portfolio roles is a major contributor to the complexity that has accumulated in an organization in the first place. But getting it right early on provides a strategic framework for reigniting the core.

To provide an example, one of our clients, a manufacturer and distributor of packaged foods ("FoodCo"), found itself with a large portfolio of wines as part of an acquisition. Customers included independent wine and spirits stores, large grocery stores, and an ad hoc selection of restaurants. The shape of the range, however, was driven less by deliberate strategic choices and instead by the influence of a few large suppliers that made up most of the volume. Absent a clear portfolio strategy, the range had become bloated with high numbers of low-margin wines. The decision for FoodCo was whether to divest this business or reinvent it, leveraging its understanding of customers and the market. It went with the latter, and as part of that challenge, assessed what it would take to split the portfolio across two distinct opportunities: a food service offering, serving high-end hotels and restaurants, where the onus would be on higher-end wines at lower volumes and with increased rotation, and grocery, which they were serving currently but with a portfolio that was not fit-for-purpose. In fact, the portfolio as it stood was not fit for either channel; ironically it had a vast array of products, but not the right ones. But having defined the categories, and the roles required of the products within those categories, the business was able to create two distinct, suitable portfolios to serve the two segments (Figure 13.4).

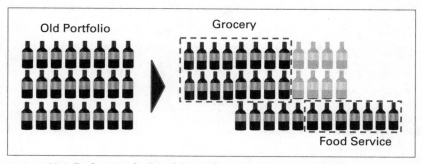

FIGURE 13.4: Reshaping the Portfolio to Serve Two Distinct Opportunities

Typically portfolio strategy falls down in a couple of key ways:

- **Segments are managed bottom-up vs. top-down.** A good product or category manager will look to optimize the mix within his or her respective area, and fight for resources to do so. But at some point these need to be squared off with (1) competing resource needs in other segments across the business and (2) the top-down corporate strategy that is laying out where to play and how to win. This has, or should have, obvious influence on segment strategy.
- **Segments are anchored around industry or subsector definitions vs. portfolio roles.** Companies serving multiple industries will naturally start to segment that way. It can be helpful to understand industry penetration and the specific

industry dynamics. But it can lead to dissipating resources across too many areas, and frequently does not translate to clear actionable objectives.

By contrast, what does a good portfolio strategy help you do? Well, as in the case of FoodCo, it can greatly inform your portfolio optimization (which we discuss next). It will also inform innovation decisions—which high growth submarkets will get the lion's share of innovation dollars over the next few years, vs. simply allocating by current revenue. Above all else, it communicates to the organization (and externally to the market, as shown in Figure 13.5) the priorities of the business and what, at a core offering level, is required to win.

In the case of Reckitt Benckiser, a well-defined portfolio strategy has propelled it to above-industry levels of performance (see Figure 13.6). Its focus: 19 "Powerbrands" that constitute 80 percent of its revenue. These include well-known names such as Vanish, Calgon, and Strepsils. The company has shown it is quick to make acquisition decisions on strong brands with incremental revenue that have high market share—speed enabled by a clear portfolio strategy. Acquiring multiple niche brands that are distinctive, and then driving global growth around them, has helped it grow both top and bottom line over the last decade.

Good Product Management Still Counts!

Although we live in an age when disruption is feasible, it is worth pointing out that the word *disruption* has taken on almost religious significance—and is overused. Wharton Professor Karl Ulrich describes two conditions for true disruption: (1) that a substantial fraction of the market must prefer the

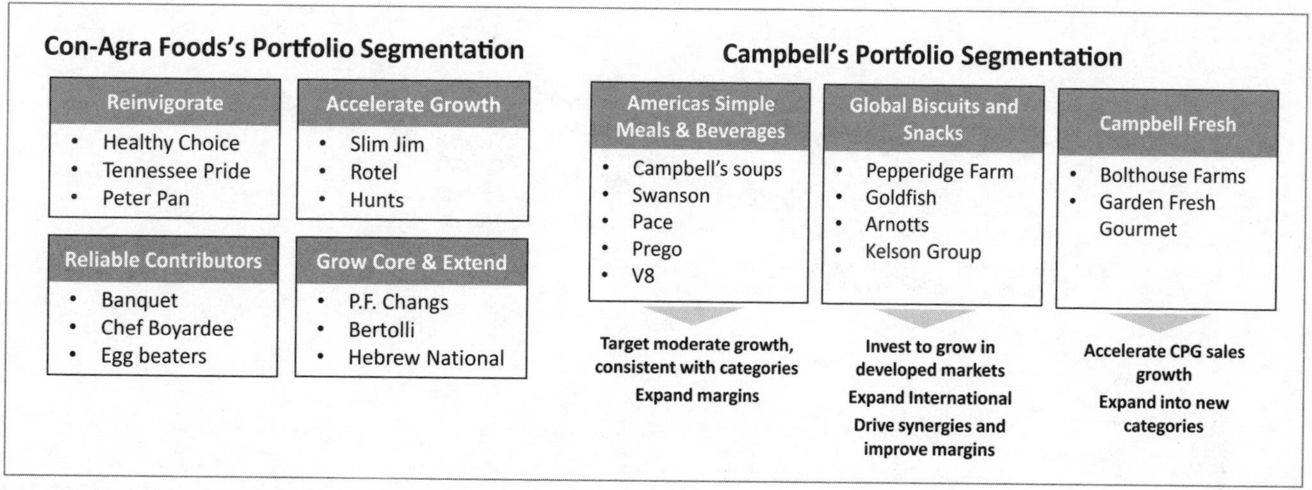

Con-Agra Foods's Portfolio Segmentation

Reinvigorate
- Healthy Choice
- Tennessee Pride
- Peter Pan

Accelerate Growth
- Slim Jim
- Rotel
- Hunts

Reliable Contributors
- Banquet
- Chef Boyardee
- Egg beaters

Grow Core & Extend
- P.F. Changs
- Bertolli
- Hebrew National

Campbell's Portfolio Segmentation

Americas Simple Meals & Beverages
- Campbell's soups
- Swanson
- Pace
- Prego
- V8

Target moderate growth, consistent with categories
Expand margins

Global Biscuits and Snacks
- Pepperidge Farm
- Goldfish
- Arnotts
- Kelson Group

Invest to grow in developed markets
Expand International
Drive synergies and improve margins

Campbell Fresh
- Bolthouse Farms
- Garden Fresh Gourmet

Accelerate CPG sales growth
Expand into new categories

FIGURE 13.5: How ConAgra and Campbell's Segment Their Portfolios

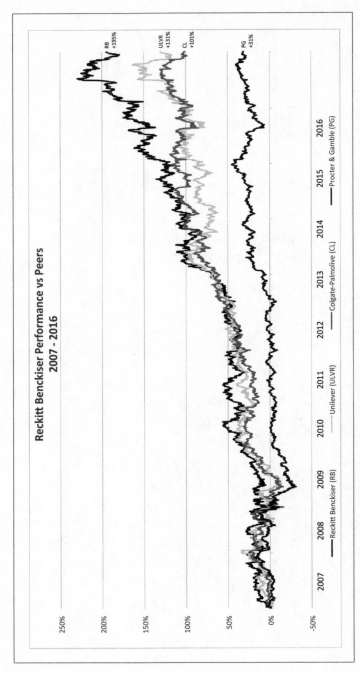

FIGURE 13.6: Reckitt Benckiser's Performance Compared to Industry Peers

product or service of the new company, and (2) that incumbents are unable to respond. Therefore, true disruption, is rare, but, he says:

> Listen to the elevator pitch of essentially any startup in a business plan competition and the template is mind-numbingly standard: [new company] will disrupt the [established industry] by [new company technology or business model]. Yet, most of them will not. If they are successful, they will find an underserved market segment, deliver a great product, garner some share, and achieve positive cash flow. That's a great outcome that will result in the creation of value. It is not disruption.[10]

The danger is that companies fall prey to what we call *the fallacy of impending disruption*, which says that: *given the frequency and likelihood of disruption, investing in sound product management and development practices is waste of time.* In fact, this may be as advisable as the actions taken by the subway worker who sank his life savings preparing for the end of the world on May 21, 2011, in line with a doomsday prophecy.[11] Fortunately for us, the world didn't end. Unfortunately for him, by May 22 he was broke. So the moral is, keep an eye open to disruption. But recognize that disruption is difficult to predict and not a strategy worthy of single-minded pursuit to the exclusion of sound product-development practices.

Reshape the Portfolio

While many companies approach portfolio optimization as simply a "chop off the tail" exercise, to truly reshape the portfolio requires a more thoughtful and holistic approach. We use a multifaceted approach that assesses the portfolio through a number of lenses. The idea: a singular view will yield a portfolio that optimizes for current profitability (for example), or customer desired breadth (alternatively), but the ideal portfolio is one that satisfies requirements across a broad range of factors.

As an example, consider Consumer Durables Co. (CDC), a large home appliance manufacturer, which had grown its revenue over several years through line introductions and extensions, but which more recently had seen its EBITDA stagnate. SKUs had grown by more than 25 percent, and engineering was barely able to sustain the pace of testing necessary for product refreshes. Prior portfolio rationalization succeeded in trimming the tail, but the benefits to engineering and profit never materialized. Management began to wonder if a further cut in products would do more harm than good and feared that a smaller portfolio would impact their ability to compete.

At the same time, they knew that the current levels of complexity were unsustainable. So the team used our approach to shed new light on the portfolio by assessing the portfolio through a number of key lenses, ultimately leading the company to a more productive and profitable portfolio:

- **Benefits.** There are many good reasons to launch a portfolio optimization, and it can bring a host of benefits. But it is vital up front to align on what you are looking to achieve from this exercise. For example, is it about improving working capital, or boosting EBITDA, or is it more to enable growth by targeting key indirect drivers such as availability and on-time delivery?
- **Portfolio strategy and segmentation.** There will always be reasons to retain or add a product; it is much harder to get people to agree to delist a product. That is why the strategic

facet is so important, as it cuts through those objections.
Many companies have allowed their strategy to evolve over
time, not as a set of deliberate decisions around resource
allocation, but in response to individual customer requests
and incremental market opportunities. This can lead to a
de facto "all things to all people" strategy that dilutes true
competitive advantage. But having clarified your portfolio
segmentation (see previous section), reshaping your portfolio
becomes much easier.

In our case example, CDC was focused on being first-to-
market in new product development and to do this used a
"good, better, best" strategy. However, over time additional
air conditioner models were added while older models were
never removed. The result was an increase from three tiers
to six, a large number of overlapping products, and a drastic
reduction in new product development speed—in stark contrast to the company's strategy.

- **Competitive requirements.** When considering the market,
traditional approaches commonly accept the competitive
landscape as a mandate that requires matching a competitor's
portfolio one-for-one. However, competition is only part of
the market context. Macroeconomic headwinds may impact
the true role a product plays within the portfolio, and regulatory requirements can add costs and burdens that often go
unaccounted.

At CDC, prior portfolio optimization efforts largely
ignored the market, as the team felt they understood competitive position. However, after initial analysis, the team
discovered that the next largest competitor had similar
revenue, but with 20 percent fewer SKUs. Management now
recognized that, in effect, they were realizing 20 percent less
scale than competitors. Additionally, the team discovered

that due to changing industry standards and customer demands the average refresh rate for each air conditioner SKU was likely to increase significantly in the near future, further stressing product development and engineering.

• **Customer coverage and substitutability.** To retain an unprofitable product, companies should have compelling evidence of substantial linked revenue (sales of one product are linked to another) or a lack of substitutability (customers are not willing to trade one product for another). What we find is that the starting assumption (corrected in our approach) is that there is 100 percent linked revenue (an overestimate) and 0 percent product substitutability (an underestimate).

In this case example, further research at CDC concluded customers neither understood nor valued the subtle differences between most air conditioners and indicated high levels of customer confusion. Products that were once considered to have zero substitutability between one another were reevaluated using customer interviews and historical sales analysis. The result was an opportunity to transition up to two-thirds of customers to other air conditioner products, removing complexity and maintaining revenue.

• **Operational and supply chain impact.** Perhaps no function feels the impact of complexity as acutely as operations and supply chain.

At CDC, previous portfolio reviews overlooked operations, but this is where a reduction in complexity can provide the greatest benefit. For the first time, the business questioned which products drove the greatest operational complexity. Analyses showed the bottom 25 percent of SKUs by volume in the air conditioner product line drove less than 5 percent of volume, while consuming 50 percent of engineering resources. Armed with this information, the team was able to focus on reshaping the portfolio to free up engineering resources, improving time to market with minimal EBITDA impact.

- **Complexity-adjusted costs and true profitability.** The financial facet provides a critical understanding of product profitability, and leverages the square root costing approach described in the previous chapter.

  While financial analysis during the original portfolio optimization exercise indicated all products were gross profit positive, further investigation at CDC revealed a very different picture. An assessment of operating profit and complexity-adjusted profitability revealed that nearly 80 percent of air conditioner SKUs were destroying at least 25 percent of operating profit.

- **Cost- and service-level breakpoints.** Benefits from portfolio optimization tend to follow a staircase pattern. On the cost side, you need to understand the chunks of cost (the fixed assets) that can be eliminated and what is required from a product consolidation perspective to get there. On the service side, you need to assess what combination of portfolio and process changes would constitute a breakthrough moment for customers—for example, same-day delivery.

All told, the results for CDC were significant. Going through this multifaceted approach highlighted customer confusion, overlapping tiers, and unprofitable products. Armed with a more comprehensive view of the portfolio, management was now able to make critical trade-off decisions. The resulting actions yielded a 7 percent increase in operating profit with 30 percent fewer SKUs, and the ability to free up 15 percent of engineering resources to focus on new product development.

Reset Priorities in Marketing, Advertising, and Promotion

With focus comes the opportunity to target investments where it counts. ConAgra moved to a much more disciplined and focused approach to leveraging its advertising and promotion spend. Nestlé now focuses 80 percent of its promotional support on its 34 billionaire brands. Said its CFO François-Xavier Roger, "It is not such a large number relative to our size and these products are growing much faster than the rest of the range and they drive a high level of profitability, so we are very focused in terms of marketing support."[12]

It's not just a matter of better use of financial resources. Focus also enables you to do more with your core brands. Said Clorox CMO Eric Reynolds, "Nothing ever gets better until you're really clear with yourself about what your brand stands for, why it even exists. At some point, someone has to say, 'Stop. We're doing all of this stuff—why? Why does it matter?'" Reynolds has focused on using data and storytelling to revive and boost sales for core products, including automated, weather-based media buying for the Burt's Bees lip balm.[13]

Realign Your Operating Model for Scale and Speed

A critical element of reigniting the core involves updating or potentially transforming your operating model. So much so, that it warrants a deep dive and a chapter of its own. For more on this, see Chapter 15, "Transform Your Operating Model."

Innovate Around the Core

For all the companies cited in this chapter, the rationale of a reignite-the-core strategy was twofold: improve profitability and free up resources to accelerate growth. This means rethinking how to innovate around the core brands. Gone are the days where incremental line extensions will carry the day. No longer can CPG companies "push" products into the marketplace; instead it's a matter of generating "pull" from consumers. As a result they are shifting resources to more fundamentally understand customer insights, to discover how consumers are using products and what latent needs remain unaddressed.

Clorox offers an example of this, where it has focused on "New faces, new spaces, new places"—looking to attract new demographic groups, looking at new consumption patterns for its products, and looking for new channels. An application of this would be how it boosted growth in its disinfecting wipes product line.

According to Clorox's research, 70 percent of consumers believe that disinfecting surfaces can keep their families healthier, but less than half act on this.[14] This gap between beliefs and behaviors represented $400 million in potential sales. Further insights showed that most shoppers prefer to buy preventative health products together and expect to find them in or near the pharmacy. So Clorox developed the "Prevent, Protect & Soothe" in-store display program and worked with retailers to colocate relevant products. In the mix were Clorox Disinfecting Wipes, Campbell's soup, Brita water filters, and Dial soap—the items you would need to Prevent, Protect and Soothe. The results were very strong. Participating Clorox brands were up 16 percent during the program, led by Clorox Disinfecting Wipes, which were up 154 percent.

What Defines the Customer Experience, Besides the Product?

Starbucks has laid claim to be the Third Place in our lives—home, work, Starbucks. To that end, it has been as much (if not more) about the experience and the space as the coffee. For many companies, with a proud product heritage, thinking *beyond* the product can be challenging. But doing so can help unlock new business model opportunities.

One way to do this can be via a Customer Journey Map, a graphical illustration of the steps your customer goes through in engaging with your company, whether it be interacting with your product, your retail experience, your service, or your website. The point being: it is rare that what defines value is simply just the product, but the experience surrounding it. Therefore, it is advisable to understand that experience, and it may tee up opportunities for business model innovation.

To achieve these types of results requires a different focus from what has worked in the past. This includes:

- **Embracing digital and a multichannel world.** Understanding how consumers shop, work, and engage with the brands to increase loyalty and glean insights. This may include the development of convenience apps, subscription-based products, an increased social media presence, and greater integration with retailers.
- **Greater focus on experimentation combined with analytics.** Leveraging the new digital platforms to test and learn

(for more on experimentation, see Chapter 10, "Improve the Odds").

- **A greater focus on ethnographic research.**

On this last point, A. G. Lafley, in his book *Playing to Win*, recalls how P&G leveraged such techniques for product development in India. Chip Bergh, then P&G's president of men's grooming, oversaw the integration of Gillette, and then its expansion into India. Bergh's first direction to his team was simple:

> *The first thing I want you to do is to spend two weeks in India. I want you to live with these consumers. I want you to go into their homes. You need to understand how they shave and how shaving fits into their lives.*

His team pushed back, why go to India? There are plenty of Indian men here in the United States, one of his colleagues challenged. But Bergh persisted.

Later, after the India trip, the same colleague sought him out at an innovation review:

> *Now I completely get it. You can look at the pictures in the books, you can hear the stories, but it's not until you're there [that you understand]. I spent three days with this one guy, shopping with him, going to the barber shop with him, watching him shave.... I was so motivated and so inspired, I designed the first razor on a napkin flying back to London.*

The new razor was built on insights that they had uncovered during the trip: that most men in India shaved with only a small cup of cold water, and without hot running water to clean the razor, hairs would clog the blade. The new razor took these conditions into account, with a safety comb designed to prevent nicks and an easy-rinse cartridge.

We have focused on consumer goods companies in this chapter to illustrate a broader point and bring the topic to life. After all, it is an industry we can all relate to, as we interact with its products—and its many, many line extensions!—on a daily basis. But of course the point is applicable to any other industry. We have seen this dynamic across the board: from the manufacturing company launching myriad products and undermining its legacy expertise in pump innovation; to the retailer who excelled at operating large-format grocery but went off-track as it tackled the convenience store market overseas; to the financial services company who mistakenly thought that complexity was free and proliferated its services. All strayed from what they did best, saw performance decline, and then had to do the work to recover the core.

For many, the Siren Song was the Expanding Portfolio. For a long time, product expansions were the default means to drive revenue, but they are just one of many adjacencies that companies can pursue. The point is not that adjacencies are intrinsically damaging, but rather that in the Age of Complexity, opportunities seem plentiful, therefore the bar should be higher than ever.

Knowing where and how to expand is the focus of the next chapter.

CHAPTER 14

Avoid the Pitfalls of M&A and New Market Entry

"As for me, I am tormented with an everlasting itch for things remote. I love to sail forbidden seas, and land on barbarous coasts."

—HERMAN MELVILLE, *MOBY-DICK; OR, THE WHALE*

Every business leader has heard the Siren Song of the Greener Pasture. Expanding beyond their organization's existing core is increasingly feasible and enticing. New product categories, increasing channels to market, significant overseas expansion . . . the language and strategy of *growth by adjacency* has become commonplace in the last decade. Most large organizations nowadays have their own in-house corporate merger and acquisition (M&A) groups, which are active and stay alert to acquisition targets.

The enticing lure, however, makes too many organizations overlook the commonsense caution that just because you *can* doesn't mean you *should*. Adjacencies and acquisitions can be powerful tools for growth, but judging by the results, they are overapplied or misapplied. Just as it's normal to overestimate the incremental revenues of product expansions and underestimate the incremental costs, so it's typical to overestimate the benefits or synergies and underestimate the complexity impacts of "no-brainer" expansions.

Part of the issue, according to Ken Favaro, a contributing editor of *strategy+business*, is that we have become "adjacency addicts."[1] He points to the airlines who launched into car rental agencies and low-fare brand extensions, to integrated steel companies who went into construction, and to pharmaceutical players that pursue the personal care market.

"In each of these businesses," wrote Favaro, "the primary motivator was slowing growth in the core business."[2] For each, the move into an adjacent territory was deemed a logical extension of the core business.

The impacts of this addiction are clear: neglecting the core and adding new layers of cost and complexity, diluting the existing advantages that a company may carry. Favaro suggests that neglecting the core is the biggest sin.

"Every one of the big adjacency moves mentioned above had to be reversed," he said. "Their promise of growth proved illusory. And the companies had to return to their core business for growth after all, often in a much weaker position than they had occupied before their adjacency moves."

That is exactly what Angela Ahrendts found when she stepped in to turn around luxury retailer Burberry. The business had a rich history, a royal warrant, and a star product in its trench coat (which British solders wore in World War 1). But the business had lost its focus due to unwise expansions, and the brand was losing its luster.

She recalls: "We had 23 licensees around the world, each doing something different. We were selling products such as dog cover-ups and leashes. One of our highest-profile stores, on Bond Street in London, had a whole section of kilts. There's nothing wrong with any of those products individually, but together they added up to just a lot of stuff—something for everybody, but not much of it exclusive or compelling. In luxury, ubiquity will kill you—it means you're not really luxury anymore. And we were becoming ubiquitous."[3]

Approaching your expansion strategy with a clear head is the subject of this chapter. We'll explore why companies get M&A right and how so many others get it wrong, and discuss the advantages of becoming an "adjacency skeptic"—a useful role for testing to ensure that whatever moves your company makes will help it become a growth leader.

The Greener Pastures of M&A

The Greener Pastures Siren is particularly active in mergers and acquisitions. Acquisitions can help you to leapfrog to a growth destination in situations where organic growth will take too long. Ironically, this ability to accelerate to a new position means that capability gaps and impacts on the core business may go unnoticed.

This notion is reflected in the fact that *M&A tends to be more reliably productive when it is pursued for profitability and scale through cost synergies as opposed to growth.* As we highlighted in our 2014 report "Diversify for Profits, Not Growth," acquisitions undertaken in pursuit of profitability focus on leveraging existing assets and capabilities to decrease the cost of doing business in new markets. In that way, revenue growth almost always follows as the extra scale (true scale) confers economic benefits that can translate to greater R&D investment, pricing, and marketing advantages.[4] In contrast, a growth-focused acquisition creates more complexity in the business, with unanticipated and negative impacts on key performance levels or customer satisfaction metrics. It can also erode management focus.

To help illustrate these points, consider Figure 14.1, which shows two examples and the final outcomes. While companies have become increasingly sophisticated in their due diligence practices, accounting for complexity is frequently skipped in deal assessments. A large Japanese conglomerate asked us to look into adding this capability as its valuations and synergy targets frequently fell short of expectations. Here's what we found: the conglomerate was:

	Stanley Acquires Black & Decker (profit-driven M&A)	Sealed Air Acquires Diversey (growth-driven M&A)
Deal	• In 2010, Stanley Works acquired fellow tool maker Black & Decker for $4.5B	• In 2011, Sealed Air Corp., a supplier of packaging, acquired Diversey for $4.3B
Stated Rationale	• Stanley's rationale for the deal was cost-focused • A total of $350 million in annual cost synergies was announced as part of the deal	• Sealed Air justified the deal by discussing how the acquisition would drive growth, with no mention of cost synergies or lowering the cost to serve customers
Results	• By 2013, Stanley had surpassed its $500M cost synergy goal with revenue synergies of $300M • Bloomberg reported this was driven by a focus on "taking the cost out in the post-close period while achieving strong new product launches "	• Just one year after the acquisition, Sealed Air took a $1.2B write-down on the acquisition due to lower than expected growth and profits • In 2016, CEO said that it would consider selling or spinning off the division

FIGURE 14.1: Profit-Focused vs. Growth-Focused M&A

- **Overestimating revenue top-line synergies.** M&A undertaken with a revenue synergy rationale is, as we discuss above, more prone to dealing with assumptions (predicting what customers will do) than profitability-motivated M&A (identifying what costs can be reduced). It's perhaps not surprising that according to a McKinsey study 70 percent of mergers failed to achieve expected revenue synergies.[5]
- **Overestimating the cost synergies by mistaking complexity costs for fixed costs.** To illustrate this issue, consider how companies traditionally look at overhead as a fixed cost, and forecast cost synergies on that basis. In fact, while the cost to produce a company's product or service is often well understood, company overhead is a murkier category.

In M&A valuations, many companies approach forecasting overhead expense as a percent of revenue, whereas overhead expense tends to be driven as much or more by complexity than size. This approach is imprecise and can drive incorrect financial projections and valuations. Overhead expenses are not truly fixed, but are (to a large degree) a function of the complexity in the business. Many times, these expenses can—and should—be directly attributed to a particular product line. Therefore, you can only accurately forecast overhead expenses once you understand how they vary with the expected growth in each of your product lines.

- **Underestimating the organizational challenge of extracting those synergies.** This issue is most prevalent among companies that are infrequent acquirers. This often impacts the timeline to capture synergy benefits. Deal teams working quickly with incomplete data may not take into account the organizational difficulty of integration, or how cultural differences can impede efforts. A good rule of thumb here is to check the sensitivity of the benefits to timing: *If it takes twice as long to capture the benefits, does the deal still make sense?* The danger of course is that the longer the integration period, the less likely it is that the hard decisions will be taken. One could point to the failure to fully integrate after previous M&A activity as the root cause for many of our clients' big complexity issues.

Across all these factors, there are steep learning curves that can make a large difference in the ultimate outcome. Not too unlike an annual vacation trip to the casino, taking a once-a-year trip to the M&A tables is unlikely to boost your fortunes.

This is clear in the data. To assess these learning curve effects, we looked at the relationship between M&A activity and stock price performance of large public companies (see Figure 14.2).[6] Bucketing by level of M&A activity from least to most, companies in the bottom fifth (little-to-no M&A activity) saw the strongest average stock price appreciation. This group of companies we labeled the *Temperate*—they generally abstain from the M&A game and walk away winners. At the other end of the scale, there are the *Professionals*, the top fifth who are the most acquisitive companies. They also delivered strong stock price appreciation. For this group, M&A is a pivotal part of their growth strategy and they have learned over time how to succeed.

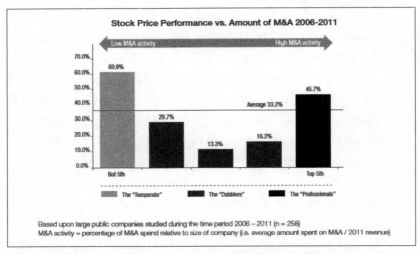

FIGURE 14.2: How Deal Frequency Impacts Stock Price Performance

Then there's the rest: the companies in the middle that take on the occasional acquisition and see significantly below average stock price appreciation. These are the *Dabblers*: they dabble infrequently in M&A and see below-average results.

In general, we found that the Temperate and the Professionals stand out in two key ways. First, they see large improvements in their profit-per-employee ratio, an indication that they are becoming more efficient over time. Second, they were able to translate these efficiency gains into significant margin expansion (they are able to squeeze more profit from each dollar of revenue they received). As you can see from Figure 14.3, the highly acquisitive Professionals on the far right are able to significantly expand margins over time (with an average of 400 basis points of expansion).

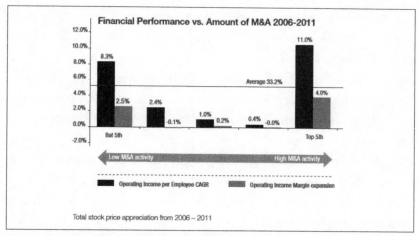

FIGURE 14.3: How Deal Frequency Impacts Operating Income

What is most striking is that despite the large amount of M&A activity that the Professionals undertake (and the added complexity it could in theory bring), they actually see the highest improvement in their profit-per-employee ratio with an 11 percent compound annual growth rate (CAGR). They get much more efficient over time, likely due to the synergies they are able to extract during the M&A integration process.

It's also interesting to note that, as impressive as their performance is, the Professionals actually have lower stock price appreciation than the less acquisitive Temperate. This may be because the Professionals deploy a large amount of capital (cash and stock) in conjunction with their acquisition strategy, which partially offsets the return they get from synergies.

On the other end of the spectrum, the Temperate with little to no M&A activity saw results similar to the Professionals. They delivered a respectable 250 basis points of margin expansion on average. They also saw very healthy improvements in their profit-per-employee ratio—likely from their ability to realize economies of scale as they subsequently grow organically. And, as mentioned above, the market rewards the Temperate with higher stock price appreciation, even though their financial performance is a bit lower than the Professionals.

Finally, we have the lagging middle section of the Dabblers. These companies engage in moderate amounts of M&A activity and actually posted strong revenue growth (5.5 percent revenue CAGR on average). Yet despite this growth, they significantly underperformed. Their margins were flat over the time period studied with many seeing their margins contract. Quite a few of these companies actually became less efficient as evidenced by their declining profit-per-employee ratio.

The takeaway here is that *two groups of companies thrive with radically different approaches to M&A—linked to how and whether they engage or avoid the Greener Pasture Siren.* The Professionals have learned to navigate safely by developing advanced capabilities; the Temperate group stays away from this rocky shoreline until they can find a safer landing point.

The third group, the Dabblers, are the ones who struggle most with M&A because they lack navigational tools (unlike the Professionals) and may not even be aware of hazards (unlike the Temperate!). Unfortunately that's where 60 percent of companies find themselves, according to our data. Given that M&A will remain an important strategic lever, but one infrequently exercised, the question becomes, *What can this third group of companies do to close the gap with the Professionals to help make their acquisitions more successful?* According to M&A professionals and private equity leaders, there are a number of best practices that can be employed to mimic their behavior:[7]

- **Switch to proactive vs. reactive deal sourcing.** Companies without clear M&A strategies approach the deal process reactively and often waste time evaluating bad deals or, worse, consummate a bad deal. In contrast, companies with clear M&A strategies are able to proactively identify and approach M&A targets with the highest potential for success. And perhaps just as important, they are able to quickly pass on poor deals that don't fit their strategy. You needn't make this a full-time pursuit, but periodically identify what an interesting acquisition target would look like and establish a standing short list of opportunities that are attractive for your business.

- **Discount your synergy estimates.** If you're driving to a new job in a new part of town, you're going to build in more buffer time than you would for a routine commute you've done for years. Approach M&A the same way, by challenging or even discounting your synergy targets along some key dimensions:
  - The time required to capture the benefits
  - Total cost synergy benefits: make sure you've taken into account the full potential costs of complexity and developed an accurate view of fixed-cost leverage that can be attained with the deal.
  - Total revenue synergy benefits: build in *realistic* projections for customer attrition and robust assumptions about growth, given the potential post-merger service-level bumps.
  - One-time costs: an area that is particularly vulnerable to underestimation for occasional acquirers.

- **Plan early for integration and define your end-state clearly.** The Professional acquirers generate the highest level of efficiency improvement over time, indicating that they are particularly good at integrating newly acquired companies. Many of them, including Danaher, Eaton, and Koch Industries, require the acquired companies to adopt their management system and culture. What these companies have recognized is that you cannot have two competing cultures in the same camp. So no matter what you're hoping to achieve through M&A—and whether you want to impose your systems and culture on the acquired company or vice versa—understand that to a large degree your eventual success and the timeline to achieve desired benefits will depend on the coherence in cultures and management systems that you create. (We discuss both of these elements in some detail in the Chapter 16.)

- **Get sufficient outside help.** The greatest dangers are the ones you don't know about. But you can hire in experience that can help shore up any gaps in your diligence, your legal support, and your integration planning. Just as with the old maxim that *nothing is more expensive than a cheap lawyer*, the benefit from investing in professional help is particularly true in this arena. Given the size and scope of most deals, any investment here will pay for itself many times over with just one successful acquisition.

The Adjacency Skeptic's Handbook

M&A has its own prerequisites for success. But whether through acquisition or organic means, the question of whether or not to pursue an entry into a new market or adjacency remains a fundamental one for growth in the Age of Complexity.

Many have found great success through adjacencies. Olam International, founded in Nigeria in 1989 and now headquartered in Singapore, has grown from a single-product, single-country company to a $13 billion giant by leveraging adjacencies. As a commodities supplier to global CPG companies, it has leveraged its capabilities, channels, and relationships to move from one commodity to the next, including nuts, spices, beans, and coffee. Once in a category, it has grown sales by moving up and down the value chain. Talking about a specific move into soluble coffee, CEO Vivek Verma laid out the adjacency rationale:[8]

> *The fact that the world needs to produce more coffee to satisfy demand has underpinned Olam's strategy of integrating our presence in the coffee supply chain. We have moved into upstream activity, setting up our own coffee estates to produce coffee on a traceable and sustainable basis. Within our core supply chain operations,* we created a specialty coffee division that capitalises on our procurement and marketing expertise *to help roasters find exceptional, certified coffees. We see a growing fit between our upstream presence and the specialty coffee marketing.*
>
> *We also moved downstream into soluble coffee to cater to the rising demand we see in emerging Asia and Central/Eastern Europe. The rationale was straightforward. Our entry into soluble coffee in 2007 was not only a one-step adjacency into* a higher value-added activity where there is a sharing of customers, costs and channels, *we were moving into a space that is equivalent to one-third of the profit pool in the bean supply chain.* [emphasis ours]

Many other companies have followed similar rationales to achieve success with M&A. Chris Zook of Bain & Company highlighted the case of how Nike built up an advantage over Reebok by leveraging a pattern of adjacency-fueled growth. First, establish a position in a target market (such as golf) through athletic shoes; then launch a clothing line, with a major athlete endorsement such as Tiger Woods; then expand into new categories; and finally launch equipment onto the market (such as golf clubs).

Other well-known names such as Disney (animation to retail), Amazon (books to "The Everything Store" and Amazon Web Services), and Apple (Macs to iPhones, Apple Stores, etc.) have all leveraged adjacencies to build revenues. Notably, these adjacencies all established self-reinforcing product and service ecosystems—see a Disney movie, then buy the merchandise; go to the store and learn about the movie.

As we discussed earlier in the book, others have fared less well. Compass Group saw international expansion as the right adjacency move, only to see it weaken the company's scale. Chiquita saw a move into consumer packaged goods as the right adjacency to leverage its brand, but the resulting investment and activity weakened the core offering (bananas).

So what separates a good adjacency from a bad one? How do you identify a winnable new market from a rocky shore of ruin? In the heat of a deliberation, it can be hard to tell one from the other, as confirmation bias kicks in: *"Sure we can do that."*

This is where *adjacency skeptics* can play a useful role. Wearing that hat will force you to ask a number of critical questions, including these six:

- Will the expansion shore up or weaken our core business?
- Will this adjacency build scale or just create complexity?
- Do we have the capabilities and operating model to execute this strategy successfully?
- What are the other alternative adjacencies?

- What tests can we run to increase our confidence in this move?
- At the end of the day, is the "juice worth the squeeze"?

Here's how the answers to these key questions can help inform a decision about whether to pursue an adjacency:

Question 1. Will This Expansion Shore Up or Weaken Our Core Business?

The most important part of this question is that term at the end: core business. This is *not* simply your legacy set of activities, products, and customers, but rather where and how your organization generates value *today* (which may be different than tomorrow).

The trouble is, many people can describe their business in the general terms of the legacy activities and niche ("we're a consumer packaged goods company"). But most are flying blind with regards to where they generate value. Unless you have addressed where you *really* make money (Chapter 12), any adjacency expansion can be risky.

Let's assume that you have done the work needed to identify your value-generators. The question then is would an expansion shore them up or weaken them? "Shoring up" would include gains such as a geographic expansion that benefits the whole network, an acquisition that impedes a competitor migrating into your space, or a select product-line extension that helps customers complete a job.

One way to assess the likelihood of *shoring up* vs. *weakening* is to question whether the adjacency leverages your distinctive capabilities. All organizations generally have one or two things they do well. By focusing on capabilities, you can avoid agreeing to just any industry adjacency. For example, discount retailers and luxury retailers are both in retail but with very different skill sets, people, and marketing strategies. If Walmart were to buy Neiman Marcus as an "adjacent opportunity," likely neither would benefit. If succeeding in the targeted adjacency—whether that be geographical, technological, market niches, etc.—requires radically different capabilities from what your organization has already mastered, then it's likely you will struggle to achieve meaningful results.

Question 2. Will This Adjacency Build Scale in Our Business or Just Create Complexity?

It is not uncommon for us to be sitting in a boardroom hearing the following: "We have seen revenue growth, but our SG&A is growing twice as fast as our top line." This is an indicator that a company is growing complexity faster than it is growing in scale.

How do you do this right? Look no further than privately owned Blue Bell Creameries, headquartered in Brenham, Texas, which has a rich history going back to 1907. One of the more remarkable aspects of Blue Bell is its disciplined approach to geographic and portfolio expansion. In fact, while it is number three in the nation in terms of revenue, its ice cream is still only available in 20 states, meaning it leads its competitors in terms of profitability.

"We're not a slave to market share," said CEO Paul Kruse. "We know what we're capable of doing, and different markets are different." When they choose to expand, he says, it's typically in a contiguous state, keeping setup and distribution costs low and giving them the ability to first understand the market. While Blue Bell doesn't have the most overall scale, it does have the highest density (scale where it competes), and that translates to profits.

Blue Bell assiduously avoids the complexity that can creep in, in the pursuit of additional revenues. "We make ice cream, we sell ice cream, and there's really probably nobody else like us because they're either co-packing with somebody else or distributing other product," said Kruse.

Question 3. Do We Have the Capabilities and Operating Model to Execute This Strategy Successfully?

With the legacy beer segment flat, we find beer companies understandably running to the craft beer market, the one segment with high growth and strong price points. However, recent product profitability studies performed for our clients have found craft beer profit margins for major beer companies to be even less than those of their legacy brands, after adjusting for the cost of the complexity. This presents brewers with a bit of a conundrum: They can't simply ignore the fastest-growing and highest-price-point category. But their operating model and capabilities are built around a product set with different characteristics (high volume, low variety).

Beer is beer, you may think. But in fact this dynamic is not that unusual: category expansions (while seemingly adjacent) may require radically different capabilities and a different operating model in order to execute on the opportunity. Trying to put low-volume, high-variety products from an acquired company through a supply chain designed for high-volume, low-variety products (or vice versa) can impact both businesses negatively.

So ask yourself, What elements of your current business are you trying to leverage with an expansion? Same customers, same assets, same channels, same capabilities? If none of the above, then you may be chasing a Siren Song.

Question 4. What Are the Other Alternative Adjacencies?

If this question is met with a long silence, it may be time to hit the pause button. Adjacency ideas can crop up opportunistically, for example, by observing customer behaviors. But committing to such a move is best made after thoroughly mapping potential opportunities for product, customer, channel, and geographic expansion. Only after these steps are completed should you then create a short list for deeper assessment. Developing "strategic alternatives" forces a rigorous discussion of benefits and risks, as well as illuminating the many paths *not* taken by committing to a particular move.

Question 5. What Tests Can We Run to Increase Our Confidence in This Move?

In Chapter 10 we discussed the importance of experimentation in the Age of Complexity. A great application of this is when considering entry into a new market: testing to learn and even testing to evaluate two or three adjacency opportunities. The testing can also lead to operational insights and help guide launch strategy.

Said Blue Bell's Kruse: "The response from the stores is going to dictate just how big our opening is. But we don't *buy it, we earn it*, we earn the consumers, so we do have a lot of consumer pull."

This is particularly important when considering geographic expansion. Consider the case of Best Buy, which entered then quickly retreated from China. Some pointed to a poor understanding of the Chinese consumer, data that could have been garnered through a series of experiments:

> *Apart from failing to differentiate its product lines, Best Buy also made the mistake of focusing on building large flagship stores, like in the U.S., rather than smaller, conveniently located retail outlets. China may have one of the highest car adoption rates in the world, but its perennial traffic congestions and lack of parking mean consumers often prefer to shop closer to their homes.* (CNBC.com)[9]

Question 6. At the End of the Day, Is the "Juice Worth the Squeeze"?

As we've mentioned several times, our rule of thumb is that *most organizations overestimate the incremental revenues from adjacency expansion and underestimate the incremental costs.* The former is driven by overlooking cannibalization of existing sales, underestimating competitive response, and delays in customer acquisition. The latter is driven by underestimating complexity costs in the new business, longer (and therefore more expensive) execution timelines, and, in the case of M&A, inaccurate estimates of cost synergies. Does the business case reflect the additional complexity costs?

Launching into a new market, adjacent or not, is rife with pitfalls. You are dealing with many unknowns. Worse, there's no way to fully anticipate them! Human psychology doesn't help. An exciting venture can cloud an accurate view of the risks and the alternatives. We hear the Siren Song: *We won at home, we will do great over there.*

Of course, one of the biggest potential risks of M&A and adjacencies is the distraction it can create from the opportunities within the core business. It is frequently easier to "do more things" than "do things better." The first creates complexity; the second creates value. But unfortunately, it is not uncommon for companies to end up returning to the core after expensive misadventures, to do the harder work of mining new opportunities by leveraging their distinctive capabilities.

We do not want to discourage nor dissuade you from pursuing adjacencies. They can be a powerful lever for growth. But before launching, we recommend ensuring that your organization is enough of a Navigator to balance your Explorer. The best approach is one that marries both: the boldness of the Explorer's mindset, which embodies the willingness to enter into new markets and leave the safety of home, with the skill set of the Navigator so you can ensure the safety of your core business, scan for both differences and similarities, challenge the idea that this particular move is the best of the bunch after a deliberate and full assessment of the alternatives, and arrive safely at your destination.

CHAPTER 15

Transform Your Operating Model

With David Toth*

"So much of what we call management consists of making it difficult for people to work."

—PETER DRUCKER

It seemed like nothing would make a dent against a dismal situation. The $4 billion company in question had missed its growth objectives over the previous several years, and had only met its earnings targets a few of the preceding quarters. In response, the business had taken action. It had launched restructuring initiatives, creating a global supply chain function and deploying a global sales structure. It announced in year-end presentations a number of programs to focus on key business issues: reducing rising SG&A costs, improving working capital, and getting pricing right. In fact, it announced the same programs, on the same issues, eight years in a row. Nothing made a dent.

---

* David Toth is a partner with Wilson Perumal & Company, Inc. and supports much of WP&C's operating model and process transformation work. Prior to joining WP&C, David worked with the firm's founders at George Group Consulting. Before that, David split his time between industry, consulting, and a start-up in various leadership roles. David received both his MS and BS degrees in industrial engineering from Purdue University.

And nothing would, until it changed its operating model. Despite being a large company by revenue, the business was actually subscale. It had fragmented itself and was, in fact, really a hundred small businesses, each with its own metrics, P&L, and focus on local optimization. Despite having moved toward global functional and product leadership roles, in reality leaders operated with limited decision-making authority, capital, and capacity. All the underlying organizations, processes, policies, and technologies were still local, independent, and different. The complexity of the operating model and resulting ambiguity in accountability kept them from realizing significant bottom line and working capital benefits while making it difficult to grow and scale the business effectively throughout market cycles.

No wonder their initiatives floundered. In the face of more than 10,000 price lists, and little in the way of controls, any pricing optimization effort would fail. Rationalizing the portfolio, to make headway against the more than 1 million SKUs the business carried, would require getting more than 500 stakeholders to agree!

It seems like madness, but the company's operating model was rooted in a belief in local entrepreneurship. Years back, this belief had helped the business grow and flourish by being customer-responsive. But the business had evolved in the years since in ways no one had predicted. It was a model that had made sense at an earlier stage in its journey, but was counterproductive today.

And that is the point: the right operating model for your business will change as conditions change. Yet many businesses operate with the same operating model they had 10, 20, even 100 years ago! Conditions *have* changed, so the time to reinvent is now. Knowing *when* to embark on a reinvention of your operating model (the triggers), as well as *how* (the road map) are critical elements in the Navigator's Skill Set, as waiting too long can put you at significant competitive disadvantage, and too many operating model initiatives get downgraded to moving names around on an organizational chart.

In this chapter, we'll define what an operating model is, discuss how models become outdated, and highlight a road map for transformation.

Understanding Operating Models

A company's operating model provides the critical link between its market strategy and the execution of that market strategy (see Figure 15.1). It defines *how* the company organizes and aligns decision making, assets, and operations to deliver value to its customers. An operating model therefore acts as both the foundation for a company's strategy and the framework for its execution. It addresses the questions of who does what, where it is done, how best to deploy assets, and how to make decisions. Just as companies cannot overcome poor execution with a well-designed operating model, they

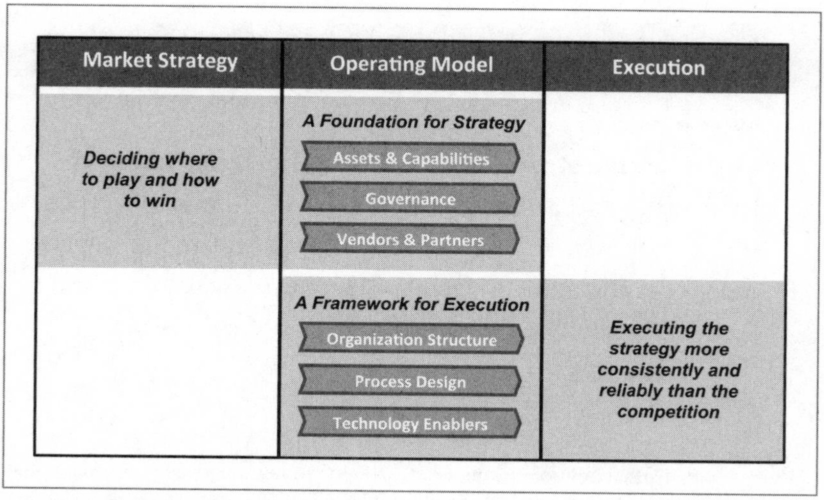

Market Strategy	Operating Model	Execution
Deciding where to play and how to win	**A Foundation for Strategy** Assets & Capabilities Governance Vendors & Partners	
	A Framework for Execution Organization Structure Process Design Technology Enablers	**Executing the strategy more consistently and reliably than the competition**

FIGURE 15.1: A Good Operating Model Impacts Strategy and Execution

also cannot overcome poor structures and governance with great execution.

There are six components that comprise an operating model:

- **Governance.** Where and how operating decisions are made and, ultimately, how the business will be aligned on a product, geographic, and functional basis; establishes the role of the corporate center; clarifies policy and process ownership.
- **Assets and capabilities.** Identification and deployment of company facilities and equipment, including offices, factories/plants, tooling, warehouses, and research labs, owned or leased; can also be the patents and intellectual property used to generate revenue or uniquely manage operations; may include data and certain competencies.
- **Partners.** Where and for what the company will rely on those outside the organization to provide; front office and operations partner roles; back office outsourcing alternatives.
- **Process design.** How the business will execute both value-chain and management processes on an ongoing basis; extent to which processes will be standardized across the business; expected process performance metrics and targets (e.g., cycle time).
- **Organization structure.*** Operating and reporting structures needed to deliver strategic and operational objectives with the chosen governance structure; group and/or department organization designs based on business volumes and specific competency needs; roles, spans of control, and

---

* When people think about operating models they frequently jump to organizational structure, with reorgs becoming focused on putting different names in boxes on the org chart. However, this is just one element of the operating model and frequently *not* what makes the biggest difference in changing how people work.

alignment of titles; relationships and metrics within and between organizations.

* **Technology.** Infrastructure, application, and data architectures employed to support decision making, operations, and compliance; considers where and how the business will need to change and scale over time.

While each of the elements of an operating model address specific aspects of a company's structure and decision-making approach, *what is most critical is how they fit together.* For example, designing an organizational structure without considering how and where assets are best located may lead to customer responsiveness issues or inefficiencies. We recently worked with a banking client that had created a new organization in London to centralize operations. Yet the company had some crucial assets—including data and analytical competency, and prime clients—located in Asia. The result was a large, centralized organization struggling to support customers amid high levels of process inefficiency and back-and-forth across continents and time zones.

Getting operating model decisions right unlocks the power of a strategy. Getting them wrong—or living with an outmoded operating model—is like a lead weight pulling you to the bottom of the sea. Said one SVP of a software company: "We languished for quite some time because we weren't structured in a way that allowed for us to implement a new strategy."

How Operating Models Become Outmoded

Part of the reason that organizations often languish with old operating models is because it can take time to realize the problem. If a particular operating model served you well at one point, it's probably not high on the list of suspects when performance starts to suffer.

Operating models become outmoded in a few key ways. It starts to happen as a company responds to new opportunities and conditions, but in an incremental fashion. Over time, the operating model slowly becomes ill-suited and stretched, which creates execution, cost, and ultimately growth issues. It is akin to building a house one room at a time versus starting with an architectural blueprint.

This happens via organic growth, as a company launches new products, enters new segments and channels, or pursues new customer adjacencies. While revenue may increase, the operating model impact to deliver this new revenue is often hidden, and costs rise unexpectedly. As an example, we worked with a client that made its money delivering large bulk products across the country, and had set up its supply chain and distribution system accordingly: full truckloads, going point-to-point. Over time, it added many new niche products, with plants innovating to customer needs. The mix shifted, and the distribution system "evolved": partial truckloads became the norm given the product variety, and products were making two, three, or four stops along the way. The assets, organizations, processes, and technologies designed for high volume and low variety became expensive and slow for low-volume, high-variety product types.

The misalignment can also occur through acquisitions. As unique cultures, processes, organizational units, technologies, and systems of governance are merged together, there is typically a period of transition. The endpoint for postmerger integration is typically defined as when the expected synergy savings have been met. Such savings are commonly from a reduction in staff and offices, rationalization of products and closure of plants, and consolidation of direct and indirect spend. However, these cost reductions are not a real indicator of integration. In our experience, there are often legacy ways of working that remain long after the designated transition period, leading to redundancy, ambiguity, and latency in the business.

But perhaps worse is when an operating model stands still, when it fails to keep up with the changing marketplace and is now no longer fit-for-purpose—when your Castle Walls are high. For example, you are a retailer but have never developed an integrated online capability; or when you have built your business and value proposition around offering breadth when what customers really want are a few items, quickly, reliably, and cheaply. When your current structure has been left behind by the industry and competitive landscape, the need to reinvent your operating model becomes urgent.

A Redesign Road Map

When redesigning your operating model, the first point is to understand that while several archetypes typically exist within industries, there is no single blueprint that applies to every company. Even within the same industry, if strategy, value proposition, offerings, asset-base, or capabilities differ, operating models can and should differ as well.

But while operating models should be different, all organizations (and the businesses or functions within) can follow the same design journey: a structured approach, rooted in a thorough understanding of current business context, which is aligned to your strategy and designed to meet specific financial and operational performance targets.

There are many factors that go into redesigning an operating model, as shown in Figure 15.2. Certainly you need a crisp understanding of the current state operating model. Laying this out explicitly can reveal shortcomings and also provides a basis for the change journey. You need a strong understanding of the target performance that the new operating model needs to deliver. We find it helpful to translate this into operational metrics. And all of this needs to be undertaken and influenced in the context of your business strategy and industry dynamics.

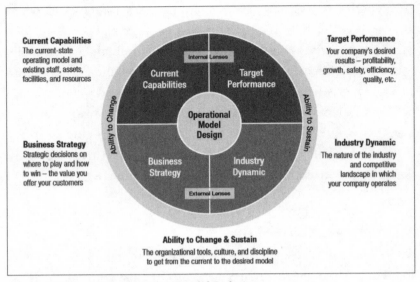

FIGURE 15.2: Inputs to Operating Model Redesign

The path forward, at either the business or functional level, will often follow a similar three-phased approach:

Phase 1: Align on the vision and analyze the current state.
Phase 2: Outline the new model and governance approach.
Phase 3: Complete the design in detail and plan for deployment.

Here is more detail on each of these phases.

Phase 1: Align on the Vision and Analyze the Current State

- Align on the vision and principles that will guide design decisions down the line.
- Define or refine the expected strategic, financial, and then operational targets to be met.

- Understand where and why change is needed (front office, back office, operations).
- Consider eventual deployment strategy and approaches.

This first step sets the table for the operating model redesign. It starts at the top of the organization. Operating model design efforts require a top-down approach in order to ensure decisions align to the highest priorities of the organization and to effectively distribute and cascade the design effort. Going through the exercise of establishing guiding principles paints a clear picture for the organization, which serves as a common reference point and aligns the executive team from the start.

Next, translating strategic objectives into operational targets provides the organization with clear design parameters and definition of success. For example, consider a company whose growth strategy is centered on new product development. The business will establish specific targets for time-to-market and percent of revenue from new products, which will help product management and development teams from the very beginning as they consider how to align and organize based on product, competency, and/or geographic dimensions.

During this time, clearly understanding current profitability and performance is paramount. For example, a successful engineered-product company was looking to update its operating model, particularly in the front office, to drive growth. The business had one sales force and three product segments serving the construction industry. The initial design assumption was to simply streamline the operating model and continue to take advantage of cross-selling opportunities. But after analysis to establish baseline performance, we determined that only 1 percent of customers actually purchased from all three of the company's segments, and only another 10 percent purchased across two segments—so 89 percent of its customer base purchased within just one product segment, and would not benefit from extensive work to take advantage of cross-selling. We also discovered, contrary to expectations, that its sales through distribution were on average larger and more profitable than its direct sales, yet there was no formal or centralized distribution management function.

This period of analysis redefined the shape of the company's operating model. What was going to be an effort to streamline turned into full-scale reengineering—with the realignment of the sales force by product segment, defining new territories, and the introduction of a new organization to formalize and drive distribution sales.

Phase 2: Outline the New Model and Governance Approach

- Define the role of the corporate center.
- Determine and agree on the proper roles of the front office, back office, and operations.
- Define specific gaps and capability needs at the functional levels.
- Assess cross–value stream impact.
- Gain a sense of magnitude of change and subsequent deployment challenges.

In this phase the needed operating model changes begin to take shape (Figure 15.3). Again, it starts at the top, gaining alignment on the scope and the role of the corporate center (Step 2.1). Will the "corporate" layer be thin, dictating targets but with responsibility otherwise distributed in business units and geographies? Or will the corporate center be much more participatory with functional leadership and support staff along with clear accountability and responsibility for results across the business? With this

Process Area L-2 Capability	Value Streams			Current Accountable	Current Gaps
	Time to Market	Issue to Resolution	Design to Build		H/M/L
1.0 Strategy Infrastructure & Product		L		Product mgmt.	◑
1.1 Market Strategy & Policy		H		Product mgmt.	◕
1.2 Product & Offer Portfolio Planning	M		L	Product mgmt.	◑
1.3 Product and Offering Capability	M			Product mgmt.	◐
1.5 Sales Development	L	L	H	BU Sales	◐
1.6 Product Development & Retire			M	Product mgmt.	◑
1.7 Prod. Marketing Comms & Promo			L	Marketing	◑
2.0 Customer Relationship Mgmt	L	M	L	Sales	○
2.1 CRM Support & Readiness			H	Finance	◕
2.2 Customer Interface Management	H	L		Cust. Srvc.	◑
2.3 Selling	M		L	BU Sales	◑
2.4 Order Handling		L		Receiving	○
2.5 Marketing Fulfillment Response		H		Marketing	●
2 ͜ ⁀tion ͜ ͜ty				͜d	◕

FIGURE 15.3: Process-Capability Mapping and Evaluation to Assess Value-Stream Impacts

highest-level decision of scope clear, functions in the front office, back office, and operations can then begin aligning on the best way to govern, deploy assets, and use partners.

A critical but frequently missed step in this phase is to step back and understand how key cross-functional value streams will be impacted. Ultimately, overall company performance is driven by how these value streams—order-to-cash, time-to-market, issue-to-resolution, to name a few—perform on an ongoing basis. In helping a natural gas company take this step, we looked at how the order-to-install process would be affected by the decision to go with a single field force managed according to geography. What we found was that "managing by geography" would create significant complexity and require significant new technology investment to maintain effective wrench-time. So instead, the business decided to organize the field force first by customer segment, and then by geography. As in this example, this step may require some rework, but it is essential to take before moving on.

At the end of this phase, the magnitude of change required becomes clear, and the business can consider how best to deploy the downstream changes being assessed, given the organization has limited capacity and resources for change.

Phase 3: Complete the Design in Detail and the Plan for Deployment

- Align process, organization, and technology in each functional area.
- Understand new roles, staffing levels, and competency requirements.
- Identify technology gaps and/or alternatives to support.
- Align functional and organization metrics to previously defined targets.
- Reassess and align on the size-of-prize and investment requirements across the effort.
- Build the detailed implementation road map.

In this phase, the design work is finally down to the department level within functions. This step only makes sense after the alignment approach, asset deployment strategy, and role of external partners (outsourcing) is decided. At this point detailed organization design takes place and organization charts are produced with titles and names.

Too often, though, we find operating model projects that have started with this step, a definite sign that the organization didn't really understand what was entailed in an operating model transformation and why the subsequent changes yielded insignificant or even dilutive results. By not recognizing and addressing all six components of an operating model, reorganizing can't really deliver transformational change.

Case Study: Making the Leap from Multilocal to Global

TMF Group is a multinational professional services firm headquartered in Amsterdam that provides accounting, tax, HR, payroll services, and provision of corporate compliance to businesses operating internationally. It became multinational via more than 50 acquisitions over the last 29 years. In fact, Alejandro Peñas, head of group operations, described its acquisition activity as a "non-stop machine." Today it has more than 100 offices operating in more than 80 countries.

"We would buy a business in a country where we were not operating before," Peñas said. "We would not turn that business onto a standard, as at that time we didn't have a common operating model." The result, he said, was a network of offices, each working in a slightly different way, each offering services to clients in slightly different ways.

This created some challenges, both operational and strategic, said Peñas, who was given the challenge of reshaping TMF's operating model. Operationally, with different roles, systems, processes, and standards, the network led to inefficiency and higher operating costs. Strategically, the network undermined what was otherwise a growing value proposition for multinational clients, where more and more contracts were served by multiple offices, and those clients needed TMF to operate consistently across those offices.

So TMF embarked on reinventing its operating model and established a structure for driving the change (see Figure 15.4). Then it defined the elements of its operating model and how each element was to be approached. The components that it defined were as follows:

- Organizational construct: the roles and structure within each office

- Governance: the key performance indicators (KPIs) used to measure the performance of offices and the ways different layers of the organization interact
- Processes, procedures, and operating standards: the internal operating policies of offices in different functional areas, such as accounting or payroll
- Systems: the technical systems that underlie different functions within offices

The organizational construct of the offices was the first element it tackled, believing that aligning the roles and structure within each office would make other operating model changes flow more smoothly. It began by looking at the biggest offices to identify good practices that could be replicated. The goal was to create a set of guidelines on the roles and structure within an office that best supported TMF in serving its customers. For example, one such guideline was that every country should have a managing director, and the delivery team should be organized in "units" under team leaders. For other roles, there was a clear need for flexibility. For example, not all offices needed a local salesperson. Some countries had more inbound sales, and others more outbound.

Midway through this effort, after seeing very little traction, the team realized that they needed to look at a wider variety of offices to capture different business situations. The first draft of guidelines for the operating construct didn't inspire much change within the organization because the team had looked at too few offices and as a result came up with a design that was too narrow. After so many years of operating relatively independently, the offices had a large degree of variety that needed to be accounted for within the recommendations. Peñas noted that finding a solution that seemed workable to a large number of the offices was more important than finding the *perfect* solution. "If it's something that the people in the

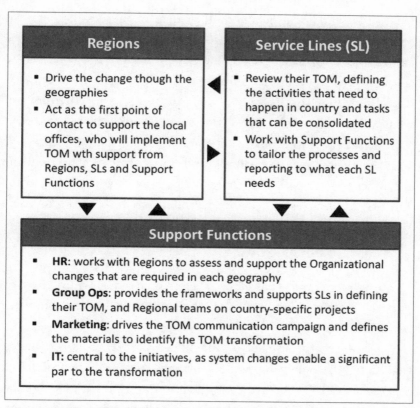

FIGURE 15.4: How TMF Organized to Implement Its Target Operating Model (TOM)

business are happy with, it's much more valuable than the 'perfect' design that remains a PowerPoint slide."

Sponsorship was another factor that made the revised set of guidelines more successful. As Peñas' team began iterating on the guidelines, they got buy-in from the head of EMEA, who then became a partner for driving change. The implementation in Europe went ahead and created a reference for others to follow.

Next the team addressed governance, which ended up being a simpler effort. They collaborated with the leadership team to define what KPIs would be used and built reports for those KPIs that were rolled out across the organization. Having already aligned the leadership roles within each office made the rollout of these standards simpler. Creating these KPIs for TMF set the stage for a successful operating model initiative by clarifying, across the organization, what was being measured and what success looked like.

The last piece the operating model transformation addressed was the processes, procedures, and supporting systems within the offices. TMF operates three major service lines: accounting and tax, human resources and payroll, and corporate secretarial. Each of these required unique processes, procedures, and systems, and each was shaped by the ad hoc nature of growth. TMF addressed these a few at a time, focusing on the areas that offered greatest opportunity based on leadership teams' willingness to partner, known organizational challenges, and clear financial opportunity.

Quantifying the impact is difficult, but TMF group estimates that so far the operating model work has had an impact of about 5 percent of EBITDA for the organization overall, with local office impact ranging from 2 to 3 percent to 10 percent depending on the size and maturity of the office. On top of the financial measures, Peñas said, there have been other benefits as well, such as risk mitigation, client retention, and business continuity.

And lessons learned? Peñas top two are: First, *remember that perfect is the enemy of good.* "Every operating model needs some flexibility. Differentiate between what must be aligned, and where there are options." Second, *be prepared to spend a lot of time communicating and ensure sufficient input is captured from the bottom of the organization.* When moving to a global operating model, sponsorship is critical at all levels. Peñas invested the time to attend regional conferences and built relationships with the managing directors. He listened to their experiences and explained what his team was working on, which made an enormous difference in facilitating a speedy implementation.

Triggers for Operating Model Redesign

It is not uncommon to pin the blame for poor performance on issues other than an out-of-date operating model. Therefore, the ability to understand and pinpoint the triggers that warrant a rethink of how you structure is a valuable part of the Navigator's Skill Set. With that in mind, we have collected below some of the typical triggers for operating model redesign—the sets of circumstances under which we would recommend that an organization at least assess the value of taking this on:

- **You've been moving from local (or multilocal) to global.** For TMF, a global operating model was central to unlocking its global support strategy for its clients. Companies frequently expand overseas in the pursuit of new revenues—the Greener Pasture Siren—and as they do, tend to do so in an incremental, country-by-country manner. Before you know it, you may have replicated costs and infrastructure across many new territories, but not fundamentally adapted your processes. The result: an expensive and inefficient operating model.

- **There's been a significant shift in your value proposition and/or product mix.** As markets shift and products go through their life cycle, it's natural to see a company's product mix shift, even as the operating model typically stays relatively unchanged. For example, consolidating, centralizing, and standardizing processes for a set of customers who demand quick response and high touch may not make sense and could create in the end significant process complexity as the business struggles with the many nonstandard requests. In contrast, having a highly dispersed, field-based organization in a market that is more cost-focused may create a structural hurdle that is hard to overcome even with the best processes and technology. Of course, it is not uncommon for a product or service to begin life as one (consultative sale) only to migrate to the other (transactional sale) over time.

- **New channels have become a bigger factor for your business.** An online presence has become a central plank for most retailers' strategy over the last 15 years. But how to bring this to reality has been a thorny question. In the early days, it was not uncommon to have a separate e-commerce team lurking in a back office somewhere. Over time the need to integrate critical customer touchpoints, supply chain, and stock management across offline and online channels became evident. But what is becoming clear to retailers—and indeed to all businesses looking to digital channels—is that this requires a fundamental rethinking of the operating model. It can't simply be a "bolt-on."

- **You are making acquisitions.** In one of our reports, we showed that there was a big difference in performance between occasional acquirers and serial acquirers.[1] Part of the difference lies in whether or not you have a scalable operating model that can quickly integrate and absorb new businesses. Companies frequently underestimate the additional complexity that accompanies an acquisition. As companies seek growth outside the core, this phenomenon increases. However, even with acquisitions of similar core-related companies, operating models may require adjustments as incremental products and services and new customers in different geographies strain the current processes and organization.

- **Your business has grown significantly in the last few years.** In pursuit of growth, many companies open the door to new organizational add-ons, and new processes, locations, and technology. Decision-making responsibility becomes loose and distributed to preserve local speed. The way you make decisions and structure the business at $100 million is different from the one you need at $500 million, let alone $1 billion. If you've seen a significant uptick in growth in the last few years, congratulations. But if your profitability hasn't grown at the same pace, look at your operating model.

Of course, any significant shift in strategy and competitive conditions should trigger an operating model review. But these developments often announce themselves more forcefully and therefore get the attention required. Macroeconomic shifts and regulatory changes can also trigger the same. And anytime you are pursuing new adjacency opportunities, an operating model review is warranted, as many times these can create far more operational complexity than anticipated. (These and other pitfalls are the subject of the next chapter.)

As TMF demonstrates, reinventing your operating model is not a small thing, but given the number of transformations and major initiatives a business typically undertakes in a two-year period, it is something you should not shy away from. Moreover, as we've indicated in this chapter, it can frequently act as a keystone, unlocking the value of a strategy or emerging market opportunity.

CHAPTER 16

Master Execution in a Complex World

"Vision without action is a daydream. Action without vision is a nightmare."

—JAPANESE PROVERB

Much of this book is focused on strategy: identifying the right options and allocation of resources to win in a competitive environment. But strategy alone doesn't generate results:

Leading Performance = Sound Strategy × Execution Excellence

Execution enables growth. Without the right strategy, you may crash onto the rocks. But without the ability to execute, you'll drift and go nowhere. Leaders recognize this gap. In a recent study of 400 global CEOs, "execution excellence" topped the list of some 80 issues that also included innovation, geopolitical instability, and top-line growth.[1] Indeed, in some ways, it seems that it is getting harder than ever to get anything done. Companies are focusing more resources on more projects, but to less effect. Complexity has eroded our ability to execute on the things that matter.

The twist is that execution excellence (or operational excellence) is more important than ever, even as it has become harder to attain. Increasing competition, fragmenting customer demand, lengthening supply chains, increasing government regulation, and expanding markets have in the past decade all combined to dramatically increase the complexity of operating a business. This increased complexity—more products, more processes, and larger organizations increasingly staffed with distributed workforces across the globe—has made execution more challenging.

Moreover, there is a vicious cycle at work, and the natural response to complexity is to add even more complexity (see Figure 16.1). In response to poor execution, companies are layering on more and more systems, programs, tools, and people, which frequently just increases complexity and impairs execution further.

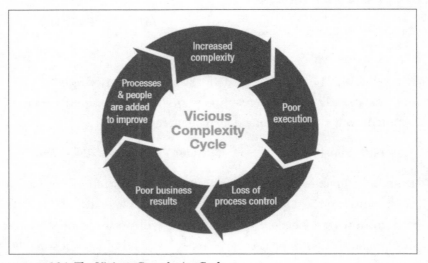

FIGURE 16.1: The Vicious Complexity Cycle

Part of the problem lies in the fact that many of the tools and programs being introduced are ill suited for today's issues. Indeed, Lean Six Sigma, Total Quality Management, the Toyota Production System, etc., all came to prominence during an era with far less complexity. Many of these tools and approaches *can* add value in an organization and *can* be effective—but generally only in defined applications and more "linear" environments. They cannot address problems such as:

- An organization with a long and complex supply chain that finds a minor delay early in the process, through a shortage of a key ingredient, which causes a ripple effect, increasing transportation cost by 100 percent.
- A flower delivery service (1-800-FLOWERS) that misses thousands of Valentine's Day orders due to weather issues, and the subsequent backlash on social media and loss of brand value resulting in a $31 million drop in market value, or about $31,000 per botched order.
- A series of low-level process failures that escalates into a catastrophe with deadly consequences, much as happened with the Deepwater Horizon explosion or the Fukushima Daiichi meltdown.

Worse still, traditional approaches to execution and risk management are not much use either. They are predicated on the ability to predict potential failure modes so that actions to prevent or mitigate the risk may be put in place. But complex systems have many interdependent variables that do not necessarily interact in linear or predictable ways. As a result:

- **Events are too complex to anticipate.** Issues that threaten execution arise due to unanticipated combinations of events, and therefore are difficult to predict. It's worth noting that with the rise of complexity and more potential combinations of events, this will happen more often.
- **Events develop so quickly that there is no time to address them.** They also leave us prone to a risk management paradox: the earlier you catch a discrepancy, the more options you have to fix it. But the earlier you try to catch it, the harder it is to see.
- **Events occur too infrequently to understand.** Each development is different, so feedback loops don't develop. This

is particularly challenging in arenas such as airlines, which have relied upon techniques such as pattern analysis to identify potential risks.

It is no wonder that execution excellence topped the list of CEO concerns!

Clearly we need a new approach for managing execution, one that accounts for new dynamics such as distributed employees, faster markets, higher complexity levels, and the enduring requirements to remain cost-efficient, safe, and fast. In our work with clients, we have originated and refined an approach that cuts through complexity and provides a foundation for execution in a complex world and is anchored around two components:

- Developing a simplified *Integrated Management System (IMS)*, which addresses the underlying framework that defines how your business functions on a day-to-day basis.
- Building a *High-Reliability Culture*, which addresses the norms and behaviors of people who operate within that framework.

These two components are complementary and mutually reinforcing. In this chapter, we'll first look at the problems that arise from typical approaches to execution, then describe what we mean by an Integrated Management System and High-Reliability Culture, and conclude by discussing how these two components can work hand in hand to enable execution.

Why Many Management Systems Are a Mess

In case you are wondering whether your organization has a management system, we have an answer for you: it does, whether you recognize it formally or not. Typical management system processes include setting goals and targets, assigning accountability, identifying and controlling risks, managing change, training employees, and auditing against requirements.* Of course, if your management system is informal, it means that you are not deliberately managing key processes—which may be an issue. But many companies go the other way, sometimes having multiple management systems— to detrimental ends. Indeed, while a few companies like Chevron, Exxon, and Koch Industries have had tremendous success with their management systems, many others have found the opposite: the management systems they've implemented to improve operations have become bureaucratic, costly, and ineffective anchors on performance, and are significant creators of complexity in their own right.

The idea of *formal* management systems has been around since the 1920s but has seen prolific growth over the last few decades. These systems cover areas such as safety, environmental issues, compliance, risk, quality, and asset management. In addition, many external organizations also prescribe management systems that businesses must follow. For example, OSHA requires companies that deal with high-hazard chemicals to implement a chemical process safety management system. Similarly, the EPA recommends implementation of an Environmental Management System. And of course, many companies require their suppliers to implement ISO 9000, a quality management system.

---

* It is important to delineate between *management system* processes and *value stream* processes. Value stream processes define what you do, while management system processes define how you manage those value stream processes. Both may represent an opportunity for improvement. In a complex system with decision-making siloes, value streams are often suboptimized and not well coordinated, and management system processes are often cumbersome, costly, ineffective, and add to the overall level of complexity. But it's important to know the difference. Many continuous improvement initiatives focus on value stream processes. But assessing or attempting to improve a process that is out of control, or poorly controlled (control being the role of management system processes) creates little or no value.

Because most management systems today are designed to achieve a single outcome (safety, compliance, quality, and so on), many companies have ended up with multiple management systems focused on singular aspects of their business. In one survey, more than 75 percent of companies reported using more than one management system.[2] Unfortunately, with management systems, it is not the case where more is better! Having multiple systems not only increases costs and complexity, but impacts risk and performance by creating potential points of conflict and confusion across the organization.

For example, for one organization with multiple overlapping management systems, we assessed potential points of conflict. In Figure 16.2, each dark square in the grid represents a point of potential conflict or redundancy in a management process, a likely generator of more complexity into the system. We list the various management system processes currently in operation on both axes. For these processes to work optimally, you would expect no overlaps or conflicts between them. In fact, the organization had 394 potential conflicts! For example, it had multiple processes that called for risk identification against a specific asset, each leveraging different risk assessment methodology, leading to conflicting conclusions and a jumble of mitigation actions.

What most companies with multiple management systems don't realize is that the vast majority of these systems contain exactly the same sets of processes. For instance, almost all management systems require processes for setting goals and targets, identifying risks, implementing procedures, training employees, and conducting audits. By implementing multiple management systems, companies unintentionally create redundant processes and needless overhead. So if a company has implemented a safety management system, an environmental management system, and a quality management system, it is likely that it has created three

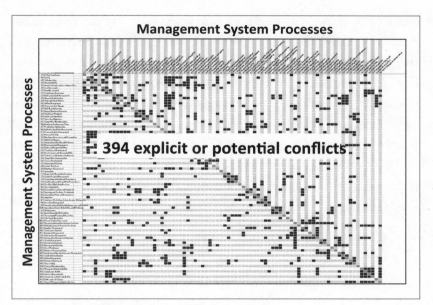

Management System Processes

394 explicit or potential conflicts

FIGURE 16.2: Example of a Mutual Exclusivity Test
Note: With a high-functioning IMS, your management system processes would
be distinct and not in conflict with each other. In this example, the client had 394
potential points of conflict.

separate sets of training processes, with three separate, redundant training requirements. It would be far more effective and efficient to create a single training process managed by a single group.

Or perhaps, you may be thinking, better to not have a formal management system at all?

After all, companies focused on growth are looking to eschew bureaucracy, and unfortunately for many, the pileup of their current overlapping management systems processes are a giant cause of bureaucracy. The temptation may be to think that the answer is informality.

The thing is, with an informal management system, a company is forced to rely primarily on "good people doing good things." As a company grows, the efficacy of such a system rapidly diminishes as visibility to what people are doing decreases and the number of things being done simultaneously increases. Consider if some of the key processes were only managed through word of mouth. It would be impossible for people to know what they are being measured against. Additionally, without assigned ownership, how do people know who is responsible and for what?

That's why some formality is needed. A formal management system, one that is intentionally devised, written, and shared with the organization, will help you more effectively:

- Communicate expectations clearly throughout the organization
- Drive standardization and consistency across divisions
- Provide the basis to hold leaders accountable for their alignment to standards and goals
- Allow for the establishment of metrics to watch for continuous improvement opportunities

While formalizing all of these things might not be time well spent for a small company with a few employees, it is essential for certain key processes in larger organizations. What you need is a "risk-based" approach that helps you prioritize the processes that could seriously impact your employees, customers, or the community, and avoid the trap of spending too much time, money, and effort managing low-value processes. That's where an Integrated Management System comes in to play.

An Integrated Management System

In order to introduce an IMS, consider how every organization can define its desired outcomes in terms of some combination of seven *value drivers*:

- Safety
- Environment
- Compliance
- Quality

- Productivity
- Yield
- Cost

Traditionally, companies have treated these value drivers as separate lenses when it comes to risk assessment and execution. They end up putting in seemingly unending key controls to prevent potential causes of failure. The result is a confusing mess (Figure 16.3).

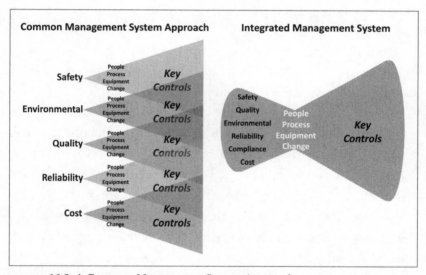

FIGURE 16.3: A Common Management System Approach

The revolutionary aspect of an Integrated Management System is recognizing that the sources of risk tend to be the same across businesses and operations, and that there are just four of them:

- People
- Processes

- Equipment
- Change

In order to transform inputs into finished goods, a company's operations act on the inputs via some combination of people, processes, and equipment. Failure by any of those may result in finished goods that do not meet the requirements of the customer. The only other way that those requirements may not be met is if there is an unexpected change, either to the inputs to the operation or the requirements themselves.

Take people as a risk category, for example. When a person or group fails to perform as expected, what caused this to happen? Usually, it's one of three issues. A person may have been unaware of what he was expected to do; he may have been unable to perform as expected; or he may have chosen not to perform as expected. That's it.

The implications are subtle yet very powerful. In terms of managing for execution, it is more direct, takes less time, and is more useful to start with the few, finite sources of risk: people, process, equipment, and change. These translate to common causes of failure—we can anticipate these common causes and build controls to defend against them (Figure 16.4). Managing to these limited potential failure modes is a lot less complex than attempting to risk-mitigate the nearly infinite outcome failures any single element can induce. This approach also recognizes that one key control may help address several causes of failure, or one cause of failure may require the support of multiple key controls.

The Seven Elements

To help make the system manageable, it is also helpful to group the key controls into seven elements:

1. Leadership
2. Employee Accountability
3. Risk Identification
4. Risk Mitigation

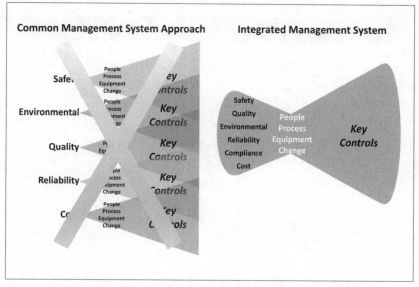

FIGURE 16.4: An Integrated Management System Eliminates Redundancy and Conflict

5. Knowledge Sharing
6. Management of Change
7. Continuous Improvement

This simplification creates a common language that facilitates communication and also provides a holistic framework for rapid assessment of a management system. For example, one such assessment highlighted a client's issue with document management—the process for developing standards and procedures. This falls under Element 5, Knowledge Sharing. In this company, document management had grown substantially over the last few years, with little consistency in how documents were used. The client was considering addressing this through an expensive IT solution, which would not have solved the problem. The key issue was that the company

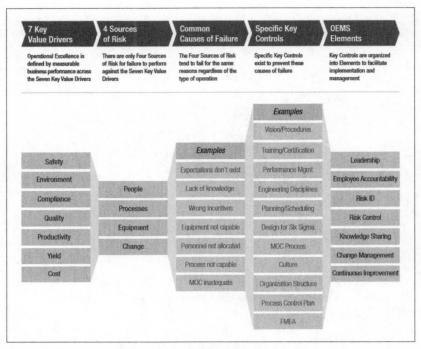

7 Key Value Drivers	4 Sources of Risk	Common Causes of Failure	Specific Key Controls	OEMS Elements
Operational Excellence is defined by measurable business performance across the Seven Key Value Drivers	There are only Four Sources of Risk for failure to perform against the Seven Key Value Drivers	The Four Sources of Risk tend to fail for the same reasons regardless of the type of operation	Specific Key Controls exist to prevent these causes of failure	Key Controls are organized into Elements to facilitate implementation and management

FIGURE 16.5: Overview of an Integrated Management System

had too many unnecessary documents! And this was rooted in how it identified risks (Element 3), developed mitigation plans (Element 4), and managed change across the documents (Element 6). New technology would have just added another process for each of these processes and thus added more complexity. In the end, the company was able to address its problems systematically by focusing on the underlying issues without the need for introducing new technology.

Further, there is a sequence to these seven elements (Figure 16.5). Often, management system transformations in large companies can become large, cumbersome, multiyear efforts that strain under their own weight. The sequence inherent in the seven elements suggests where to focus, as each element builds on the previous. For example, it doesn't make sense to focus on getting better at controlling risks if you are not sufficiently capable or getting better at identifying risks in the first place.

High-Reliability Organizations (HRO): A Culture of Execution

An Integrated Management System is a critical but insufficient lever for execution excellence in a complex world. It provides a simplified structure and framework for execution that cuts through organizational complexity. It also elevates the critical processes in your business, and acknowledges which ones require less definition. This clarity creates a much leaner, cost-efficient operation.

A management system is the "hardware," but it still requires the "software" of human performance for optimal performance: culture. Culture is the means by which an organization can execute in increasingly complex, uncertain conditions.

Complex systems require a different kind of culture to operate. Emerging conditions make work instructions insufficient; high-risk industries are dealing with the fact that in today's world there has been a geometric increase in ways that catastrophe can potentially occur; global organizations may be operating with distributed workforces making it harder to monitor employees' actions.

More specifically, so-called "Black Swan" events—the highly improbable events with catastrophic outcomes—are becoming more common. These events, such as the Lehman Brothers collapse or the Fukushima disaster, sit outside the normal range of expectations and are therefore not anticipated. They are easy to understand—after the fact!

New cultural models are required to deal with the potential of these events. The focus needs to be on learning and developing behaviors and mindsets that can deal with the unexpected. The organizations that adopt these practices and develop these capabilities are known as High-Reliability Organizations (HROs). HROs operate simplified and integrated management systems, but they go further by leveraging culture. As a result, *they operate consistently more effectively and safely than other organizations.*

Perhaps the most well-regarded HRO is the U.S. Naval Nuclear Propulsion Program (the "Nuclear Navy"). In its more than 60-year history operating nuclear reactors with young operators in harsh environments, the organization has *never* had a reactor accident. The reason: a system for operational performance and safety it calls "defense in depth," which relies on three layers of defense:

- **Robust and well-tested and maintained equipment**, while recognizing that even the best equipment will at times fail.
- **Rigorous procedures**, while recognizing that it is equally impossible to devise procedures that cover all contingencies.
- **Well-trained operations**—the last line of defense—that have a thorough understanding of the plant and its capabilities and are steeped in a set of *Cultural Pillars* that enable them to deal with new situations as they arise.

It is the last element—what the Nuclear Navy calls the "Pillars of the Program"—that speak directly to creating a culture that is adapted to unpredictable and complicated situations. They are:

- **Integrity.** People can be relied on to do what they say they will do, and to do what is expected of them, whether someone is looking or not. They have the courage to do what is right and to hold everyone accountable, including themselves.
- **Level of knowledge.** People understand not only what they do, but why they do it. People are continually expanding their understanding of systems, processes, and hazards of their workplace so that they can identify abnormal conditions and potential hazards, react effectively to unanticipated situations, and be able to back each other up.

- **Questioning attitude.** People anticipate problems and are alert to unusual conditions. They are constantly asking themselves: What could go wrong? Has something changed? Am I sure things are as they seem? What do I not know? What might others be missing? Having a questioning attitude does not come from a lack of trust of others or a belief that you or your fellow employees are ill-prepared to complete the task at hand. Rather, it comes from vigilance and a sense of chronic unease: a belief that there may be better ways of doing things.
- **Formality.** Employees follow authorized processes. They conduct their work as planned and communicate information in a disciplined manner. They recognize they are part of an organization made up of other people, facilities, equipment, and processes that must work in concert. If something can be improved, they use the appropriate channels to formally make those changes; they don't develop "work-arounds." They communicate with one another in a consistent and defined manner to ensure that information is reliable and understood.
- **Forceful watch team backup.** People actively back each other up, and they speak up when potential problems are recognized. The concept of forceful watch team backup is rooted in everyone's understanding that they are part of something larger than themselves, they must work in concert to be effective, and no one person is ever perfect. They actively look for what a coworker may have missed and expect others to do the same in return. They have the courage to step in—the courage to care.

The Cultural Pillars are mutually reinforcing. For example, a strong level of knowledge is the basis for a questioning attitude, as without it, how can one recognize abnormal conditions? (See Figure 16.6.) These pillars emerged from the learnings of a storied

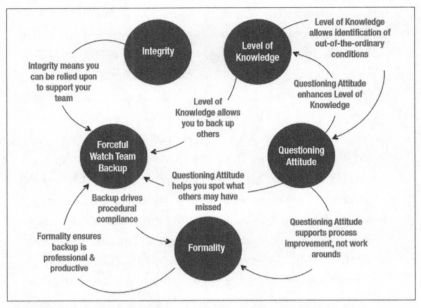

FIGURE 16.6: HRO Cultural Pillars Are Mutually Reinforcing

organization, adapting to extreme conditions. But we can all benefit from them because they are applicable across any industry, ranging from high-risk industries such as oil and gas, to retail, where the Cultural Pillars translate to a consistent customer experience, and even healthcare. Indeed, hospital systems are one area that is currently very HRO-focused, where cost pressures, regulatory pressures, and new technology are creating unprecedented levels of complexity.

In our work, formalizing, adapting, and deploying these pillars to other organizations, we have seen their power. We have also gathered a lot of benchmark data on numerous companies, as well as formally measuring the pillars within the U.S. Nuclear Navy (see box below on how we measure culture through our yardstyck™ approach). HROs by definition outperform non-HROs, and HRO cultures align with the Cultural Pillars. For example, employees in

HROs are more closely aligned across levels in their view of what the target culture is (what good looks like). And HRO cultures are much closer to their desired target culture than non-HROs.

Measuring Culture with Yardstyck

Culture is key to performance, reliability, and profitability. It also directly shapes the customer's experience, as the frontline behaviors reflect cultural norms. Unfortunately, "culture work" has frequently been devoid of metrics and data: with no baseline, it is hard to understand issues and progress. In response to client needs, WP&C developed, then automated, a system of measuring culture as a springboard for improvement: yardstyck (Figure 16.7).

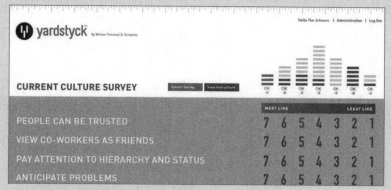

FIGURE 16.7: Yardstyck Is Entirely Web-Based and Uses a Forced Ranking Technique

Yardstyck is a tool that we developed to help our clients assess their culture and the gaps to excellent execution, using our benchmarks for how HROs perform across the Cultural Pillars.

How it works:

1. **Baseline the current culture.** The first step of the process solicits employees to respond to a survey, providing leaders with data and insights into how employees describe the current culture based on 40 different indicators aligned to the Cultural Pillars. Yardstyck provides a baseline that future progress can be measured against.

2. **Define the target culture.** Next, participants describe the target culture. This helps leaders understand what employees want the culture to be like, the degree of alignment, and the size of the gap between current and target cultures.

3. **Benchmark against HRO culture.** WP&C has conducted yardstyck assessments with HRO organizations like the U.S. Nuclear Submarine Force, allowing us to provide organizations with world-class benchmark comparisons.

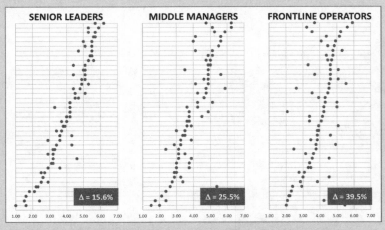

FIGURE 16.8: Yardstyck Reveals How Perceptions of Culture Vary by Level

Using yardstyck, leaders are able to *measure* their culture, whether they have 40 or 40,000 employees, and answer questions such as:

- Do all our employees experience our culture in the same way? Is it different by level or site (Figure 16.8)?
- Do all our employees understand what our target culture is?
- How do we compare against best-in-class organizations with healthy cultures?
- Where should we focus our culture change efforts? How are we progressing on our journey?

This data is valuable as it pinpoints key disconnects, but also provides a platform for tracking progress as you work to adapt your culture. The benefits are significant, not just from a risk and execution perspective, but also from a profit improvement perspective (Figure 16.9). Consider how one of our clients, a $10 billion refinery, launched a cultural transformation to embed the pillars. The intent was to leverage culture as a barrier to catastrophic risks. It achieved this with a 75 percent reduction in "loss of containment" events in just nine months. But notably, it also achieved reliability gains worth $200 million in EBIT improvements in just one calendar year.

It is worth noting that the pillars not only provide a means to adapt to new and emerging issues (given that it is impossible to anticipate and design for every potential failure). They also work hand in hand with a simple management system to capture learning. As the mastery of a complex system cannot be designed into the operation from the start, it must be discovered "bit by bit." HROs harness best-known approaches and leverage a simplified management system as a framework for learning. They learn from every "event" and develop a new, deeper understanding of the operation, before rapidly disseminating this knowledge throughout the

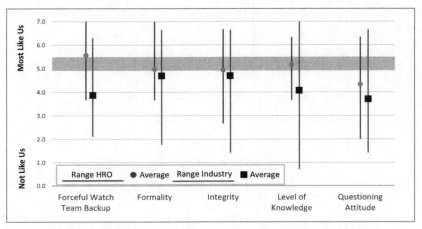

FIGURE 16.9: Non-HROs Underperform HROs and Are Less Aligned with Cultural Pillars. The chart shows aggregated data of HRO companies, as well as non-HRO companies who are just starting HRO programs. *Yardstyck* data reveals that HRO companies are distinctly aligned with the Cultural Pillars, unlike their non-HRO peers. Source: WP&C client output from *yardstyck* cultural assessment

organization. This is why it is possible to say that every submarine that goes to sea in the U.S. Nuclear Navy represents the cumulative learning of over 6,200 years of reactor plant operations.

The Organizational Genius of Admiral Rickover

Much of our thinking regarding culture and Operational Discipline is inspired by the late Admiral Hyman Rickover and the United States Navy. In the wake of World War II, then Captain Rickover was the first to recognize the enormous potential of nuclear-powered submarines and surface ships. He embarked on his quest to build the Nuclear Navy before there was even a commercial nuclear power plant on the drawing board. As a consummate engineer, he was keenly aware of the enormous technical challenges to be overcome. Indeed this would be the most technologically complex undertaking of its day: reducing the size of a nuclear reactor so it would fit inside a submarine, and building an organization capable of operating it safely. The vision: a navy that could go further and go longer, without the constraints of fuel and batteries, conveying enormous tactical advantage.

The results speak for themselves: Since its inception over 60 years ago, the U.S. Nuclear Navy has operated more nuclear power plants than any other organization in the world, and has done so without a single reactor incident. Further, the navy does this with young personnel, high turnover, and while operating in remote, dynamic, and often harsh and unforgiving environments at sea.

Rickover's real genius lay in his understanding of the significant organizational challenges involved: how do you put something as complex as a nuclear reactor on a boat, under the ocean, and operate it safely with a crew of young sailors? He recognized that doing so meant eschewing the traditional military culture that had existed for centuries: follow orders, do what you are told, and don't ask questions.

Rickover knew that to achieve the Naval Nuclear Propulsion Program's dual objectives of continuity of power and reactor safety, his operators would have to operate in a different way. He would have to build a different culture, one founded upon what has come to be known within the Navy as the Pillars of the Program: Integrity, Level of Knowledge, Questioning Attitude, Formality, and Forceful Watch Team Backup.

Rickover expected even his most junior sailors to question things, to have an integrated understanding of how the entire plant worked, to back up not just each other but also their officers, to operate with painstaking formality, and to be able to be relied upon. Key to arresting the development of problems was identifying when small things were not quite right, which required everyone in the crew to continuously examine and question things. But to do so required a keen level of knowledge to be able to spot when something, even minor, was wrong.

Mastering Execution

In our work with leaders, we have seen that most recognize that their outdated cultures need work. However, tackling culture change can be overwhelming. Similarly, overhauling a management system may feel like a gargantuan task. So, in the end, nothing gets done. But there's a method for tackling the task top-down that can cut through the complexity so you can master execution:

1. **Diagnose and measure the current context and baseline.** Establish a measurable baseline and understand the existing circumstances. This can be via top-down approaches such as with a seven-element Integrated Management System diagnostic and the yardstyck culture assessment that can rapidly diagnose your execution capabilities. Take the time to understand your execution issues, the strategic context, and the business case for mastering execution in your organization, and you'll save a lot of time later, and build an irrefutable case for change.

2. **Define the required execution capabilities and then design your future state.** What new or improved execution capabilities are required to meet your strategic objectives? How do an Integrated Management System and HRO culture support those execution requirements? This is the critical design work, detailing what a new Integrated Management System and

culture look like, in the specific context of your business, and it requires alignment across the executive team. It is important to define this with some specificity, as—for example—not all management system processes carry the same importance.

3. **Communicate the vision and the road map, and select your starting point very carefully.** Restarting a major change initiative because the initial starting point was wrong is significantly harder than getting going the first time. Align the organization on the new culture in terms of real-world behavior expectations. Overcommunicate, and then communicate some more.

4. **Ensure executive sponsorship.** CEOs, put this on your agenda. It is not without challenge to execute a large program that is designed to address issues in execution! A way to shore this up is through senior executive sponsorship and the bright light that shines upon it. This cascades down. Understand clearly who is responsible for the changes at your company; managers may be tasked with executing, but senior leaders cannot expect to just "hand the project off to the team." Ensure that the new culture is supported through the management and rewards systems.

5. **Begin the change journey and stay flexible and positive!** Be transparent with course corrections and plan changes. Expect meaningful course changes to be required during the effort, and communicate that this will be the case from the beginning. Of course, don't forget to take every opportunity to celebrate and affirm desired changes when you see them; don't wait for the big wins, small wins add up.

Together, the two components of an Integrated Management System and HRO culture can transform an organization's ability to execute its strategy reliably, consistently, safely, and at lower cost in a highly complex world. Developing the right management system and changing culture are difficult tasks requiring significant leadership will and commitment. The journey to excellence will look different for every company. But what is clear is that the necessity to develop new execution capabilities is significant for most organizations as they adapt to a very different environment.

CALL TO ACTION

Build Out Your Navigator's Skill Set and Become a Growth Leader

Opportunity:

In the final section, we defined the critical capabilities required to navigate successfully to profitable growth in the Age of Complexity. Few organizations find themselves strong in every capability, and where you should focus depends on your current competitive situation; however, all else being equal, understanding where you really make money is a good place to start as it will help set priorities.

Key questions for discussion:

Navigator's Skill Set	Discussion Questions
We know where we really make money.	• To what degree do we believe our standard costs? • What decisions would be impacted with an accurate view of costs?
We are deliberate in how we manage our portfolio.	• What is the current state of our core brands? Our portfolio generally? • What opportunities exist to reignite growth by focusing on the core?
We approach new markets and targets with discipline.	• In M&A, are we Professionals, Temperate, or Dabblers? • How can we improve our assessment of adjacency opportunities?
Our operating model is fit-for-purpose.	• When did we last overhaul our operating model? • Does our operating model enable or impede our ability to execute?
We execute efficiently and consistently.	• Does our management system cut through or increase complexity? • To what degree do we have a culture of execution?

Areas to investigate:

- Based on additional review, plot where you sit on the Navigator's Skill Set axis.
- Estimate where competitors may be positioned relative to you.
- Combine with your Explorer's Mindset coordinate to plot where you sit on the two-by two grid.
- Assess the opportunity and what it would look like if you were a Growth Leader (top right).
- Chart a course! Consider what it will take to become a Growth Leader.

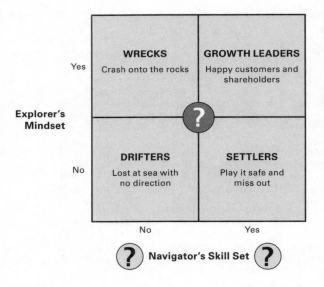

ACKNOWLEDGMENTS

Getting to publication has been a journey for us, one we've taken alongside our clients as they wrestle with what it means to compete and grow in the Age of Complexity. We've been helped and inspired along the way by the many conversations, insights, and challenges posed and thank our clients for their encouragement.

We also want to thank our many colleagues who have made substantive contributions to the book, including David Toth, Ernie Spence, Megan Beck, Scott Stallbaum, Andrew Dorin, Rob Turell, Tom Hamnett, and Chris Seifert.

We are indebted to the team at McGraw-Hill: to Knox Huston, our first editor, with whom we started this journey, and Cheryl Ringer, who has helped us get this across the finish line. Also, our appreciation goes to Sue Reynard for her editorial support.

Our thanks to Frederik van Tuyll and Alejandro Peñas of TMF Group for their thoughtful contributions around what it takes to deploy a global operating model.

We also would like to acknowledge Mike George and Andy Beal, who have acted as inspiration and counsel for us over the years.

Last but not least, we wish to thank our families for their support and understanding as we learned firsthand the time demands of writing a book while running a business, which doesn't leave time for much else.

NOTES

CHAPTER 1

1. Livingstone was a medical missionary who famously and obsessively sought out the sources of the River Nile.
2. Richard Foster Innosight study.
3. Jim Collins, *How the Mighty Fall*.
4. Steve Jobs iPhone Keynote at MacWorld 2007.
5. Ibid.

CHAPTER 2

1. Wilson and Perumal, *Waging War on Complexity Costs* (McGraw-Hill, 2009).
2. Bill Sweetman, "A Billion Here . . . Rand Report Dismisses Joint-Program Savings," *Aviation Week & Space Technology*, December 30, 2013 / January 6, 2014.
3. Sievanen, Suomala, and Paranko, *Activity-Based Costing and Product Profitability* (Tampere, Finland: Institute of Industrial Management, Tampere University of Technology, 2001).
4. "The Forbes 400: The Richest People In America," *Forbes.com*, September 2013.
5. "2010 IBM Global CEO Study," IBM, May 2010.
6. "The Focused Company," Bain & Company, June 2012.
7. "9th Annual Global CEO Survey," PricewaterhouseCoopers, 2006.
8. Maury Klein, *The Power Makers* (New York: Bloomsbury Press, 2008).
9. Andy Kessler, *Running Money* (New York: HarperCollins, 2004).
10. Maury Klein, *The Power Makers*.
11. Ibid.

CHAPTER 3

1. John Rapley, "The New Middle Ages," *Foreign Affairs*, May/June 2006.
2. Ralph Peters, *Wars of Blood and Faith* (Stackpole Books, 2007).

3. Notwithstanding amazon.com, which is stretching the definition of "longer term."

4. Bill Greenwald and Judd Kahn, *Competition Demystified* (Penguin Group, 2005).

5. According to a recent survey of 25 McDonald's owners conducted by Janney Capital Markets, quoted by *The Huffington Post* in "McDonald's Store Owners Fear Fast Food Chain Becoming Too Slow," May 17, 2013.

6. Leslie Patton, "McDonald's Seen Overhauling U.S. Menu from 145 Choices," Bloomberg, May 16, 2013.

7. The outbreak of *E. coli* at multiple Chipotle restaurants was not a function of menu simplicity, but rather related (ironically) to issues arising with its core selling point—its use of fresh ingredients vs. frozen (Bloomberg news).

8. Quoted in Bloomberg article, "McDonalds Seen Overhauling U.S. Menu."

CHAPTER 4

1. Translated by S. H. Butcher and Andrew Lang, 1906.

2. Xiang Wan, Philip T. Evers, and Martin E. Dresner, "Too Much of a Good Thing: The Impact of Product Variety on Operations and Sales Performance," *Journal of Operations Management*, 2012.

3. Geoffrey Colvin, "How Rubbermaid Managed to Fail from Most Admired to Just Acquired," *Fortune*, November 23, 1998.

4. Ibid.

5. Ibid.

6. Bo Jackson, retired baseball and (American) football player.

7. Chiquita Investor presentation, December 2013.

8. "Chiquita Seeks New CEO as 'Undercover Boss' Exits," *Wall Street Journal*, August 7, 2012.

9. Ely Portillo, "Chiquita Exiting Grape Business," *Charlotte Observer*, October 18, 2012.

10. Jim Collins, *How the Mighty Fall* (JimCollins, 2009).

11. Tali Sharot, *The Optimism Bias: A Tour of the Irrationally Positive Brain* (Vintage, 2012).

12. Interview with the *Globe and Mail*, February 1, 2013, https://www.youtube.com/watch?v=dR-GfEGpuCc.

13. Interview with WP&C, February 20, 2014.

14. Jim Collins, *How the Mighty Fall*.

15. Inditext: 2012, *HBR* case (Rev. March 7, 2014). Case study by John R. Wells and Galen Danskin.

16. The last new car to be factory-equipped with a cassette deck in the dashboard was a 2010 Lexus. "For Car Cassette Decks, Play Time Is Over," *New York Times*, February 4, 2011.
17. J. E. Kaufmann and H. W. Kaufmann, *The Medieval Fortress* (Da Capo Press, 2004).
18. Niccolò Machiavelli, *The Art of War* (Chicago, IL: University of Chicago Press, 2005).
19. "Die Another Day: What Leaders Can Do About the Shrinking Life Expectancy of Corporations," BCG, July 2, 2015.
20. *Harvard Business Review*, October 2013.
21. Steve Denning, "What Killed Michael Porter's Monitor Group?," Forbes.com, November 20, 2012.

CHAPTER 5

1. Translated by S. H. Butcher and Andrew Lang, 1906.
2. According to CEO Kruse, one such flavor is coconut. He said: "Ninety percent of the people hate coconut but the 10 percent that love it just go crazy. We did enough for three months, but it was gone in five weeks." Interview with Paul Kruse, CEO of Blue Bell Creameries, by WP&C, August 2011.
3. "80 Percent Retailers Not Ready for Omnichannel Supply Chain," FierceRetail blog, September 16, 2015, quoting an HRC Advisory study.
4. Chief Strategy Officer Conference, London, 2014.
5. "Despicable Me 2 Producer Knows How to Win the Box Office," *Bloomberg Businessweek*, September 23, 2013.
6. Matthew Garrahan, "Chris Meledandri, the Man Who Has Made Millions from Minions," *Financial Times*, January 5, 2014.
7. "Despicable Me 2 Producer Knows How to Win the Box Office." *Bloomberg Businessweek*, September 23, 2013.
8. Jillian D'Onfro and Eugene Kim, "The Life and Awesomeness of Amazon Founder and CEO Jeff Bezos," *Business Insider*, February 11, 2016.
9. Jaydon Song and Kyungmook Lee, *The Samsung Way* (2014).
10. In a private dinner with Dr. Kwon, president, Samsung Electronics, Dr. Kwon emphasized to both of us the importance of speed in the digital age: he bemoaned European competitiveness because of slow decision making; pointed out that American tech firms were leading the digital age because of the speed of decision making in American tech culture, after which Samsung is modeled; and pointed out that Japan's culture of consensus renders them uncompetitive in the digital world. He added that the areas where Japan is competitive, which are photography and printing, the core technology is analog rather than digital.

11. We have seen this work the other way as well, where high-growth items displace investment that could extend the life of a legacy business. Frequently, companies underestimate the complexity costs associated with these high-growth businesses, or fail to see that they require a different operating model to support than the one currently in place.

12. A code we have cracked. See Chapter 12 for a discussion on Wilson Perumal's Square-Root Costing.

CHAPTER 6

1. For more on the Belgian atrocities in the Congo, see Adam Hochschild, *King Leopold's Ghost* (Houghton Mifflin, 1998).

2. Norman Sherry, *Conrad's Western World* (Cambridge University Press, 1971).

3. Robin Hanbury-Tenison, ed., *The Great Explorers* (Thames & Hudson, 2010).

4. Geoffrey Colvin, "How Rubbermaid Managed to Fail from Most Admired to Just Acquired," *Fortune*, November 23, 1998.

5. For a great reference, and read, see *Longitude*, by Dava Sobel (Bloomsbury Press, 1995).

6. Dava Sobel, *Longitude*.

7. October 2, 2013.

8. *What does a petabyte look like? Computer Weekly* tried to answer this by providing some examples (http://www.computerweekly.com/feature/What-does-a-petabyte-look-like). For example, one petabyte is enough to store the DNA of the entire population of the United States—and then clone them, twice. If you had one petabyte of songs on your iPhone, it would take 2,000 years to play them all.

9. Andrew McAfee and Erik Brynjolfsson, "Big Data: the Management Revolution," *Harvard Business Review*, October 2012.

10. Different leaders develop different approaches to deal with this. One executive told us that he knew that after 10 a.m., his day would be consumed with operational activities. So if he had four hours of strategic thinking he'd come in at 6 a.m.; five hours, he'd come in at 5 a.m., etc. In retail, it's not uncommon for the executive team to be out of the office on Fridays to spend the day in stores with customers and staff, to anchor on what's important as well as create headroom for perspective.

11. Johnson's breakthrough moment for Target came during one of his many trips to Europe. He was at a housewares show where Italian company Alessi was presenting its pots and juicers as works of art. "It was like walking through a museum," he says. "They weren't there to

make money; they were there to make great products." This impressed upon him the value of design, which became a big part of Target's success. Jennifer Reingold, "Ron Johnson: Retail's New Radical," *Fortune*, March 7, 2012.

12. "Apple Extends Lead in U.S. Top 10 Retailers by Sales per Square Foot," *Fortune*, March 13, 2015.

13. Das Narayandas, Kerry Herman, and Lisa Mazzanti, "Ron Johnson: Retail at Target, Apple, and J.C. Penney," *Harvard Business Review* case, April 24, 2015.

14. Quoted in Brad Tuttle, "The 5 Big Mistakes That Led to Ron Johnson's Ouster at JC Penney," *Time*, April 9, 2013.

15. Jennifer Reingold, Ron Johnson: Retail's New Radical, *Fortune*, March 7, 2012.

16. Max Chafkin, "How Failed JC Penney CEO Ron Johnson Is Redeeming Himself with Enjoy," *Fast Company*, October 26, 2015.

CHAPTER 7

1. For many people "entrepreneurial" simply means working in a small company, or having the opportunity to do many things, or not having to wade through a bunch of bureaucracy. For others, it means having the potential for significant upside. Still for others it means being recognized for all of their unique talents, which obviously they must have. While all these may exist in an entrepreneurial company, we believe these are all as far from really defining entrepreneurship as is having borrowed a lot of money. Few people it seems know what really makes entrepreneurship entrepreneurial.

2. Peter H. Diamandis and Steven Kotler, *Bold* (Simon & Schuster, 2015).

3. PayPal was the result of a merger between two startups, one cofounded by Thiel and the other by Musk.

4. Thiel, *Zero to One: Notes on Startups, or How to Build the Future* (Crown-Business, 2014).

5. Vivienne Walt, "Amazon Invades India," *Fortune*, December 28, 2015.

6. Churchill's comment on Clement Atlee: "A modest man, who has much to be modest about."

7. The authors said that these strategies were identified through multiple conversations and in-person interviews, combined with over 200 hours of video footage. The researchers categorized the ideas from this research and then analyzed from there.

8. Diamandis and Kotler, *Bold*.

9. George Bernard Shaw, *Man and Superman*.

10. Diamandis and Kotler, *Bold*.

11. Quoted in Diamandis and Kotler, *Bold*.

12. Matt Rosoff, "Jeff Immelt: GE Is on Track to Become a 'Top 10 Software Company,'" *Business Insider*, September 29, 2015.

13. Jeff Immelt, "Reflections from Washington" (blog), September 29, 2016, https://www.linkedin.com/pulse/reflections-from-washington-jeff-immelt?trk=mp-reader-card.

CHAPTER 8

1. Walter Isaacson, "The Real Leadership Lessons of Steve Jobs," *Harvard Business Review*, April 2012.

2. Ernst F. Schumacher, British economist (1911–1977).

3. The budget should reflect the company's strategy, not the other way around. In practice, however, often the objective of the budget-setting process is to get to a budget, rather than to reflect and support the strategy.

4. "Let My Fritos Go: The Pepsi Challenge: Keep the Company in One Piece," *Economist*, March 1, 2014.

5. Michael Hitt, R. Duane Ireland, Robert Hoskisson, *Strategic Management: Competitiveness and Globalization: Concepts and Cases* (South-Western Cengage Learning, 2009).

6. Cheryl Knight, "New Global Initiatives Help Pfizer Inc. Save More Than $30M," Fleet Financials, July 2010.

7. Tricia Duryee, "Everything You Need to Know About eBay and PayPal's Split," Geekwire.com, July 1 2015.

CHAPTER 9

1. "Is the Pace of Business Really Getting Quicker?," *Economist*, December 5, 2015.

2. Note: Exits from the Index were due to either a drop in value or acquisition. While some acquisition targets were good news for shareholders, most exits were another milestone in decline, including some famous names: Circuit City, Bear Stearns, Solectron, Radio Shack, Kodak, Palm, Sears, and the *New York Times*.

3. Gilvan C. Souza, Barry L. Bayus, and Harvey M. Wagner, "New-Product Strategy and Industry Clockspeed," *Management Science* 50, no. 4 (April 2004).

4. Endorsement for *Waging War on Complexity Costs*, by Stephen A. Wilson and Andrei Perumal (McGraw-Hill, 2009).

5. Emily Pope, "How General McChrystal Captures the Magic of Small Teams at Scale," General Assembly Blog, October 8, 2015.

6. Stanley McChrystal, David Silverman, Chris Fussell, and Tantum Collins, "General Stanley McChrystal: How the Military Can Teach Us to Adapt," *Time*, June 9, 2015.

7. Frederick Taylor was a mechanical engineer and is regarded as the father of *scientific management*. He is famous for developing time and motion studies to improve factory efficiency.

8. "Kelly's 14 Rules & Practices," http://www.lockheedmartin.com/us/aeronautics/skunkworks/14rules.html.

9. Daisuke Wakabayashi, "Apple Engineer Recalls the iPhone's Birth," *Wall Street Journal*, March 25, 2014.

10. McChrystal, Silverman, Fussell, and Collins, "General Stanley McChrystal: How the Military can Teach us to Adapt."

11. Scott Engler, "A Journey of Leadership: 7 Lessons from Gen. Stanley McChrystal on Network Leadership," LinkedIn, January 4, 2016.

12. "Retired U.S. General Stanley McChrystal Talks Leadership Strategy," MIT Sloan, February 18, 2015.

13. 2015 Reckitt Benckiser Group plc (RB) Annual Report and Financial Statement.

14. General Stanley McChrystal, *Team of Teams: New Rules of Engagement for a Complex World* (Portfolio, 2015).

15. *Harvard Business Review*, January-February 2014.

16. Jaeyong Song and Kyungmook Lee, *The Samsung Way* (McGraw-Hill Education, 2014).

CHAPTER 10

1. Cited in Phil Simon, *Too Big to Ignore* (Wiley, 2013).

2. "Hal Varian on How the Web Challenges Managers," McKinsey Commentary, January 2009.

3. Eric Schmidt and Jonathan Rosenberg, *How Google Works* (Grand Central Publishing, 2014).

4. Daniel Cohen, Matthew Sargeant, and Ken Somers, "3-D Printing Takes Shape," *McKinsey Quarterly*, January 2014.

5. Zac Hall, "Apple Stores Recruiting Fashion/Luxury Experts Ahead of Apple Watch Debut," *9to5Mac*, December 8, 2014.

6. John Geraci, "What I Learned from Trying to Innovate at the *New York Times*," *Harvard Business Review*, April 7, 2016.

7. Kevin J. Boudreau and Karim R. Lakhani, "Using the Crowd as an Innovation Partner," *Harvard Business Review*, April 2013.

8. The graphics at the beginning of each of the four parts of this book were sourced through a crowdsourcing contest, with the winner competing with illustrators from around the world.

9. Michelle Caruso-Cabrera, "3M CEO: Research Is Driving This Company" CNBC, June 10, 2013.

10. Mark W. Johnson, Clayton M. Christensen, Henning Kagermann, "Reinventing Your Business Model," *Harvard Business Review*, December 2008.

11. Kim Wagner, Andrew Taylor, Hadi Zablit, and Eugene Foo, Boston Consulting Group, BCG survey: "The Most Innovative Companies 2014," October 28, 2014.
12. Arun Sundarajan, "From Zipcar to the Sharing Economy," *Harvard Business Review*, January 3, 2013.
13. Michael Schrage, "Q&A: The Experimenter," *MIT Technology Review*, February 18, 2011.
14. Mat Honan, "Remembering the Apple Newton's Prophetic Failure and Lasting Impact," *Wired.com*, August 5, 2013.
15. Joyce Bedi, "Thomas Edison's Inventive Life," Smithsonian Institute, April 18, 2004.
16. Rita Gunther McGrath and Ian MacMillan, *Discovery-Driven Growth* (Harvard Business Review Press, 2009).

CHAPTER 11

1. One was that memory chips were Intel's *technology drivers*—"What this phrase meant was that we always developed and refined our technologies on our memory products first because they were easier to test. Once the technology had been debugged on memories, we would apply it to microprocessors and other products." The other belief was that Intel's salespeople couldn't do a good job without a full product line.
2. Andrew S. Grove, *Only the Paranoid Survive* (Crown Business, 1999).
3. Martin Peers and Nick Wingfield, "Blockbuster Set to Offer Movies by Mail," *Wall Street Journal*, February 11, 2004.
4. Ibid.
5. Quoted in Rick Newman, "How Netflix (and Blockbuster) Killed Blockbuster," *U.S. News and World Report*, September 23, 2010.
6. "The Last Kodak Moment?," *Economist*, January 14, 2012.
7. Schumpeter, "How Fujifilm Survived," *Economist*, January 18, 2012.
8. Claudia H. Deutsch, "At Kodak, Some Old Things Are New Again," *New York Times*, May 2, 2008.
9. Kana Inagaki and Juro Osawa, "Fujifilm Thrived by Changing Focus," *Wall Street Journal*, January 20, 2012.
10. David Goldman, "How the Surface Lost $1 Billion and Lived to Tell the Tale," *CNNMoney*, March 31, 2015.
11. Grove, *Only the Paranoid Survive*.
12. Richard Foster and Sarah Kaplan, authors of *Creative Destruction* (Doubleday Press), discuss the second and third points as contributors to "Cultural Lock-in."
13. An exception to this would be Mike McNamara, CIO of Target Corporation and formerly CIO of Tesco Stores in the United Kingdom. Not

long after taking on the new job, McNamara told CEO Brian Cornell that his budget was too big, as reported in the *Star Tribune* (Kavita Kumar, "Target's IT Chief Set a New Direction, Starting with Smaller Budget," July 30, 2016). "For the first time perhaps in my career, I had someone walk into my office and say, 'Brian, I've got too much capital to spend,'" Cornell recounted incredulously to Wall Street analysts at a meeting in New York. McNamara explained, "We were just doing too many things." The company has since cut the number of projects from 800 down to 80. Says McNamara: "Even a company as big as Target doesn't have 800 priorities."

14. Brad Stone, *The Everything Store* (Little, Brown and Company, 2013).

15. Rita Gunther McGrath, *The End of Competitive Advantage* (Harvard Business Review Press, 2013).

CHAPTER 12

1. The company's standard cost figures did not go down to operating profit. For this analysis, the standard cost figures were translated down to the operating profit level by adding SG&A costs allocated evenly as a percentage of revenue.

2. The profit figures in this example have been altered to protect our client and are therefore illustrative.

3. These costs are technically variable costs in that they vary with volume, but they are very different from traditional variable costs that vary *proportionally* with volume. We will use the term *variable* to refer to traditional variable cost.

4. Technically, not all complexity costs follow the square root of volume relationship. Although most do, some of what we call complexity costs can follow the variable or fixed cost relationships, but those are already covered in those categories. More correctly, we could call these square root of volume costs, but that is much more cumbersome than calling them complexity costs, which is nearly as correct and a much more informative term.

5. By design, SRC cost figures are simply polynomial expressions (Cost = $Ax + Bx^{1/2} + C$) making it rather straightforward to develop cost and profit scaling curves.

CHAPTER 13

1. Seth Godin, "But What If This Was Your Only Job?" (blog), December 28, 2014, http://sethgodin.typepad.com/seths_blog.

2. Serena Ng, "P&G to Shed More Than Half Its Brands," *Wall Street Journal*, August 1, 2014.

3. Jennifer Reinhold, "Can P&G Find Its Aim Again?," *Fortune*, June 9, 2016.

4. Demitrios Kalogerpoulos, "Procter & Gamble Co. Stock at $90: What's Next?," *Motley Fool*, April 8, 2017.

5. Lindsay Whipp, "P&G to Cut Costs by Another $10B," *Financial Times*, February 18, 2016.

6. Alexander Coolidge, "P&G Reports $7.9B Profit, Ups Key Sales Outlook," *Cincinnati Enquirer*, January 20, 2017.

7. Rick Kush, "The Hershey Company: Aligning Inside to Win on the Outside," *Ivey Business Journal*, April 2012.

8. P&G internal blog, "The Strategy is Simple . . . ," December 24, 2010, http://news.pg.com/blog/company-strategy/strategy-simple%E2%80%A6.

9. Nestlé 2017 CAGNY Presentation, February 23, 2017.

10. Karl Ulrich, "The Fallacy of 'Disruptive Innovation,' " *Wall Street Journal*, November 6, 2014.

11. "New York Man Spends Life Savings Ahead of May 21 Doomsday," Foxnews.com, May 14, 2011.

12. Nestlé 2017 CAGNY Presentation, February 23, 2017.

13. Drew Neisser, "Clorox CMO's Five Building Blocks of a Better Brand," *Advertising Age*, March 8, 2017.

14. John Karolefski, "Clorox Leverages Shopper Insights to Power Seasonal Promotions," *CPG Matters*, April 2012.

CHAPTER 14

1. Ken Favaro was formerly CEO of Marakon Associates.

2. "The Dangers of Adjacencies Strategy," S+B blogs, *strategy+business*, January 30, 2014.

3. Angela Ahrendts, "Burberry's CEO on Turning an Aging British Icon into a Global Luxury Brand," *Harvard Business Review*, January/February 2013.

4. WP&C's *VantagePoint* 2014, no. 2.

5. Scott A. Christofferson, Robert S. McNish, and Diane L. Sias, "Where Mergers Go Wrong," *McKinsey Quarterly*, May 2004.

6. As detailed in our VantagePoint report, "Avoiding the Pitfalls of Being an Occasional Acquirer: How Infrequent Acquirers Can Learn from the Professionals to Execute a Successful M&A Strategy."

7. WP&C interviews and research.

8. Vivek Verma, Managing Director & CEO, Olam internal blog, "Entry into Soluble Coffee," Issue 2, 2016.

9. Shaun Rein (managing director, China Market Research Group), "Why Best Buy Failed in China," CNBC, March 7, 2011.

CHAPTER 15

1. "Avoiding the Pitfalls of Being an Occasional Acquirer," *VantagePoint* 2013, no. 4, available at www.wilsonperumal.com.

CHAPTER 16

1. Cited in Donald Sull, Rebecca Homkes, and Charles Sull, "Why Strategy Execution Unravels—and What to Do About It," *Harvard Business Review*, March 2015.
2. "Only 1 in 4 Businesses Do This Well" (blog), Wilson Perumal & Company, http://www.wilsonperumal.com/blog/blog/only-1-in-4-businesses-do-this-well#more-3822.

INDEX

ABOUT THE AUTHORS

Andrei Perumal is managing partner and cofounder of management consultancy Wilson Perumal & Company, the leading advisor to companies on how to thrive in a complex world; and coauthor of *Waging War on Complexity Costs*. He advises senior executives and government leaders on issues of strategy, complexity, and operations, combining significant consulting, management, and technical experience. He excelled in the U.S. Navy's nuclear propulsion program, as a strategy consultant with Bain & Company, and later as a principal and leadership team member with George Group Consulting's operations strategy practice.

Andrei has held industry roles with Beal Aerospace Technologies, where he drove the development and operation of a hydrogen peroxide rocket propellant plant, and later was handpicked by Andy Beal (#42 on Forbes list of wealthiest Americans) to be head of strategic operations for Beal Bank, the most profitable bank in the United States. Also, as a young intern with Rockwell's Space Systems Division, Andrei independently developed novel analysis that helped avert a major space shuttle launch delay. Andrei holds an aeronautical engineering degree from MIT.

Stephen A. Wilson is managing partner and cofounder of management consultancy Wilson Perumal & Company. He works with senior leadership teams in businesses and private equity firms in North America and Europe, advising them on critical strategy, operations, and innovation questions. Stephen has 20 years of experience working across industry, and in particular supports clients in consumer goods, industrial goods, services, and retail. He has written extensively on the topics of growth strategy, cost-competitiveness, and organizational development, and on the issue of how to compete in today's complex world.

He is coauthor of *Waging War on Complexity Costs* and *Conquering Complexity in Your Business*, both published by McGraw-Hill. He has also written articles for *Agenda* (a *Financial Times* publication), *Chief Executive* magazine, *Investor's Business Daily*, and CNBC.com. Stephen previously worked with strategy firm Marakon, and later became a principal and leadership team member with George Group Consulting. He holds an MBA in finance and strategic management from the Wharton School.

Wilson Perumal & Company is a leading international management consultancy, with operations in North America and Europe. We work with leading corporations, private equity firms, and governmental organizations on some of their toughest strategic, organizational, and operational issues. Our focus is helping these organizations develop and execute strategies for competing in a complex world.

For more information, go to www.wilsonperumal.com.